Applied Linguistics and Language Study

General Editor: C. N. Candlin

The Classroom and the Language Learner

Ethnography and second-language classroom research

Leo van Lier

Longman
London and New York

Longman Group UK Limited
Longman House, Burnt Mill, Harlow,
Essex CM20 2JE England
and Associated Companies throughout the world.

© Longman Group UK Limited 1988

Published in the United States of America by
Longman Inc., New York

First published 1988

BRITISH LIBRARY CATALOGUING IN PUBLICATION DATA
van Lier, Leo
   The classroom and the language learner:
   ethnography and second-language classroom
   research. – (Applied linguistics and
   language study).
   1. Language and languages – Study and
   teaching – Research 2. Second language
   acquisition
   I. Title II. Series
   401'.9   P53.8

LIBRARY OF CONGRESS CATALOGING IN PUBLICATION DATA
van Lier, Leo.
   The classroom and the language learner.
   (Applied linguistics and language study)
   Bibliography: p.
   Includes index.
   1. Language and languages – Study and teaching.
   2. Second language acquisition. 3. Sociolinguistics –
   Research. I. Title. II. Series.
   P53.V36 1988   418'.007   87-3692

Set in 10/12 pt Linotron 202 Erhardt

Produced by Longman Singapore Publishers (Pte) Ltd.
Printed in Singapore

ISBN 0-582-55264-8

Contents

Acknowledgements

We are indebted to Newbury House Publishers for permission to reproduce an extract from page 168 of H Trueba *et al.* (eds.) *Culture and the Bilingual Classroom: studies in classroom ethnology*. Also to Professor Rita Dunn for permission to reproduce the diagram (p. 32) 'Diagnosing Learning Styles' from page 11 of *Theory into Practice*, Vol. XXIII No. 1; and to Frederick Erickson for permission to reproduce the diagram (p. 118) 'Social and Cognitive Model for making a point' from page 112 of 'Talking Down: some cultural sources of miscommunication in inter-racial interviews' published in A Wolfgang (ed.) *Research in non-verbal communication*, Academic Press, New York; also to Oxford University Press for the diagram (p. 231) from M P Breen and C N Candlin 'The Essentials of a Communicative Curriculum in Language Teaching' published in *Applied Linguistics*, Vol. 1 1980, page 90; and for the diagram (p. 218) 'The Transition from Controlled to Free Practice' from P Hubbard *et al. A training course for TEFL*, page 192. We are also grateful to TESOL Central Office for permission to reproduce the diagram (p. 220) from S Gaies 'Learner Feedback: A Taxonomy of Intake Control' published in J C Fisher, M A Clarke and J Schachter (eds.) *On TESOL '80*, page 95.

Preface

Leo van Lier identifies a set of premisses for his contribution to the *Applied Linguistics and Language Study* series. They begin with a declaration of our limited knowledge of the process of teaching and learning in second-language classrooms despite the major industry that such teaching represents globally. Accordingly, he argues, it is the responsibility of researchers into second-language acquisition and language teachers themselves, to augment this knowledge not only by collecting classroom data but also to interpret that data in the context of its occurrence, namely the second-language classroom itself. It is, however, in wishing to accept this responsibility that the problems in so doing first become clear, and through an understanding of them an awareness of perhaps why it is that the database is so restricted.

This book then exists to argue a case; it is not a state-of-the-art survey, as provided for example by Mitchell's admirable account (1985) in the abstracting journal *Language Teaching* (although it is noteworthy how she emphasizes the lack of a coherent research tradition and underlines the fragmentary state of the still largely descriptive one-off studies that characterize the field). Dr van Lier's concern is twofold: firstly, to define the problems I refer to above of the place of classroom research within second-language acquisition study and, more generally, within social science. Secondly, to offer teachers primarily, but also researchers, a well-documented guide for the conduct of such research in the contexts of classrooms. These two concerns are interwoven in the text; problems arise out of the descriptive methodologies and objects of focus he has identified through his own empirical research. Incidentally, since the data for analysis and the object of learning in such classrooms is language, the book also makes a contribution to the application of discourse analysis and pragmatics to an area of human discourse which is particularly suited to the ethnographic and qualitative approach to data which he advocates. The overall approach is, then, classically applied linguistic: it begins from local and quite practical problems of making a relationship between classroom behaviour and language learning, and through an exploration of what such problems imply requires the reader to confront major issues in research, both of its practical management and its intellectual bases. As such, the book joins others in the series in defining the nature of its discipline.

What then are the problems that the book identifies? Let me take each of Leo van Lier's chapters in turn, and identify what appear to me to be those key issues we must address.

In his Introduction appears a key contrast which surfaces throughout the book, that between 'understanding' the processes of teaching and learning, and striving for some causal or 'proof' relationship between patterns of behaviour. As Mitchell points out in her account, 'the relationship between instruction and the learner's classroom experiences on the one hand, and the L2 learning process on the other, remains largely obscure'; so it is for van Lier and it is the object of his book to show what research is needed to lessen this obscurity. The central procedure for him is that of interpretation in context, using micro-ethnography as a means and with greater understanding as a goal. Here of course, he is most closely allied to United States research by Erickson and Mehan, but also to British research of Stubbs and Delamont, Adelman and Walker and, in terms of more general curriculum theory and research, the work of Stenhouse whose concern for evaluating 'worthwhileness' of classroom activity makes the connection to macro-ethnography and social theory which van Lier also underlines. This contrast, then, directs the book towards the issue of judging the effectiveness of classroom instruction in language teaching, and for that to be attempted we need a greater clarity of what is meant by 'context' in such a study, and what the role is of 'interpretation' by the various participants of their place and activity in such a context.

The second-language classroom in context is, appropriately, the topic of Chapter 1, and Leo van Lier identifies at once the central problems: firstly, the procedural one of obtaining detailed case-study information which focuses on utterances in the context of their production, the importance of 'going into classrooms' I highlighted earlier in this Preface and listing their salient characteristics. Secondly, and as an immediate consequence, the problems surrounding inference and extrapolation from that data, especially when, as here, a stand is taken against too superficial a global scanning in the interest of obtaining what the author would, rightly in my view, regard as premature generalizations. In Chapter 1, therefore, the author takes the view that not only is understanding language learning his prime concern but that to do so he must engage in speculative research grounded in detailed micro-analysis.

In Chapter 2, on the aims of second-language classroom research, we see another contrast sharply and problematically opposed, this time within the procedures of classroom description themselves, namely the taking-down of participant accounts as an alternative to category-coding by the outside observer. This issue masks a more fundamental problem, however. Where does classroom research as a data-gathering and problem-posing activity stand in relation to theory? Like the author, readers may also find it curious that much theorizing in second-language acquisition studies ignores the second-language classroom as a relevant source of data and as a relevant place to apply its findings. Despite the current movement towards a coming together of classroom research studies and second-language acquisition research (noted, for example, in Dick Allwright's recent contribution to this series) Leo van Lier's point must be well-taken; second-language acquisition as a research field has separated itself from classroom research. No doubt there are historical as well as practical reasons for this separation, but it seems quite counter-productive given the interests both areas have in such relevant topics for both teaching and acquisition as: learner interlanguage, classroom inter-action, learner strategies, instructional evaluation, learner/teacher behaviour variation etc., all of which the author refers to as significant in the language classroom.

I referred at the outset to the methodological focus of this book as a counterpoint to its theoretical significance. In his third chapter the author returns to the issue of illuminative understanding raised in his Introduction and sets out clearly the central problem:

> ... how to identify, describe and relate, in intersubjective terms, actions and contributions of participants in the second-language classroom, in such a way that their significance for language learning can be understood ...

Answers to this problem must begin from an analysis of language learners' language, using such data as a means to explore what we might call the meaning-potential of second-language classrooms for an understanding not only of language-learning processes but also the effectiveness of instruction. In his focus on ethnography Leo van Lier offers the reader an account of relevant studies seen from the perspective of their methodologies, and in so doing underlines his point that understanding classroom language behaviour not only requires a particular set of linguistic descriptive tools drawn from discourse analysis but also an openness to the contribution that can be made by a variety of relevant disciplines. Classroom research is thus an interdisciplinary endeavour though without yet a comprehensive and clearcut boundary. As he makes clear, here in respect of methodology of research, there is no successful integration yet of ethnographic and experimental research in second-language acquisition.

Any analysis of classroom language learning must take account of the social facts of classrooms as particular social institutions in which the local contexts of particular participation must be connected to the broader social forces governing the school as a predominantly 'languaged' institution. As the author remarks, 'before the lesson the learners come from somewhere and after the lesson they go somewhere else', and as a consequence any approach to classroom behaviour, especially one that is ethnographic in character, must make such a link between the classroom as a social setting which is illustrative of, and contributes to, higher-order social forces. This is a common problem in discourse and pragmatic analysis, that of determining how, at what point, and to what extent such connections between traces in the described text and these social forces can be made. Although in this book van Lier cannot fully examine this important issue, his references to the work of Thompson and Giddens are salutary, especially since in second-language acquisition studies at least (though happily less so in, say, bilingual education research) such connections have been relatively unexamined. Perhaps of greatest importance for the teacher reader in the fourth chapter is his emphasis on linking the choice of relevant phenomena and the appropriate choice of research methodology to prior assumptions not only about language learning but also, as I have made clear, about the role and purpose of the classroom itself in such a process.

The three succeeding chapters constitute very much the descriptive core of the book, in that they identify three appropriate phenomena in the sense I indicate above. Interaction, participation and repair have been specifically chosen as vehicles to explore particular classroom issues, while at the same time, through their treatment, offering the reader worked-through examples, as it were, of a usable methodology. As elsewhere in the book, therefore, theory, problem and practice are carefully interwoven.

I have referred earlier to the central issue of the link to be made, albeit indirect, between the observable behaviour of learner and teacher language and the extent of learner language development. Chapter 5 makes the important case for combining quantitative and qualitative approaches to the study of interaction, looking not only on the distribution of turns themselves but also on the options for turn taking and the extent to which these were taken up by different participants. Actual performance, therefore, must be correlated with options and initiatives if it is to be meaningfully evaluated. One can immediately see how the linguistic tradition of discourse analysis must be associated with a social psychological one lest data that exist be misinterpreted and data which do not 'exist' in transcription be discounted. This emphasis on initiative not only offers additional modes of connecting interaction and intake, it also has clear implications for the distribution of rights and duties between teachers and learners, and among learners, in the classroom. It thus has pedagogical as well as acquisitional significance and provides a further example of the relevance of this book to programmes of teacher inservice education. From interaction, then, we pass logically to Chapter 6 and its emphasis on participation. Here the author not only clarifies various modes of teacher-learner relationship but also offers a usable classification of different activity types in which these participants engage. The introduction of activity-type not only makes a connection to the work of Levinson and Erickson but also compels the reader to evaluate the varying roles these participants play and the balance that is struck between teacher control and learner initiative. Once again the issue of the microcosm of the classroom and the macrocosm of social life is raised and debated, using the author's own data as helpful stimuli and local context.

Chapter 7 poses four key questions to the topic of repair and its organization, each of which highlights in its way the central issues of this book:

1. Who should repair and when, teacher and/or learner?
2. What constitute legitimate repairs?
3. How does repairing help the language development of learners?
4. How distinctive is second-language classroom repair?

The first, of course, emphasizes the issue of control and initiative we have just referred to in respect of the discussion of Chapter 6. It focuses on the classroom as a venue for the exercise of power and underlines the asymmetries of any instructional milieu. The second addresses both the issue of discoursal coherence as well as that of pragmatic appropriateness. In so doing, incidentally, it makes the case for a pragmatic and dynamic approach to the analysis of discourse, where the rule-governed succession of utterances is to be evaluated not only in terms of local exchanges but against the backdrop of the whole discourse of which the extract in question is but a part. Such a question, of course, also tangentially addresses the issue of power in that we may add as a rider, 'legitimate' to whom? The third question centrally addresses the essential connection between action and learning that Mitchell, as I indicated, rightly finds still obscure. Perhaps one way forward to clarifying this issue is to take up immediately the consequences of the fourth question and ask to what extent repairing is beneficial in other-than-classroom contexts to the clarification of positions and knowledge, minimal prerequisites one would have thought for that understanding upon which learning must be based. If, as Leo van Lier maintains, repairing is a characteristic classroom activity, it will surely be useful to examine what the features and functions of repairing are in such non-classroom environments. Obliquely from other contexts we may come to estimate the peculiar character of classroom language and also be more able to judge as a result what it can uniquely contribute to classroom purposes. Such a comparative study would provide illumination to current debates on the merits of instructional and non-instructional language learning and also assist teachers to organize their classroom activities in terms of their real-world communicative potential.

It is this link to pedagogy and classroom management which suggests the theme of 'Connections' as a title for the final chapter. Throughout, the book has been implicative for teaching behaviour, and by extension, for teacher education. In Chapter 8 Dr van Lier argues the case for teaching improvement being bound up with action research in the classroom, conducted by teachers as well as by sympathetic researchers. This is, in a way, the final problem of the book; how to develop participatory research involving teachers, learners as well as researchers, which is part and parcel of the practice of teaching. It is a current debate, and this important book shows not only how it may be accomplished but, much more significantly, what approach we need to take to the classroom as a social institution and, accordingly, what research methodologies we should prefer.

Christopher N. Candlin   *Lancaster*
General Editor   *December 1986*

Introduction

Of course, we all 'know' why the children and the teacher are there in the classroom. We know because we have learnt about schooling by taking part in the game. We have all learnt to play in the 'pupil' position. Many of the readers of this book will have played in the 'teacher' position too. For us this has become invisible knowledge, invisible because we take it for granted. It is hard to recover invisible knowledge and see it afresh: how would we perceive a classroom if we had never seen it before? All we can do is to play the anthropologist. We can pretend to look through ignorant eyes and ask questions about what Mrs. Jones says to her pupils, and why they respond as they do. But to frame the questions and answer them we must grope towards our invisible knowledge and bring it into sight. Only in this way can we see the classroom with an outsider's eye but an insider's knowledge, by seeing it as if it were the behaviour of people from an alien culture. Then by an act of imagination we can both understand better what happens and conceive of alternative possibilities.

(Barnes 1975, pp. 12–13)

Since the above lines were written there has been a slow but steady increase in classroom studies which aim to understand what goes on in classrooms and why, in the same way that anthropologists aim to understand unknown cultures. Most of these studies describe maths, reading and other lessons in classrooms where the language of instruction is the learners' native language, or in bilingual classrooms. Such studies describe how learners take turns to speak, how questions are asked and answered, how certain learners participate more or receive more attention than others, and so on. A common characteristic is that considerable attention is paid to the *social context* of that which is described, and this is one of the main differences between such research and the more common studies which use coding, tabulation, and experimentation, and often compare classroom behaviour with performance on tests.

The type of research Barnes refers to can be done in many different ways, and addresses many different questions. The terms *process-oriented*, *sociolinguistic*, or *ethnographic* are often used to describe it, but the labels cover a very heterogeneous range of research activities which do not easily fit into a single theoretical framework. To bring these various endeavours together under the common denominator of *classroom research* (CR) in practice means simply that the focus of the investigation is all or part of what happens in actual classrooms.

Research into second-language (L2) classrooms is to date, though there are a few exceptions, still very much conducted with the aim of finding cause-effect relationships between certain actions and their outcomes. This aim leads to a concern with strong correlations, levels of significance, definability and control of variables, and all the other requirements of scientific method. The price that is paid for scientific control is an inevitable neglect of the social context of the interaction between teachers and learners. Without this social context it is difficult to see how classroom interaction can be understood and what cause-effect relationships, if they can ever be conclusively established, really mean. At the risk of oversimplification, research can be divided into a type which wants to obtain *proof* and a type which wants to *understand*. So far, research into second-language classrooms overwhelmingly leans towards the former type of research, and this creates an inbalance because of the limitations inherent in it. In this book I propose a focus on the second type so that the balance can be redressed and, furthermore, I advocate that CR should be *open* rather than *closed*, that is, formulated and designed in such a way that it can be used to maintain a dialogue between the two types of research. Ideally, experimental and interpretive research should be convergent rather than parallel or divergent lines of enquiry.

In order to show the purpose of the book I will, rather than just summarize points which will be made at length in the text, quote some salient extracts from the literature, which provide reasons for approaching the study of L2 classrooms from an interpretive and contextual rather than an experimental and causal point of view.

1. On the importance of social context, Breen says the following:

> The classroom may be a relatively 'inefficient' environment for the methodical mastery of a language system, just as it is limited in providing opportunities for 'real world' communication in a new language. But the classroom has its own communicative potential and its own authentic metacommunicative purpose. It can be a particular social context for the intensification of the cultural experience of *learning*.
>
> (Breen 1985b, p. 154)

Classroom research must investigate if the assumption that the classroom is both inefficient and limited is warranted. As teachers (and learners) we may not wish to accept this at face value. We need to study the communicative potential and the metacommunicative purpose (the pedagogical purpose of language learning) of the classroom in order to establish to what extent they offset and counterbalance any inherent limitations. Breen, it appears, is thinking of a genuine second-language learning environment in which language development primarily occurs outside the classroom, but can be intensified and consolidated inside it. If this is so, we need to examine how language development can be promoted also in classrooms in foreign-language settings, where outside exposure to the target language may be minimal.

2. Sanday provides a strong argument for the use of ethnography in classroom research:

> The well written ethnography has the capacity of reaching an audience in a way no other scholarly product can possibly aspire to. Similarly, the sensitively conducted presentation to teachers of videotaped interaction has the capacity to change behavior in a way that a manual for proper conduct cannot. It is important that we keep this in mind as we continue to explore the ethnographic paradigm. It would be a mistake to sacrifice the art and the empathy that characterize the ethnographic endeavor on the altar of science. If ethnography becomes a brief-lived fad among educational researchers, it will be because the quantitative-experimental paradigm overruled the desire to uncover the content and texture of behavior. I do not believe ethnography will go out of style as long as anthropologists continue to explicate this approach.
>
> (Sanday 1982, p. 253)

Sanday makes an interesting suggestion for teacher training, which relates to Barnes's statement that teachers must create some distance from their classroom activities in order to look at them in a fresh light. Ethnographic analysis of classroom interaction can be used as part of teacher training, to create awareness of and sensitivity to teachers' and learners' actions, and by practising teachers to explore the effectiveness of their own lessons.

3. The relationship between cognitive and interactive work is of particular importance in ethnographic research, since the observable interaction must provide clues to the cognitive processes which determine language learning. The following two quotations illustrate this relationship:

> In considering how talk unites the cognitive and the social, we have seen that 'social' has two inter-related meanings: the microsociological meaning of the situation of which talk is a part, and the macro-sociological meaning of stratifications within society – by class, ethnicity, sex, etc. Research on classroom discourse that can contribute

to increased equity as well as increased quality needs to consider both
sets of variables.

(Cazden 1985, p. 458)

The younger the children the more likely it will be that much of their
activity will be accompanied by speech intended for no one else, i.e.
giving themselves instructions or supplying a running commentary which
is meaningful only in the context of the activity (. . .). Older pupils will
do much or all of this in their heads and (. . .) *the quality and complexity
of this speech will be highly dependent on the quality of their experience of
speech with others.* (emphasis added)

(Rosen 1969, pp. 128–9)

Cazden's distinction between micro- and macro-context interestingly
mirrors the two different directions classroom research appears to be
taking, with some researchers focusing primarily on the immediate
context of interaction (Erickson, *passim*; Long and Sato 1984), and
others recommending a wider social context which takes account of
social theory and institutional ideologies (Rampton 1987; see also
Fairclough 1985 for relevant theoretical arguments).

Cazden's suggested link between the cognitive and the social is
explicitly stated by Rosen who relates the quality of interaction with
the quality of 'inner speech', an issue of obvious relevance to L2
classroom research.

4. Ethnographic classroom research directly illustrates classroom
methodology, and is therefore of immediate relevance to classroom
teachers. This relevance is twofold: firstly, reports of ethnographic
research will give teachers insights into what happens in classrooms,
so that they can compare this with their own classrooms and,
secondly, it is research that can be conducted by teachers themselves
in classes which they are currently teaching. The following quotations
illustrate this:

. . . [T]he findings of classroom-centered research may be more directly
applicable to teachers' needs than other types of second language
research. Ultimately these findings will help teachers and researchers
alike to better understand the teaching and learning process, thereby
facilitating that process in all its complexities.

(Bailey 1985, p. 118)

There is a need for a description of the manner in which and the extent
to which communication is focussed on in different second language
classes in current general programs. For example, what types of
communication activities are used? What are student and teacher
reactions to these activities? To what extent are these activities
integrated with other aspects of the syllabus? It would be particularly

interesting to observe those (unstreamed) classes that are considered by program personnel (e.g. second language consultants and teachers) to be especially successful in the second language program to find out how skilled the learners are in communication with native speakers and how the syllabus and teaching methodology used in such a class differ from those used in less successful classes.

(Canale and Swain 1980, p. 37)

If this chapter has emphasized the importance of an 'informal' approach and reciprocal classroom roles for students and the teacher, this is not because these are the only ways to ensure successful learning but because ordinary conversation is in many ways the most natural type of discourse and because there has been so little of it in classrooms. The pendulum should not swing too far, however, for 'formal' language teaching based on planned discourse will continue to be of great importance for many language learners.

(Ellis 1984a, p. 216)

There are many unanswered questions about L2 classrooms, and the above quotes raise a number of them. We do not know how to identify a successful classroom even though we may have strong ideological and methodological opinions about what is good, better, bad or worse. We do not know if a classroom that tries to be as little a traditional classroom as possible is necessarily more effective than a more structured and regimented one. Judgements about classroom effectiveness and quality often reflect personal preferences and current fashions, as much as they do critical arguments and data-based findings. Issues concerning authenticity, naturalness and formality of classroom proceedings and classroom language remain as yet relatively unexplored, and the concepts themselves therefore largely undefined.

This book examines in depth the scientific principles underlying an ethnographic approach to L2 classroom research, and will therefore be of interest to researchers who wish to embark on such research or to compare different views of research methodology.

More centrally, however, the book is intended for teachers and trainee teachers who are interested in increasing their professional awareness through a better understanding of classroom interaction and an active involvement in classroom research. This is arguably the most important and productive way to achieve improvements in second-language development in classrooms.

This book would not have been possible without the generosity of all the teachers and learners who allowed me to observe and record their classes. I hope the work will benefit them and their peers. I wish to thank several colleagues for the help they have given me in different ways. In the first place, I am indebted to Chris Candlin whose advice and encouragement over the years have been invaluable. His detailed comments on the various drafts, his patience and insights have shaped this book to a very large extent.

Much of what I know about classroom research I owe to Dick Allwright, who first introduced me to the subject. I appreciate the discussions and conversations we have been able to have.

Other colleagues have commented on some of the issues discussed, or on some draft material, and in doing so have assisted in the clarification of a number of points. I am grateful to Craig Chaudron, Hywel Coleman, Steve Gaies, Claire Kramsch, Quique Lopez, Richard Rossner, Larry Selinker, John Smith and Aida Walqui for opportunities to discuss various relevant matters or for comments on earlier versions of parts of the book.

To Aida, Jantje and Marcus, thanks for helping me to keep a proper perspective on things.

Leo van Lier   *Salinas*
                                                                                 1986

1 The second-language classroom in context

Introduction

This book is about second-language (L2) classroom research (CR) and the topic itself suggests the two areas that are relevant: the *L2 classroom*, and *research*. The book presents an in-depth look at both aspects and treats them as two sides of the same coin. Chapters 2 to 4 examine the central issues of research: the *Why*, *How* and *What* questions, and Chapters 5 to 7 examine several aspects of L2 classroom work from different angles. The ways of study and the angles of vision are grounded in the preceding research-methodological chapters. This dual core of the book is flanked at both ends by chapters which provide context and connections – hence the titles of this chapter and Chapter 8.

I have avoided cluttering the book with too much procedural detail and have therefore included an appendix about observation and transcription techniques.[1]

Although relevant research by others is discussed where it is deemed appropriate, most of the content reflects my own research and thinking on the issues. Therefore, this book is not a state-of-the-art survey or a comprehensive treatment of the literature, but one attempt among several to come to grips with the successes and the problems the L2 classroom presents to learners and teachers.

Context and relevance

CR is research in a contextually defined setting, and in this respect it can be compared to research in courtrooms, doctors' consultation rooms, family dining rooms, and so on. All such research shares some basic features, one of which is that considerations of context and purposeful interaction are central.

This need to focus on the context of interaction creates specific problems for research. Many researchers are tempted to begin by asking the question: which aspects of the context are relevant? Often the answer given to this question is: those aspects that are common to all L2 classrooms. The reason for this interpretation of relevance is that it is felt that what is said about one classroom is of interest only to the extent that it can also be said about (at least) a number of other L2 classrooms as well. After all, it is argued, this is necessary for the formulation of testable hypotheses. This reasoning, however plausible, is not likely to benefit our understanding of what goes on in L2 classrooms in the long run. The classroom researcher must consider all aspects of context, and relevance, in the last analysis, must be defined as that which is relevant to the participants themselves. The particular is therefore as relevant as the general, *in the context of the interaction*.

CR as context-based analysis can therefore not have as its primary aim the immediate generalizability of findings.[2] The first concern must be to analyse the data *as they are*, rather than to compare them to other data to see how similar they are. If we are too concerned about the latter we will start sifting the data too soon, selecting similar bits and discarding dissimilar (or apparently dissimilar) ones, looking for concepts that can be readily identified, named and classified, and becoming pressured to define those concepts in clear, unambiguous but, unfortunately, superficial and misleading terms. Early generalizing can be detrimental to classroom research: it often prevents depth of analysis.

Hymes has said that 'educational research has tended to define problems in terms of variables common to all schools' (Hymes *et al.* 1981, p. 11). There has been almost unanimous pressure to choose topics for research that can be readily generalized to larger populations. Most of our effort has gone into showing how some feature in our sample compares with that same feature in the relevant population as a whole, and we have therefore focused on the common rather than the unique, the general rather than the particular. We have been encouraged – and in some cases allowed – to look only for those things that are generalizable; we are told that the unique and the particular are not generalizable, hence not relevant.

As Hymes points out, the situation is very different in anthropological research (and possibly in many other areas as well):

> If someone finds out something new about the Navajo, say, it is proper to publish it for just that reason. It counts as knowledge, and it counts as part of the scholar's bibliography. Greater understanding of the Navajo is a legitimate activity.
>
> (Hymes *et al.* 1981, p. 11)

We are all agreed that greater understanding of language learners is also a legitimate activity. The usual habitat of the language learner – when he is being a language learner – is the classroom. Of course, we can argue, as some do, that successful learners learn more on the street than in class, but if we take that argument to its conclusion, ESL classes are unnecessary and EFL classes useless; in that case the profession is untenable. Before accepting that we will want to make a concerted effort to show that classrooms are viable places for language learners to spend time in.

Experimental research and CR

There are two basic facts that most, if not all researchers will agree to: we know very little about what actually goes on in classrooms, and it is essential to find out. The question is *how* to do the finding out and, since it seems that experimental research coupled with statistical tests of significance have so far failed in making much progress, basically two options are open:

1. find better experimental methods and better statistical tests;
2. find alternative ways to study the classroom.

I believe that both options must be pursued vigorously since neither holds the exclusive key to progress. Some people naturally incline towards option 1, and have expertise and training to contribute to this option. Others incline towards option 2, and also have expertise and training to offer. For this two-pronged (or multi-pronged, more likely) approach to work, some conditions have to be agreed on:

1. There must be a dialogue between the different approaches, i.e. everyone must be concerned that others *understand* what was done, how and why. I am particularly concerned that there are many research reports that summarily report complex statistical manipulations (multiple regression, factor analysis, analysis of variance, cross correlation, etc.) without showing why these techniques were chosen and what they are supposed to tell us. Similarly, on the other side of the fence, ethnomethodological and anthropological terminology is displayed without much respect for the interested audience. We all need and use help from outside experts during our research, and we should pass that help on to our colleagues.
2. The sequence and process of researching should be reported, including false moves, blind alleys, problems encountered along

the way and how they were dealt with. Let us admit that, as a profession doing part-time research, we are in search of the right ways of going about it, and have much to offer to others about what we have learnt from our mistakes as well as our successes.

3. There must be respect for the others' ways and views. The prevalent view in L2 research that humanistic or speculative approaches are useful only to the extent that they may prepare for experimental work is fundamentally misguided. Understanding may be arrived at in many different ways, and understanding is a necessary companion of theory formation. The dichotomy between normative and interpretive approaches has existed for many centuries and is unlikely to be resolved by L2 researchers. Its continued existence indicates that both approaches are necessary and complementary and that they, particularly in our field, deserve equal attention and status.

4. In consequence, journals must pay balanced attention to different approaches to research and promote an *openness* that allows teachers and researchers to assess the relevance of diverse approaches to study. The recommendations made here may imply that papers will be longer than many of them are now. However, editors should note that the reading public will prefer to read two longer papers which are well-explained, well-documented and hence instructive and comprehensible, rather than four shorter papers which have been condensed into some summary bare-bones format due to the dictates of editorial policy.

The data base

The central data base for this book is a small core of lessons recorded in Great Britain and the USA, added to sporadically from different sources. Essentially, when classroom research is conducted *in* the classroom rather than *about* the classroom, the set of data must be kept small. One lesson may yield as much useful information as ten lessons, and probably a good deal more than fifty lessons, except if we have unlimited time at our disposal. Small amounts of data can provide powerful analyses, as is shown for example by Harvey Sacks' classic paper 'On the analyzability of stories by children', which uses as data just two sentences:

The baby cried
The mommy picked it up

(Sacks 1972)

On the basis of this 'story' Sacks builds a detailed and exhaustive analysis of everyday story telling.

Behind the data set, however small, the researcher brings to the task whatever insights and experience may have accumulated over the years, and this is of crucial importance. This knowledge constitutes the *base line*,[3] a sense of common ground between observer and setting, which underlies efficient descriptive and analytic work. Most of us have, as teachers and as learners, considerable experience of classroom life, and this gives us a participant's perspective which is useful. In addition, however, a detached stance is needed at the time of observation and analysis since as learners, but especially as teachers, we are often too involved in the process to do much memorizable noticing apart from the usual anecdotes. This, as we shall see, is in fact one of the main reasons for teachers to engage in their own classroom research.

The diversity of second-language classrooms: context in research

One of the problems with L2 classroom research is that there is such a tremendous variety of L2 classrooms. The profession has a range of abbreviations at its disposal to refer to some of the diversity, such as EFL, ESL, ESP, EAP, and so on (for a listing of current abbreviations, see Rossner's editorial comment in *ELT Journal* **40**(1), pp. 1–2), but this does not begin to capture adequately the range of differences. To my knowledge no serious attempt has been made to organize all the variables that make classes different into one single scheme, and of course such an undertaking, if it were possible at all, might not be considered by everybody to be worth the effort. However, one important benefit would be to draw attention to the varied contexts of language learning.

An area where much work has been done in classifying variables, including contextual ones, is bilingual education. A classic example is Mackey's typology of bilingual education, yielding 90 different types (Mackey 1970).

Bilingual education research is a good example of the necessity to take contextual information into consideration. In both practical and theoretical terms, bilingual education is a highly heterogeneous enterprise, and it is notorious that methods which work well in one situation may fail dismally in another. As an example, the reader may study the debate about the applicability of the Canadian immersion model in the United States (see, e.g. McLaughlin 1985). Factors that are central in this debate are differences in socio-economic status of children, home support of L2 immersion, relative status of the two languages, and others. Another, rather worrisome, feature is the apparent ease with which one single phenomenon or popular assumption can be used to argue both for and against a particular educational model. For example, it is a common assumption that if the language at home is different from the language at school, academic retardation will result (the 'linguistic mismatch' assumption). This assumption is used by proponents of bilingual education to demand instruction in the home language, and by opponents to pressure for the use of the school language at home. In actual fact, as Cummins shows (1984, p. 109), research indicates overwhelmingly that this assumption is false.

Both bilingual education and second-language acquisition are surrounded by popular opinions, folk wisdom, and lay theorizing, as much as by serious research. In settings where societal and political pressures enter into the picture, public opinion and official policy may be swayed predominantly by such folk wisdom, and not by appropriate research. Indeed, given that research itself is often put in the service of particular ideological tendencies, e.g. through a process of selection of variables, methods and evidence, it becomes a tool for ideological factions. This is inevitable in an emerging, immature field of science, where there is no strong tradition of research, although it also happens in long-established sciences when the demand for action outstrips accumulated understanding.

The diversity of contexts of language development is part and parcel of research into bilingualism and first-language acquisition and it is one of the reasons why progress in these areas is painfully slow. On the other hand, L2 acquisition research still largely operates on an unstated assumption that L2 development is a uniform process, with the result that hypotheses and models are proposed which are supposed to be universally valid. Thus the morpheme acquisition studies lead to proposals of a natural order of acquisition, and a distinction between conscious learning and unconscious acquisition results in across-the-board recommendations to forget about structured syllabuses and concentrate on comprehensible input. As Ellis points out: 'The danger of over-generalization in a field which has, perhaps, been overready to insist on the universal properties of language acquisition is apparent' (1984b, p. 284).

The search for universal tendencies is valuable and necessary. However, it must be supported and accompanied by a search for and awareness of diversity. Indeed, universals can only be identified when the diversity is understood, as general linguistics clearly tells us.

Language development, both first and second, goes on all over the world in several thousand different languages, in numerous different settings, in people of all ages, in classrooms, homes, factories, streets and fields. Even if we limit the field of enquiry to one single facet, English-as-a-second-language development in classrooms, the potential for variation is enormous. It includes groups of Arab graduate engineering students in a university in Texas, French tourists on the south coast of Britain, children in a Peruvian kindergarten, Vietnamese refugees, Turkish migrant workers, Chinese secondary school children, Japanese diplomats, and so on.

So far we have assumed that, however varied their background, all learners in the classroom are engaged in the learning of the same second language. However, we increasingly find classrooms in which only a few, or maybe just one, of the learners speak a native language which is different from the language of instruction. For these learners every classroom is an L2 classroom, and unless they are left to sink or swim, every teacher in such a classroom is at least a part-time L2 teacher. The presence of minority children in majority classrooms is becoming the rule rather than the exception in the United States, and I expect that it will become increasingly common in other countries as well. This situation creates complex problems, and L2 research must share a responsibility within the educational community to help find the imaginative solutions that are needed.

In all the different L2 classrooms things go on that may appear similar or very different, and I assume that the same can be said for what goes on inside the learners in terms of development. As yet we know too little about all the variables that play a role in all the classrooms to be able to make rash recommendations about methods of teaching and ways of learning. An encouraging sign is that recently several researchers have begun demanding increased attention to the *context* of L2 development. So far this is largely limited to programmatic statements (Breen 1985b; Long and Sato 1984), though attention to context is increasingly evident in theoretical models which take social factors into account, such as the *acculturation model* of Andersen, Huebner, Schumann, the *social-psychological* focus of Giles, Lambert, Gardner and Beebe, and the *variable-competence model* of Ellis (see further Chapter 4). Of course, what is meant by context can vary greatly. I shall come back to this in subsequent chapters, but basically one can take a *micro* or a *macro* view (or both, of course). Long and Sato (1984, p. 274) take a micro view: 'the context second-language speakers create for themselves and the context created for them by their interlocutors'. The macro view would be inclined to look at home-school relations, L1-L2 relative status, learners' attitudes and reference groups, and so on. The former might be described as discoursal or interactive context (or context-in-performance), the latter as socio-cultural context. A slightly elaborated – though by no means complete – listing of contextual factors is provided in Box 1.1

BOX 1.1   Aspects of context

setting	– availability of L2 outside class (exposure)
	– status of L2 relative to L1
	– functions of L2 in community
	– societal/institutional expectations
content	– test/exam-oriented
	– discrete-item/form-oriented
	– interaction-based
	– task-based
	– subject-based
interaction	– teacher-learner recitation
	– conversation
	– group activities
participants	– age
	– sex
	– size of group
	– peer relations
	– attitudes/expectations
	– prior schooling
	– socio-economic status
	– preferred learning styles
method	– teacher/learner roles
	– learner autonomy
	– type of syllabus
	– criteria for quality and success

An examination of contextual features such as those mentioned in Box 1.1 can give us much necessary information about the L2 classroom and the people in it. At some point all these different factors must be taken into account, for all are relevant, many are related, and as yet we know little about their potential contribution to L2 language development. In the classroom they all come together and produce that undefinable quality, the _dynamics_ of classroom work. It is clear that, unless we are to oversimplify dangerously what goes on in classrooms, we must look at it from different angles, describe accurately and painstakingly, relate without generalizing too soon, and above all not lose track of the global view, the multifaceted nature of classroom work. A theory of L2 classroom development, one that allows us to address the questions, e.g. Does it make a difference? How effective is it? How can we improve it? will not develop overnight. Along the road we must answer the questions: What kind of world is the class-room? What is its place in society? How does it turn out the way that it does? How differently can it turn out in different circumstances?

Going into the classroom: research in context

In L2 classroom research (CR) the central data derive from things that go on in the classroom. This seems self-evident, yet much research goes by the name of CR which gets its data from other sources, such as simulated conversations, tests, interviews and so on, data which do not actually tell us anything about classroom dynamics, though they may tell us much about learners, learning and teachers (van Lier 1985). It thus seems necessary to restrict the scope of operations. I would suggest that CR requires that the researcher spends most of the time during the data-gathering phase(s) of the project inside actual, regular, ongoing classrooms that have not been specially set up for the purpose of research. We may modify to some extent in admitting as valid data-gathering time also viewings and hearings of tapes recorded in such classrooms.

Classroom data may have much in common with other kinds of data, but they also have their own set of unique characteristics. These will influence research both in terms of what is investigated and how the investigating is done. Some salient characteristics are listed below.

1. In a classroom, actions occur in a context. What is said and done is influenced by what happened before, and influences what happens next. This can be described in purely interactive terms by saying, for example, that an elicitation (e.g. a question, or a prompt) calls forth a response, the response in turn calls forth an evaluation, and so on. At a deeper level, however, we can also say that every action illustrates both interpretation (of what went before) and intention (to comply, to influence future actions, and many other things, most of them hard to get at). This already gives us two layers of analysis, but there is much more.
2. Some instances of classroom interaction occur because they have been planned to occur that way, others because circumstances at the moment demand action or reaction. Often the teacher's actions

are a result of prior planning, and the learners may be aware or unaware of the nature of the plan. Planned discourse can be very different from unplanned discourse, and discourse that is planned by one but not the other participant(s) results in asymmetry.

3. When things are done along similar lines a number of times, they turn into routines in which all participants know what is likely to happen next. This leads to activities which are similar to rituals in which everyone knows what to do next, and the only surprise is when unexpected things happen.

4. Given appropriate models, briefs, scripts or instructions, learners can produce impressively complex linguistic strings which in ordinary L2 interaction they are quite incapable of, either before or after the performance in class. So, after being drilled extensively in answers such as 'I've already . . .(past participle). . . it/them', the learner, that same evening, may happily and effectively reply to a room-mate's complaint: 'It's your turn to wash the dishes' with: 'I wash already, see?' In-class performance can therefore not always be equated with actual competence.

5. The teacher who emphasizes cognitive language learning may aim to make learners do a lot of thinking by asking tough questions in the hope that language use accompanied by cognitive work will result in more language development. Yet often tough questions can be answered in few words and, conversely, simple questions may beget long answers. Amount of cognitive work is therefore not directly measurable in terms of amount of language production, and here a possible conflict arises for the teacher. Do I want them to think a lot or to talk a lot? Preferably both, but how?

The list can be added to, but the examples should be sufficient to make it clear that the researcher cannot take isolated utterances, categorize them, add them up and compare them in a straightforward manner. Minimally, they have to be studied in the context of their production. How wide that context should be is a major issue of debate. Classroom researchers doing on-the-spot coding with check-lists can usually not go beyond the immediately preceding and following utterances. This may be totally inadequate as Walker and Adelman's anecdote in Box 1.2 illustrates.

Context may be regarded as extending, like ripples on a pond, in concentric circles from any particular action or utterance. At some point we will have to draw a line and say: this is as far as we shall look. What we are doing when we examine an utterance in context is basically of course *explaining* the occurrence of that utterance at the same time as *describing*. We therefore engage in explanation, and

BOX 1.2 **Strawberries**

One lesson the teacher was listening to the boys read through short essays that they had written for homework on the subject of 'Prisons'. After one boy, Wilson, had finished reading out his rather obviously skimped piece of work the teacher sighed and said, rather crossly:
T: Wilson, we'll have to put you away if you don't change your ways, and do your homework. Is that all you've done?
Pupil: Strawberries, strawberries. (Laughter)

How would a classroom coder deal with such an apparently meaningless response? When Adelman and Walker later on asked what 'strawberries' meant it turned out that the teacher often criticized pupils' work for being like strawberries: 'good as far as it goes, but it doesn't last nearly long enough'.

(Walker and Adelman 1976)

in that sense a distinction between descriptive and explanatory research is simplistic: it is not possible to do one without the other.[5] As soon as we begin to look at context, we decide to select, and we select on the basis of decisions of *relevance*. Relevance is decided on the basis of an emerging framework, however fragile and tentative. My crucial point is that, once we decide that context is essential in the examination of interactional data, we engage, of necessity, in explanatory work. And we describe to explain, and explain to understand. These mental activities are of course part and parcel of ordinary, everyday scrutiny of people's actions and talk, and all people, not only researchers, engage in them. The essential methodology therefore includes 'common sense' as one of the tools-of-trade.

In L2 research, as in other areas of educational or social science research, it is predominantly assumed that explanation must ultimately come from proof of cause-effect relationships, and that the only way to obtain such proof – or at least levels of probability and prediction – is through the administration of statistical tests to suitably circumscribed samples following controlled treatment. It is perhaps worth pointing out that this elaborate procedure is developed for no other reason than that it is notoriously difficult to obtain proof and to control, administer and observe treatment in educational settings. Biologists and physicists, the role models for the hard-nosed scientific side of our profession, do not need statistics nearly as much as we do. The statistical apparatus, and its quasi-experimental source, is a remedial programme for a borrowed scientific procedure, and is fraught with problems. Many of these problems are illustrated in the work of one of the pioneers of quasi-experimental research, Donald Campbell (an excellent recent survey is Brewer and Collins 1981; for a detailed critique see Cronbach 1982). I do not wish to disparage quasi-experimental research or the use of statistical measures, but it is necessary to point out that it is one tool among several for obtaining knowledge and understanding. The problems that confront education, including language education, demand a variety of approaches and a dialogue between them. With the important caveat that quasi-experimental methodology and quantitative research are not identical, I find myself in substantial agreement with Ellis:

> Quantitative research often screens important variability or misses significant interactional processes. But there is no need to oppose qualitative and quantitative research. Each is capable of 'critical thinking' and each has its place in IL (interlanguage) studies. The danger is in imagining that enquiry that does not involve quantification is not scientific or in failing to acknowledge the contribution that can be made by 'hybrid' research (i.e. research that employs both qualitative and quantitative procedures).
>
> (Ellis 1984b, p. 284)

As I shall argue throughout this book, the issue is not between quantitative and qualitative methods (or rather, tools), but rather an open-mindedness about different ways for arriving at understanding, without assumptions of differential scientific value. Such open-mindedness can lead to a fruitful combination of research methods to address particular problems and questions.

The place of CR in second-language research

The need for research into classrooms is by now an acknowledged fact in the L2 profession. The number of papers in the area is increasing steadily and it features prominently in many conferences. As the popularity of CR increases it becomes necessary periodically to assess, and reassess, its contributions, its methods and its relationships to other aspects of L2 research.

At the broadest level of *orientation* one may label research as linguistic (e.g. morpheme studies, error analysis), psycholinguistic (research into interpretive strategies, cognitive processes, learning styles, etc.), sociolinguistic (interactional analysis, ethnography of communication), sociological (e.g. home-community relations), or pedagogical (evaluation of teaching methods, teacher training, etc.).

Any and all of the orientations mentioned may use a variety of *methodological* approaches and *tools*, ranging from controlled experimentation to diary writing, and from complex statistical batteries to anecdotal description, so that one specific orientation cannot be linked to any particular research methodology or set of tools. However, there may be preferences or intrinsically more appropriate procedures for certain approaches, e.g. psycholinguistic research into cognitive processes may tend to employ introspection or retrospection (verbal protocols), and research into communication strategies often uses transcribed dyadic conversations between learners as data.

Many researchers advocate the use of *triangulation*, that is, the inspection of different kinds of data, different methods, and a variety of research tools (see Box 1.3). All this means that research cannot be easily classified and pigeon-holed, since it is often eclectic. CR is itself a hybrid activity, and may fit on different occasions into any of the orientations mentioned. Its defining characteristic, as I have suggested, is that it focuses on the classroom as a source of data. In terms of method it can be argued that it cannot be restricted to a specific set of procedures, though perhaps some are more appropriate than others, given the setting.

BOX 1.3   Triangulation

In addition to the use of multiple methods, there are at least three other varieties of triangulation. *Theoretical triangulation* involves the use of several different perspectives in the analysis of the same set of data. *Data triangulation* attempts to gather observations with multiple sampling strategies. Observations on time, social situations, and persons in various forms of interaction can all be gathered. The use of data triangulation insures that a theory is tested in more than one way, increasing the likelihood that negative cases will be uncovered. *Investigator triangulation* is the use of more than one observer in the field situation. The advantages of multiple observers are obvious: tests on the reliability of observations can be quickly made, and observer bias can thus be judged. *Methodological triangulation* can take two forms. The first is *within-method* and the second is *between-method*. The former is seen when an investigator employs varieties of the same method; for example, three different scales measuring other-directedness. Between-method triangulation is stressed by Zelditch.

   The combination of multiple methods, data types, observers and theories in the same investigation is termed multiple triangulation. While it may be difficult for any single investigation to achieve this full combination, it is certainly possible to utilize multiple data levels and methods.

   These remarks suggest a standard for evaluating studies: the greater the triangulation, the greater the confidence in the observed findings. The obverse is equally true. The conclusion is evident: Sociologists must move beyond single-method, atheoretical studies.

(Denzin 1970, p. 472)

In this book I advocate *ethnography* as a method, and an *understanding* of what goes on in classrooms as a goal. I do this since I believe it is essential for the classroom researcher to *respect* the classroom as a setting. If we go in with the specific purpose of finding 'good' or 'bad' aspects of teaching, learning or interaction, or of locating specific examples of behaviours prespecified as being of interest, we are in danger of losing that respect, which is in effect essential to ethnographic work as a method in anthropology.

What characterizes CR is therefore a focus on a particular setting which is crucial to the profession: the classroom, and a commitment to respect the integrity of that setting. We can expect of the classroom researcher, in terms of skills and knowledge minimally the following:

a) skill in techniques and strategies of observation and recording;
b) expertise in the transcription of complex, multi-party interaction;
c) attention to holistic as well as particularistic aspects of classroom interaction;
d) a good ability to develop a base line (see p. 5), grounded in depth and width of experience.

There are other research characteristics which are currently hotly debated, such as a distinction between theoretical and applied, or quantitative and qualitative research. I suggest that these distinctions are, from the classroom researcher's perspective, of secondary importance. Some research is done in order to solve specific problems and is therefore applied, but it may contribute to the common stock of understanding and theory formation just as much as research for the sake of research. All research may or may not employ quantification as a tool, and the value of this can only be determined by inspection of results. There is nothing intrinsically superior to quantification, speculation or description, as I have already pointed out.

What then is the place of CR in second-language research? It is not a separate orientation, nor can it be pinned down to any particular research method. As I see it, it is a commitment to go into the classroom and find out what goes on in it. It is probably the most difficult place to do research in, as witnessed by its long history of neglect and its status as a 'black box' between input and output measures (Long 1983a). Researchers have tended to avoid it as a particularly 'messy' source of data, and walked around it in the hope that, eventually, its walls would come tumbling down. My aim is to show that viable research can be done inside the classroom, and that this can be of crucial benefit to the profession, i.e. that it can fit in with other research and add to cumulative understanding. Ideally it will be a catalyst for other aspects of L2 research because, ultimately, any findings will have to be made relevant to the possibilities and limitations of the classroom. I therefore see a central role for classroom research in the future, not least in terms of the applicability of research findings that come from other data sources.

In addition, CR is central in another sense. The ever-present danger of a widening gap (of trust, relevance, understanding) between research and practice can only be avoided if the concerns of learners and teachers are kept on centre-stage. This can be done through classroom research, especially if teachers (and learners) themselves take an active part in it and thus use research as a central aspect of teaching praxis. There are many additional benefits in this, but at the very least it can assure that a dialogue between actors, directors and critics is maintained.

CR and second-language development

The success of a course of language studies in a classroom is judged in terms of the *product*, that is, the learners' terminal proficiency. To do this a number of tests and examinations are available which measure that proficiency, or aspects thereof, and allow it to be compared to a norm or to the population of language learners at large. The classroom itself can also be evaluated in this way: if its learners score higher or lower than some comparable norm, it may be said to have been respectively more or less successful. However, this cannot be taken as a direct measure of classroom success, since other variables may have played a decisive role as well, such as individual effort and aptitude of learners, social and cultural factors, exposure unrelated to the classroom, some element of 'group chemistry', and so on.

The examinations themselves can never inform us of the role that classroom work played in the scores obtained. Further, even if we can identify the classroom as a major factor of success, the examination will not tell us *how* the success was obtained. It will therefore not tell us how we might eventually be able to discriminate between 'good' and 'bad' classrooms: for that information we will have to go to the classroom itself.

In the classroom interaction occurs: interaction between teacher, learners and materials (or content matter of any kind). This is the essential element of the classroom. A group of people in a room not interacting at all for the entire scheduled period of time would hardly be called a classroom; we would probably refer to it as a self-study session. Somehow, from the researcher's point of view, classroom success must be studied on the basis of the public and observable interaction that takes place in it. This is difficult, since as Faerch and Kasper (1980) point out, the processes of interlanguage formation occur in the learners' heads, and we cannot observe them directly. It requires the making of inferences, and the assumption that observable interaction provides useful clues about mental processes that go on concurrently. This is of course a tenuous connection, but one which is not necessarily unwarranted, given our knowledge of language use in social contexts.

Classroom research is thus a sensitive enterprise: it must always be on guard against high-risk inferences and against the temptation to extrapolate from chance occurrences. For this reason I advocate an ethnographic approach to the issue, since it explicitly aims to provide safeguards against misinterpretation. As I shall show later on (see Chapter 3), ethnography is based on the principles of *holistic* and *emic*[6] enquiry. Both these principles require constant attention to the context of actions and to the viewpoints of the participants themselves, as a group and as individuals. These requirements are difficult to implement, and much of the discussion in the following chapters therefore focuses on context and interpretation.

The ethnographer is always on the lookout for patterns and regularities, and, beyond that, for underlying patterns that connect. This means that both in-depth study and global scanning are needed; metaphorically speaking the ethnographer needs both microscope and telescope, and uses them alternately to view the same landscape. The classroom researcher inspects a here-and-now process. However, the ultimate aim is to show cumulative language development, and this means that classroom research must eventually become longitudinal. The microscopic, here-and-now analysis and description is essential to provide depth and substance to longitudinal work which would otherwise skate over the surface.

As teachers, learners, teacher trainers and researchers, we assume that language development can and does occur in classrooms. At present, however, this is little more than an assumption, and it is necessary to gather hard evidence to substantiate it. In this book I hope to show that this evidence can be found in the classroom itself, and particularly that teachers themselves can play a decisive role in the investigation which, after all, is crucial to the profession. In the process we will find, of course, some indications for areas of improvement of classroom interaction. By focusing on our own territory we, as teachers, can ensure that it commands the respect it deserves.

Notes

1. Transcription is central to ethnographic research. However, many other tools are available to the classroom ethnographer, such as interviewing and scaling techniques, observation checklists, statistical measurement, etc. An excellent and very readable introduction is Cohen and Manion 1985.
2. I am not suggesting here that generalizing is not important in theory formation. However, it must be well-founded, and thus cannot be a central aim in the initial stages of research. Furthermore, we must distinguish between *conceptual* generalization (of constructs and phenomena) and generalization *from sample to population*. The concern is that the latter is often attempted without being firmly rooted in the former.
3. The term *base line* is used here in its anthropological sense. It is a problematic notion interpreted in different ways, but what is essentially meant here is a touchstone of sorts which guides the ethnographer's observation and interpretation, a system of information and beliefs to which specific things the researcher sees and finds are *compared* and, indeed, which *selects* that which is seen. To give an example of its importance, if the ethnographer's baseline is only derived from native-culture values and experiences, an *ethnocentric* interpretation will result.
4. Chapter 4 will provide brief descriptions and selected references. However for excellent surveys of SLA theories see Ellis 1985; Larsen-Freeman and Long forthcoming.
5. I am not suggesting that description and interpretation are identical activities, but rather that, at least in context-based research, they cannot be kept entirely separate.
6. As Hymes points out, 'Pike's conceptual distinction, *emic:etic*, has become a standard, if much debated, part of general anthropology' (1969, p. 361). One of the clearest statements of the original intended meaning of the terms is made by Brend:

   > The emic and etic standpoints are alternate ways of viewing the same reality. The etic standpoint is a view from outside, either random in its selectivity or with a set of presuppositions that have only a chance relationship to the scene being described. The emic standpoint is a view from within that notices just those features of the scene that are marked as significant by internal criteria (1974, p. 3).

   In practice, of course, emic and etic considerations tend to mix (as they do in phon*etic* and phon*emic* studies of sounds), and this mix is determined by the researcher's base line, as described in note 3.

2 The aims of second-language classroom research

Introduction

The next three chapters will address the *Why*, *How* and *What* questions of L2 classroom research respectively. In this chapter I shall examine the reasons for doing CR in the wider context of second-language acquisition research.

As suggested in Chapter 1, CR derives its primary data from the interaction in the classroom. These data, consisting mostly of verbal and non-verbal behaviours, can be treated in a variety of ways. In the past they have been examined in linguistic terms, e.g. for the number and variety of errors manifested, the number of complete or error-free T-units produced, the occurrence of certain grammatical morphemes, and so on. They have also been studied in social terms, to assess the climate of the classroom, the relations between teacher and learners, social networks between groups of learners, etc. Other focuses of interest have been cognitive demands on learners, aspects of discipline and management, experimental applications of certain methodologies, and much else. Broadly speaking, efforts to characterize classroom work have fallen into two categories: anecdotal description based on field notes, and coding based on predetermined checklists of categories. Box 2.1 illustrates typical examples of each. Both types of classroom analysis have come under heavy attack: the first because of its potentially selective and subjective, possibly even fictional treatment of goings-on, the second for its mechanical tabulation of superficially identifiable features, leading to mostly trivial findings. A third type of approach, input-output studies, has circumvented the classroom by focusing only on what learners knew before versus what they knew afterwards, by means of pre- and post-tests. This can therefore not be called CR in any real sense of the term.

Criticisms of all three approaches are no doubt well-founded and must be taken seriously since each one, in isolation, cannot provide an adequate description, let alone understanding, of what goes on

BOX 2.1

a) Extract from Boggs:

Debra has her hand poised at the board. She is figuring in her head, and her hand makes quick, intense gestures. Mr Miller stares at her intently. You can feel the tension.

Mr Miller, irritated: 'Wait a minute. Wait a minute.' His voice softens, as if he has caught his irritation. 'That's okay, Debra.' He adds brusquely, 'Sit down.' He erases everything at the board and rewrites the same problem. 'We must find the common denominator. What is it, Debra?'

'Twelve' explodes as a conclusion to the intense fear and constraint. It is a tone and a loudness I had not heard before in the room.

He requires Debra to go beyond the limits of Cherokee propriety, to forget the rest of the people in the room. To disassociate one's self from those present without cause is unthinkable and unpardonable, but it is what the teacher requires and he does it with ease.

(Boggs 1972, p. 354)

b) Flanders' 10-category schedule

Teacher Talk	1	Accepts feelings
	2	Praises or encourages
	3	Accepts or uses ideas of pupils
	4	Asks questions
	5	Lectures
	6	Gives directions
	7	Criticizes or justifies authority
Pupil Talk	8	Pupil response
	9	Pupil initiation
	10	Silence or confusion

Procedure: Note one of the 10 behaviours every three seconds during a lesson. At the end, add up all the occurrences of each category, and compare.

(Flanders 1970)

in some specific classroom or set of classrooms. However, this does not mean that as *methods*, used in combination, they cannot be very useful or even essential. Chapter 3 will look in some detail at different ways of getting information from classrooms, but the first question that needs to be asked is *why* we need information from the classroom directly. Once the purpose of research is made explicit it will be easier to assess which methods may lead to the desired results, and which research tools are appropriate for carrying out the research.

The purpose of the second-language classroom

Language development, first and second, goes on both inside the classroom (as part of a formal establishment, school or institute) and outside it. The classroom is generally considered a formal setting, and in consequence most other environments are informal in terms of learning. In environments where informal language development plays a significant part, it is possible to regard the formal classroom as supplemental, complementary, facilitating and consolidating. So far as second-language development in such environments is concerned, the informal settings can be regarded as primary, the formal classroom as ancillary. The L2 lesson then becomes a language arts lesson, focusing on special language skills and cognitive/academic growth, much in the same way as the L1 lesson, refining and building upon development already achieved in the informal settings. L2 development, in this view, is thus not necessarily uniquely a classroom responsibility.

Second-language acquisition research to date, however, cannot indicate the circumstances in which we can rely on the informal settings to provide (sufficient) opportunity and/or stimulus for successful L2 development. For the overwhelming majority of L2 classrooms, therefore, it will be essential to assume and to demonstrate that L2 language development can and does occur in the classroom for, if it does not, the language lesson will be limited to learning *about* language, not learning the language itself.

Some argue that, given the nature of the L2 classroom as a formal setting, it is not an environment conducive to language development (in its strongest form this view would hold that language development in the classroom is impossible). Others maintain that, if the classroom provides (i.e. mirrors) the conditions that make language development possible in the outside world, it can be successful. Both views imply that the L2 classroom, in order to allow for L2 development, must be as 'unclassroom-like' as possible. Whether right or wrong, this is a basic issue in second-language acquisition research, by no means resolved as yet, and indeed a key issue that CR must address as a long-term goal. When we study and practise CR the role and purpose of the L2 classroom in terms of L2 development will inevitably be foremost in our minds.

A note on theory

The well-known ethologist Lorenz, in his 'A Scientist's Credo' (Lorenz 1971) says that there are two main reasons for engaging in research: wanting to know, and wanting to help. This distinction is similar to the more superficial one between basic and applied research, which periodically causes heated debates and acrimonious exchanges between 'pure' researchers and shop-floor problem-solvers. It relates to the role of scientific theory in a certain area of human endeavour. A basic question that can be asked of a theory is: Is it more important that it be well-constructed and internally solid, or that it enables certain problems to be tackled in an efficient way? In down-to-earth terms, a teacher may ask: What is a theory good for, anyway?

Let us assume that we do not have a theory of classroom L2 development, and that we are seriously concerned to improve teaching and learning in classrooms. We can further assume that we do not actually know exactly what goes on in L2 classrooms, from moment to moment, and that we therefore have no solid basis for arguing which moments are better and which are worse. This means we have a problem, since we cannot suggest how improvements may be made. We may have ideas and hunches that suggest that, e.g. lists of explicit rules, are highly beneficial, or that carefully sequenced substitution drills are the answer, but we find that other people have other ideas and hunches, and who is to say that ours are better than theirs?

Ideas, hunches and assumptions are useful (they are the stuff that most theories start with), but they are insufficient. At this point we need a theory: something that puts our ideas and intuitions on a solid footing so that we can provide strong arguments in our favour. A theory is a reliable and coherent account of *what is*, as well as a valid *blueprint for further action*.

This dual description of what a theory is embodies the two basic purposes that theory can serve:
a) theory as *tool*, that is, as an aid in directing empirical investigation; this may be called the *heuristic* role of theory;
b) theory as *goal*, that is, the interpretation and ordering of empirical laws; an economical and efficient way of abstracting, codifying, summarizing and storing information.

Both purposes are of necessity complementary. As far as CR is concerned, the role of theory can be considered from two angles, firstly the initial role of theory in guiding the conduct of research, secondly the part that CR may play in the development of second-language acquisition theories. It is this second role which needs to be considered when we examine the reasons for doing CR.

CR can be undertaken for either or both of Lorenz's reasons for doing research: wanting to know, and wanting to help. CR can thus be seen as a knowledge-gathering or as a problem-solving activity, or both. The former can be regarded as a theoretical pursuit, the latter as programme evaluation, programme improvement, curriculum development, and so on. However neat this distinction may look on paper, in practice both purposes are usually present in any piece of research, though with varying degrees of prominence and emphasis. In terms of the *effects* or *benefits* of research, any project may of course contribute to both theoretical advances and the solution of problems regardless of any stated aims. Indeed, were this not the case, the relevance of theory to praxis would be in constant and serious jeopardy.

It must be stressed that the *purpose* (helping or knowing) of the research says nothing at all about the scientific *conduct* of the research. In order to see this clearly, the distinction between theory as *tool* and theory as *aim* is crucial. It may be that in practice problem-solving research is often conducted with greater haste and less scientific rigour than basic theoretical research (which, after all, does not need to come up with immediately applicable results), but both types can be conducted following the same research-methodological principles derived from a *theory-as-tool*.

In the following sections I shall group the reasons for doing L2 classroom research under three headings: *scientific*, *linguistic* and *pedagogical*. I shall not make a constant distinction between *wanting to know* and *wanting to help*, assuming that these purposes intermingle, as I think they should, in the work of all teachers and researchers.

The scientific argument

Observation is central to all science. This much is uncontroversial, the problem being *what, when, how often* and *how* to observe. For second-language acquisition research, it is clear that we must observe second-language development in action. If we wish to claim that the L2 classroom is an important place where this occurs, then that classroom must be observed. This may seem a very straightforward and obvious fact, but in practice, as, e.g. Long (1983a) has pointed out, the classroom has often been treated as a black box. Researchers appear to have argued that, if a process is difficult and cumbersome to observe, it is sufficient to observe the results (exit tests) and to assume that the process led to the results. This is clearly inadequate since it will not tell us what the process is and what it does.

The reader may object at this stage and point out that classrooms are being observed all the time, first of all by the participants in them, the teachers and learners, and secondly by large numbers of supervisors, inspectors, evaluators, teachers-in-training, and so on. This is, of course, true, but for a number of reasons these kinds of observations have not led to an appreciable growth in our knowledge and understanding of classrooms. Some of these reasons will be explored in Chapter 3, but here we must note that mere presence in the classroom, either as participant or as evaluator, does not constitute systematic study (scientific description, analysis, interpretation) of classroom processes.

Any theory of second-language acquisition which does not explicitly take into account classroom data, either in the form of using such data for theory construction, or in terms of being relevant to the analysis of such data, is seriously incomplete. This, it seems to me, is irrefutable if we hold that the L2 classroom promotes L2 development. At this moment in time there is no lack of second-language acquisition theories, in fact, as Ellis suggests, there may be 'a superfluity of theorizing' (1985, p. 248). Ellis describes seven of the most prominent theories in some detail, and we may note that five out of these seven make no specific comments about classroom learning, either as relevant data or as relevant application. Of the remaining two, the Monitor Model suggests implications and applications of its various hypotheses for classroom procedures, and only Ellis's own Variable Competence Model explicitly uses classroom data as analytical evidence (see Ellis 1984a). We thus have the curious situation that most second-language acquisition theorizing ignores the L2 classroom as a relevant source of data *and* as a relevant place to apply findings.

This reluctance of second-language acquisition theorists to consider classroom data and classroom interaction threatens to make the study of L2 development a very one-sided one. The scientific validity of second-language acquisition research requires that due attention be paid to L2 classroom procedures, and a classroom-research component is thus a theoretical necessity for any serious theory-building effort. It further depends on the particular model of theory construction adopted (e.g. inductive, deductive, functional, and so on) whether classroom research is to be regarded as an initial conceptualizing and hypothesis-generating exercise, as a data testing ground, or as an integral aspect of an interaction between data and conceptualization.

The alternative to this integration is for CR to proceed with its own efforts at theory formation independent of other second-language acquisition theories and models, and to leave attempts at fusion for some unspecified future time. This might result in much duplication of effort, though it might also lead to insights not easily available otherwise. The latter is particularly true if CR can succeed in applying research-methodological principles and procedures and methods of theory construction which are different from the statistical-inference models that currently dominate second-language acquisition research. Such a different approach is available in the form of ethnographic research.

In contrast to current second-language acquisition theories, class-room ethnography, as advocated in this book, takes the educational environment (with the classroom at its centre) as the crucial data resource and thus strongly emphasizes the social context in which language development takes place. It is thus, at the very least, an essential complement to such theories. At best it is also a powerful theory-generating approach in its own right.

The linguistic argument

Current second-language acquisition theories get their evidence largely from the linguistic production of L2 learners. While this should come as no surprise, the way the data are collected is significant. Overwhelmingly the data derive from oral or written tests, or from pseudo-conversational data collected in settings especially constructed for the research: elicitation measures, conversations with researchers, simulated conversations between learners or between learners and native speakers, and so on. Ethnographers of exotic cultures of course traditionally rely heavily on specially trained informants, but the dangers of this approach, however necessary, are spelled out in every introductory textbook on anthropological field work.

Very few studies, mostly longitudinal in nature, have addressed speech naturally occurring in classrooms, i.e. not elicited by the researcher (see Felix 1981; Ellis 1984a). Some researchers have observed naturally occurring speech outside the classroom over a period of time, usually of one single learner, e.g. Schumann 1978; Huebner 1983. The longitudinal, naturalistic studies cast some doubt on the natural order of acquisition proposed by studies of morpheme production in obligatory elicited contexts (see particularly Huebner 1983), and show that the entire process of L2 development is vastly more complex than earlier order-of-acquisition studies suggest.

The classroom-based studies by Felix and Ellis do suggest that the overall sequence of language development (minor and usually temporary variations in order notwithstanding) is almost identical in formal-instruction and in informal-development contexts. The evidence is tenuous, however, and many more contextually based studies in both formal and informal environments are needed before well-founded statements about the universality of the route of development can be made.

If it turns out that classroom instruction cannot influence the route of development, and that learners go through the same stages of learning in the same sequence, regardless of differences in grammatical sequencing of input or presentation of rules, this will by no means provide an argument against the effectiveness of instruction. At most it will argue against specific orderings of linguistic input as traditionally proposed in many pedagogical grammars and teaching textbooks.

Advocates of classroom L2 development may look towards evidence that classroom instruction accelerates the *rate* of development, as well as allowing learners to reach a higher *level* of proficiency. There is as yet no clear evidence in this regard, mainly because researchers looking at this possibility have, by and large, equated *effect* of instruction with *duration* of instruction, rather than with *quality* or *intensity* of instruction, or any number of other variables which might come to light if classroom instruction *itself* had been a source of data.

It is clear that CR is required in order to shed light on issues of *route* and *rate* of development, especially since it places L2 development in the social context without which it cannot occur and cannot be understood.

There are a number of other linguistic issues which CR can shed light on, but limitations of space prevent a detailed discussion of them (see Ellis 1985 for a thorough and very lucid account of second-language acquisition research). I will merely enumerate here the role of planned and unplanned discourse in L2 development, the modification of input which occurs in settings where native and non-native speakers interact, the possible benefits of explicit study of linguistic rules, and the ways in which learners vary their linguistic output according to circumstances.

Classroom interaction is not all of one kind: at various times during lessons learners are called upon and call upon themselves and each other to communicate in the target language in a great variety of ways. This produces a rich and diverse source of data for second-language acquisition research which, in spite of the logistical difficulties inherent in the setting as a locus for research, offers opportunities for the study of learners' interlanguages that no amount of experimentation or elicitation can match.

The pedagogical argument

CR is probably the one branch of second-language acquisition research which speaks directly to the teacher. Second-language acquisition theory is replete with discussions about core and periphery grammar, markedness and unmarkedness, nativization and denativization, analysed and unanalysed knowledge, and so on. The L2 practitioner may be forgiven for not knowing what to do with such information at nine o'clock on Monday morning when facing, say, a class of Qatari engineers. Second-language acquisition theorists cannot concern themselves directly with issues pertaining to the nine o'clock class since they must forge ahead in the quest for knowledge of second-language acquisition. The teacher meanwhile must decide whether a diagram-labelling exercise, a cloze passage, a discussion of physical-exercise equipment for middle-aged business people, or a review of two-part verbs is the best way to proceed. The teacher must get on with the job and cannot wait for second-language acquisition knowledge to eventually come trickling down from various theoretical quarters.

It is clear that now, more so than ever before, there is a danger of a rift occurring between theory and practice. As researchers find that they have important clues to knowledge, viable methods for research, and vital theoretical positions to uphold and defend, they concern themselves less and less with the practical concerns of day-to-day teaching. Many years ago, authorities such as Sweet, Jespersen, Palmer, West and Jones spent considerable time and effort in making practical suggestions about classroom teaching, resulting in primers and textbooks that at times sound remarkably modern alongside present-day methods books.

Many of today's journals are filled with articles containing information that no practising teacher could possibly know what to do with, and reports of research that only a handful of specialists can understand. It should be no surprise, then, that language teachers 'express impatience, bordering on hostility, with researchers and their work', as Seliger and Long note (1983, p. v).

The widening gap between the researcher and the teacher can only be bridged by efforts to make research relevant to practice. Since it is unlikely that researchers will be able to turn or return to being classroom language teachers, we may explore the possibilities of teachers becoming researchers, in order to help themselves to the benefits of research. In addition, the scope of second-language acquisition research can be expanded to include CR as an essential component of research. There is little doubt that this will happen in some way, but given strong prevalent research-methodological preferences, the danger is that data will be taken from the classroom without being returned in some enriched form. As Shirley Brice Heath recommends, teachers must learn to ask of visiting researchers: 'Okay, and what will you do for me in return?' (Heath 1986).

A classroom researcher who adheres to the ethnographic principle of respect for context will naturally engage the teacher and the learners as participants of the research, and as a next step is likely to share emerging findings with them (see, e.g. Carrasco 1981; Hymes *et al.* 1981 for examples of such sharing).

The scope of classroom research

In the above I have in general terms argued for the necessity of CR for second-language acquisition research and for the teaching profession. While it would be foolish to claim CR as a new panacea capable of resolving problems inherent in other research sites and methods, it is clear that the classroom is a necessary complement both as a source of data and as a criterion of relevance of findings. In the remainder of this chapter I shall consider some of the perennial themes in language learning and teaching and suggest how CR might help investigate them.

Some themes that I see as central are:
1. the nature and development of *interlanguage*;
2. the role of *communication* and *interaction*;
3. the use of *strategies*;
4. variations in *learning*: styles and modes;
5. the centrality of *evaluation*, including feedback and knowledge of results.

I shall briefly consider these themes in turn.

Classroom research and interlanguage

In the L2 classroom as elsewhere learners use a language which, according to some, is somewhere along a continuum between their native language and the target language (Nemser 1974; Corder 1981;

Davies *et al.* 1984). In so far as this language exhibits regularities which are neither derived from L1 nor entirely from L2, but which point to an inherent systematicity, this language can be called an interlanguage. As a developing system this interlanguage can be studied in the same ways as other such systems, notably pidgins and creoles in processes of creolization and decreolization (Andersen 1983), and a child's acquisition of the native language. Classroom observation and description can, in longitudinal studies, focus on stages of development, and, in shorter-term studies, on instances of hypothesis formation and testing. In the L2 classroom, ideally at least, learners stretch their powers of learning to their limits and may be seen to experiment with their interlanguage hypotheses, whereas outside the classroom they might be inclined to play it safe and rely on tried and trusted recipes.

The L2 classroom is also a place where language is explicitly *modelled* so that learners can take advantage of it as input. The function of this modelling, which may comprise both authentic samples of the L2 as well as metalinguistic information, tends to be played down in communicative approaches, but needs to be investigated closely before judgements can be made. In Box 2.2 an example of learners trying out a new word, and of a teacher modelling the target form, is illustrated.

In the L2 classroom learners do many things which demonstrate their processes of hypothesis formation and testing. They do this in a pedagogical context which officially warrants experimentation and trial-and-error application. In addition, the classroom explicitly undertakes to provide linguistic fuel for the extension of the learners' interlanguage, and the success (or otherwise) of this must be assessed in the context of its occurrence.

Classroom research and communication

In recent years we have been urged to ensure that learners genuinely communicate in the L2 classroom, rather than go through endless successions of meaningless drills and abstract explanations. The work of sociolinguists such as Labov and Hymes has given us important clues as to what the construct of *communicative competence* may involve, and second-language acquisition researchers have provided insightful descriptions in terms of language learning (e.g. Canale and Swain 1980). Yet, it is clear when we look around us, that there are many different ways in which we can and routinely do communicate. One of the most pervasive assumptions in L2 methodology is that the exist-

---

BOX 2.2

learners are describing things found in kitchens

```
 1  L1    ehm ... cocking ...      cooker an: (refrijadillo)
                                                  ((Span. pron.))
                          ᶜ
 2  T             the cooker                              ᶜthe?
 3  L1    (frecksidets)
 4  L2    (fishan)ᵗ
 5  L            (frishen) ᵗ
 6  L                  (frish) ᵗ
 7  L                         (frisian)
 8  T     fridge      fridge      or- refrigeratorᵗ
 9  LL       ᶜfridge    ᶜfridge              (refridg-)
10  T     shall we try it? refrigerator
11  LL    ((chorus)) refrigerator
```

A running commentary of this episode might proceed as follows:
In turn 1, L1 attempts to say *refrigerator* by using some modified
cognate form derived from his native language (Spanish). In 2 T the
teacher requests clarification, and L1 tries again, attempting an
'anglification' of the Spanish term. Four learners offer other
possibilities, 6 L perhaps coming closest to the English clipping
fridge. At 8 T the teacher begins modelling, which the learners
spontaneously exploit by imitation. In 10 T the teacher explicitly
suggests further modelling and chorus repetition (which continues
for a number of turns beyond 11 LL).

---

ence of an 'information gap' is a prerequisite for communication to
occur. As a result many activities are based on the transmission of
information from one speaker to another, involving explanations,
descriptions, instructions, and so on. However, if we examine the
purposes and contexts of most of our verbal interaction during an
average day, we will probably come to the conclusion that the transmission of information is a very minor concern compared to such vital
tasks as creating and maintaining social relationships, establishing
accommodation between speaker and hearer, getting people to do
things for us, making sense of the situation we are in, creating a good
impression of ourselves, and so on.

The classroom does not provide the same motives for communicating as participating in the outside social world does. The prepon-
derance of information-exchange activities which we find in
applications of the communicative approach tend to transform classroom communication into a rather narrowly focused enterprise. I
suggest that this is largely so because we have failed to consider the

communication potential of the L2 classroom *itself*, and the authentic resources for interaction it has to offer. Classroom authenticity may not exactly mirror world authenticity, but there may be sufficient correlates for the former to be viable as a training ground for the latter (see Willis 1981 for interesting suggestions for using the classroom-as-is as communicative input; see also Breen 1985a).

Classroom research and strategies

When we communicate we interact with another or others. Our communicating depends therefore only partially on the things that we ourselves do. We use strategies in order to ensure that the effect of our communicating on the interlocutor(s) is as close as possible to what we want it to be. These strategies involve, among many other things, manipulating the code systems (linguistic, prosodic, kinesic) in certain specific ways. This is more difficult to do if we are speaking an L2. Strategies are ways of dealing with problems, thus, the more problems, the more we need to use strategies.

Much work has been done in this area (see Faerch and Kasper (eds.) 1983), but usually in interviews or simulated conversational settings rather than in the actual classroom setting. Yet the L2 classroom can be a particularly rich data source for the study of strategies, particularly if its communication potential as a social context and as a purposeful learning environment is realized. The learners will then exploit their own and one another's presence fully to try out their interlanguage, and it is likely that the use of strategies (whether as on-the-spot tactics or as planned sequences to solve predicted problems) will be frequent.

The area of strategies is at present confused and plagued with terminological insecurity. In addition to the classic descriptions by Dunkin and Biddle (1974), Smith and Meux (1962), and others, of classroom strategies and tactics, distinctions are currently proposed between communication, learning, discourse, interpretive, productive, conversational and other strategies (see Box 2.3). There is no general agreement on the role of consciousness and of planning (to name but two ingredients) in the description of strategies. CR may provide an observational methodology which can be equally applied inside and outside the classroom, and can act as a counterbalance to more speculative psycholinguistic work, thus assisting in the clarification of the cognitive and interactive processes learners engage in.

BOX 2.3 Some views of strategies

1. Smith and Meux 1962, p. 3:
   strategies: patterns of acts that serve to attain certain outcomes and guard against certain others
   tactics: smaller movements, tactical elements of strategies (logical operations)

2. Dunkin and Biddle 1974, p. 323:
   strategies: 'the extended and substantive properties of the exchanges among teachers and pupils'
   tactics: 'details of communication among classroom members ... immediate give and take ... as they concern themselves with but a single topic'.

3. Faerch and Kasper 1983, p. 36:
   'Communication strategies are potentially conscious plans for solving what to an individual presents itself as a problem in reaching a particular communicative goal.'

4. Tarone 1983, p. 65:
   'The term communication strategy ... relates to a mutual attempt of two interlocutors to agree on a meaning in situations where requisite meaning structures do not seem to be shared.'

5. Bialystok 1983b, p. 105:
   Ll-based strategies: a) language switch
                          b) foreignizing
                          c) transliteration
   L2-based strategies: a) semantic contiguity
                          b) description
                          c) word coinage

Classroom research and learning

Educational and psychological research is paying increasing attention to the ways in which people learn. As a result, second-language acquisition workers are beginning to realize that different people may have different ways to learn second languages. This realization considerably weakens dogmatic methodological approaches such as behavioural, cognitive, naturalistic, even communicative ones. There may not be one common denominator under which to fit the 'good' language learner (Naiman *et al.* 1978; Rubin 1975). Do those who generate lots of input in observable ways (Seliger's 'HIGs', Seliger 1983) always have the edge over the silent eavesdroppers, the dictionary and grammar book analysts, the compulsive translators? The common methodological assumption is still that whatever is a good method is a good method for everyone.

CR can shed much light on this issue by looking at the ways in which learners in classrooms approach tasks and activities, and the ways in which they attempt to solve their communicative problems. This is however an area in which it will become particularly useful for observational and descriptive methods to team up with other ways of looking, e.g. learners' diaries (see Bailey 1983; Schumann and Schumann 1977), interviews, and self-reporting.

There is now a considerable amount of literature on learning styles (see particularly a thematic issue of *Theory Into Practice* on this subject – Dunn 1984), so that classroom researchers can find specific guidance on what to look for in the identification of different styles, and also on how classroom methodologies and activities may favour certain styles over others. This may be of crucial importance for the multi-cultural classroom where learners from different backgrounds may have different ways in which they can best do their learning. We must always remember that teaching never causes learning, but rather creates (or fails to create) the conditions in which learning can occur.

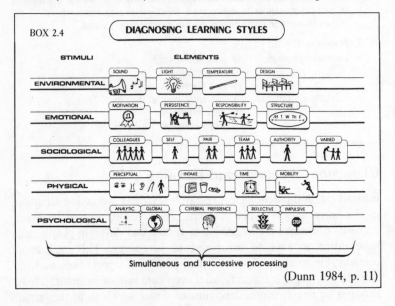

BOX 2.4   DIAGNOSING LEARNING STYLES

Simultaneous and successive processing

(Dunn 1984, p. 11)

Classroom research and evaluation

Everyone involved in language teaching and learning will readily agree that evaluation and feedback are central to the process and progress of language learning. As suggested in Chapter 1, there are two aspects of evaluation that CR must address. In the first place, learners continually ask themselves and others the question: 'How am I doing?' The classroom is a place where continuous feedback and evaluation naturally occur, but the ways in which they occur vary greatly. Engaging in classroom activities demands some form of 'pay-off', or knowledge of results. Learners' contributions are routinely evaluated, often by the teacher in the form of praise or correction, less often perhaps by the learners themselves in terms of self-monitoring, judging the effects of talk, or self-correction. Chapter 7 will address this aspect of classroom performance in some detail by looking at the *repair* of problems of talk.

In addition, of course, learners are frequently evaluated by means of various tests which can be very important to their future careers. The extent to which such tests actually measure the complete range of a learner's L2 capabilities is still very much an issue of debate in language testing circles (see, e.g. Candlin 1986). An argument can be made for the assessment of proficiency on-site and on-task, in interaction with peers on conceptually challenging tasks, and role plays demanding socio-cultural appropriacy. While such assessment is, no doubt, difficult to conduct and problematic in terms of reliable and objective scoring, some pioneering work (e.g. Brown *et al.* 1984) indicates that it is not impossible and that it can provide a valid counterpart to traditional tests.

The second aspect of evaluation CR must address is the evaluation of programmes and of classrooms. Teachers also continually ask, 'How am I doing?', and are often not able to reliably assess if or why a class is going as well as, better, or worse than could be expected. A major reason for this is that they are too involved in the ongoing and absorbing process of teaching to be able to step aside and take a cool look at what actually happens in the classroom. However, it is often true that the best people to evaluate a classroom are the people who participate in it, namely the teacher and the learners. Therefore teachers can use CR to evaluate their own classrooms, preferably together with the learners, and several suggestions are made in subsequent chapters that I hope will promote this. If an outside observer enters the classroom for the purposes of research, I think it is essential that the participants are involved at all stages, not as objects to be watched and scored, but as informants, co-researchers and beneficiaries.

Conclusion: the focus of classroom research

Focus refers to the direction of research, that is, where we want the research to lead. It is determined by our ideas of what findings are desirable, and by our aspirations as researchers. Sometimes the focus is evident from the scoring sheets or the pre-formulated hypotheses we carry into the classrooms, but I suggest that this is not necessarily the best way to embark on a CR exercise.

Inevitably, much subjective reasoning goes into our decisions of research direction, whether we admit it or not. Basically, through research we want to get to know, understand, or even prove something that we do not yet know, or understand, or are not yet able to prove. The wish to find out may be due to plain scientific curiosity or to a desire to improve things in the relevant area of work, i.e. a wish to help, as my earlier discussion of Lorenz's two reasons for research suggests. These two reasons may be combined (e.g. I can only help more if I know more), or they may be in conflict: helpers may regard knowers with suspicion, knowers may turn up their sophisticated noses at the more mundane helpers. This issue of focus causes a lot of trouble in second-language acquisition, as it does in all science. Grassroots workers (in our case teachers) may feel intimidated by researchers, and unfairly scrutinized or discriminated against by their presence and by interference in their work. Researchers, on the other hand, may regard teachers as recalcitrant, unwilling to cooperate, unappreciative of efforts to improve their work. There is thus always a tension between the theoretical and the applied, and this is dangerous, especially in an essentially service-oriented field such as second-language acquisition. One of the problems is that second-language acquisition is often unquestioningly appendaged to linguistics, and some linguists question the appropriateness of this association. While I feel that second-language acquisition research and linguistics are of necessity related, it is no doubt true that another essential link, to educational research, is often insufficiently exploited.

The relationship between linguistics and second-language acquisition aside, I have argued earlier in this chapter that CR is probably the branch of second-language acquisition that is most likely to be able to prevent a rift between theory and practice. By necessity it involves close contact with the actual 'shopfloor', it depends vitally on good relations between teacher, learners and researcher, and indeed, as I have suggested, it is the one area where the roles of teacher and researcher can most easily be combined. Another powerful argument is that CR can provide direct and almost instantaneous feedback useful to the classroom teacher, as the extract from Carrasco in Box 2.5 shows.

BOX 2.5

The Taped Scene. Briefly, what they saw was Lupita performing and interacting outside of teacher awareness during free time. After having finished the Spanish Tables instructional event task (she was the first to finish the task), Lupita decided to work on a puzzle in the rug area. She was soon joined by two other bilingual girls, each independently working on their own puzzles. Lupita was immediately successful in placing a few pieces back on the puzzle template. Then Marta, a bilingual child assessed by the teacher as a very competent student, asked Lupita for help in placing her first piece on the template. Lupita not only helped but also taught her how to work with it by taking Marta's hand and showing her where and how it should be placed. Lupita continued to help her for a short while and then returned to her own puzzle. A few moments later, Lupita disengaged herself from her puzzle work and became interested in what a boy, who had just entered the scene, was doing with a box of toys. Lupita asked him if she could play with him, when suddenly the boy was interrupted by the classroom aide who asked him if he had finished his work at the Spanish Tables (trying to convey to him that he shouldn't be there). The boy did not quite understand, perhaps, what was being asked of him. Lupita turned around and told him that he should go back to finish his work. He left and Lupita continued working on her puzzle which was almost completed. Marta again asked for help after not having accomplished very much since the last 'help.' Lupita helped Marta for a short time, then returned to her own task. The teacher then entered the scene, moved past them toward the piano, and played a few notes to cue the children that the event would be over in two minutes and to begin to prepare for the next event. Lupita speeded up her effort while Marta continued to have trouble. Lupita finished her puzzle, then helped Marta with hers, while the third child in the scene (who was sitting next to Marta) approached Lupita's side with her puzzle and nonverbally indicated that she also needed help. Lupita told Marta to continue to work on hers alone while she helped the third child and asked if she could help them finish the puzzle. Lupita, working quickly with the third child's puzzle, directed Graciela to go help Marta since she needed the help. After Lupita and the third child put away their finished puzzles, Lupita looked around and noticed that Graciela and Marta were still at theirs. She quickly approached them, knelt down in front of them, took command and helped them finish in time for the next lesson. This tape scene clearly showed Lupita's competence as a leader and teacher, as well as her ability to work puzzles. Moreover, it seemed to reveal how Lupita's peers perceive her as compared to how the teacher perceived her.

(Carrasco 1981, p. 168)

3 The methods of classroom research

Introduction

In the last chapter I suggested three sets of grounds for doing classroom research: scientific, linguistic and pedagogical. In addition, a distinction was made between research which directly aims to improve a condition or solve a problem, in other words, which sets out to help, and research which aims to construct, strengthen or test theories in order to improve our understanding of the issues involved in the research field.

Classroom researchers start out with certain ideas, values, assumptions of significance and relevance, a set of preferred procedures, and hopes for certain results. Out of all this initial baggage, which we may loosely call the researcher's *assumptions*, a *frame of reference* grows, and a research *framework* is constructed. How much of this we see in the final report varies, but very often a great deal remains implicit and unreported. Of course, the researcher's assumptions do not stop the moment the research begins, rather, they change and mature as the study progresses. Assumptions therefore shape and give direction to research, and are important enough to deserve reporting and close study. They tell us much about what researchers think the classroom is, and reflect ongoing decisions made in response to the real (rather than assumed) characteristics of the research setting.

This 'subjective side' (which includes the application of common sense – or unexamined reasoning) is common to all science. Indeed, classroom research has, in principle at least, the full array of scientific options at its disposal in the same way as any other setting. The crucial issue is that, in practice, certain things are more appropriate than others, some things are possible, others not. In biology, medicine and psychology some issues can be successfully investigated through experiments with rats in laboratories. However, if an ornithologist wants to study how cuckoos find nests, lay eggs, and so on, there is little alternative to going out into the woods with a pair of binoculars and trying to be inconspicuous.

In between these two extremes, the true experiment, and surreptitious observation, lie a host of possibilities all of which can be useful and appropriate at different times and in different places. In all cases we want to find out something and need specific skills and techniques to reach our goal. The researcher's choice depends on the above-mentioned assumptions, established views in the profession (and, possibly, outside funding agencies, supervisors, employers and others), and the possibilities and limitations provided by the research setting.

In this chapter it will not be possible to do justice to all the possible approaches and methods for doing classroom research (the interested reader may consult several excellent surveys and textbooks on the subject, notably Dunkin and Biddle 1974; Good and Brophy 1984; Cohen and Manion 1985). Rather, I shall concentrate on an approach loosely referred to as ethnography, which, as we shall see, can itself use a number of research tools which are normally associated with other approaches to enquiry. To justify my focus on ethnography I can explicitly refer to the following assumptions which provide a rationale:

1. our actual knowledge of what goes on in classrooms is extremely limited;
2. it is relevant and valuable to increase that knowledge;
3. this can only be done by going into the classroom for data;
4. all data must be interpreted in the classroom context, i.e. the context of their occurrence;
5. this context is not only a linguistic or cognitive one, it is also essentially a social context.

Ethnography can be conducted in many ways. In anthropology, the ethnographer observes a little-known or 'exotic' group of people in their natural habitat and takes field notes. In addition, working with one or more informants is often necessary, if only to describe the language. Increasingly, recording is used as a tool for description and analysis, not just as a mnemonic device, but more importantly as an *estrangement device*, which enables the ethnographer to look at phenomena (such as conversations, rituals, transactions, etc.) with detachment. The same ways of working are applied in classrooms. However, recording (and subsequent transcription) is of even greater importance here than in anthropological field work, since many more things go on at the same time and in rapid succession, and since the classroom is not an exotic setting for us but rather a very familiar one, laden with personal meaning. Recording as an estrangement device is thus extremely vital.

A requirement frequently made of classroom observation is that it must be non-judgemental or objective. This is a problematic notion which I shall come back to, but we may note here that no observation can be truly objective, nor theory-free. However, a recording can mediate between the selectivity and subjectivity inherent in all on-the-spot observing, and the demand for detachment.

It is clear that an anthropologist must strive to be neutral as regards the group that is studied. Neither excessive admiration and idealization, nor any hint of ethnocentrism, are acceptable in scientific descriptions of cultures. The same can be demanded of classroom researchers, but it will be much more difficult to achieve, simply because we are studying a setting that is already familiar. Anthropologists know that they cannot make statements about how a culture should function or how people ought to behave on the basis of what they themselves are used to, but classroom researchers by and large have strong and explicit opinions about how classrooms should function and how learners and teachers ought to behave.

This problem pervades CR and is particularly evident in studies which, by virtue of their procedures, isolate certain behaviours for quantitative treatment. For example, researchers who believe that interaction should be meaningful at all times may code and add up all questions asked by teachers and learners in terms of their true information value and find, unsurprisingly, that in classrooms large numbers of questions are asked which are quite different from questions in ordinary conversation. Yet such a finding in itself does nothing to confirm or disconfirm the original assumption regarding the value of meaningfulness of interaction. In order to address the assumption itself, other work needs to be done, and broadly speaking two options are open:

1. study the effect of different questions through some programme of *intervention*, e.g. setting up an experiment involving differently trained or instructed teachers in separate classrooms, and measuring the effect through tests;
2. examine the occurrence of different types of questions *as they naturally occur*, through observation, description and analysis.

Both these approaches have their advantages and disadvantages, may yield different kinds of information, and can be complementary. The second approach, one which I advocate as the central methodology for classroom research, may bring us closer to understanding why interaction occurs the way it does; the first one may show (if the focus is on what happens in the classroom, not just on test results) what the effect of changes in interaction patterns can be.

Whatever the methodology of research involved, it is clear that *observation* of classrooms is a central aspect of CR. The precise role of this observation in the investigative process, and the ways in which it should be carried out, need much further exploration. In addition, the relation between CR and *evaluation* must be clarified. CR is often conducted with the express purpose of evaluating teachers and programmes, and this purpose has significant consequences for the procedures used and the relations between evaluator and evaluated. Moreover, as I have suggested, evaluation may tacitly influence even those studies which do not explicitly evaluate, by virtue of the researcher's assumptions, including curricular preferences. In the following sections I shall examine the roles and methods of observation, and the relation between evaluative and descriptive CR.

Observation

Most learners and teachers in L2 classes are very familiar with the phenomenon of the observer. In the best of possible scenarios, they have come to accept and largely ignore the presence of a person in the back of the room scribbling away and trying to blend into the woodwork. What this person actually does, however, remains for the most part a mystery. Learners, for whom the L2 classroom after all is a public stage, by and large take such visits in their stride after a while. The teacher, on the other hand, may well find the presence vaguely threatening, and conduct lessons differently because of it. This in turn will have some effect on the learners, so that an observer may never be able to observe a natural, undisturbed lesson. This vexing issue, termed the *observer's paradox* by Labov (1972, p. 209), needs to be dealt with in practical and sometimes ingenious ways.

An important initial step is the image that the observer presents. Sometimes, no doubt, observers are perceived, as Rosen vividly puts it, as 'sinister figures in the wings, faintly contemptuous, armed with the paraphernalia of expertise and tapping ominously their research findings' (Rosen 1978, p. 55).

Such an image would be totally incompatible with ethnographic research which crucially depends on a relationship of trust. If the classroom ethnographer is regarded as an evaluator or inspector, the entire enterprise becomes impossible. This is of central importance to CR, and the classroom researcher who wishes to employ an ethnographic approach must note the concern voiced by Kirshenblatt-Gimblett (Box 3.1).

BOX 3.1   Ethnography as spying?

Practitioners have recently expressed an interest in how
ethnographies of the classroom could provide supervisors with a
better basis for identifying problems and evaluating teachers. It is
applications such as this that could give ethnography a bad name.
To use an essentially non-judgmental research strategy for the
purpose of making judgments would violate the moral integrity of the
ethnographic enterprise and jeopardize the validity of the results.
Ethnography is based on trust; if ethnography were to be the basis
for evaluation and attendant decisions regarding firing and hiring,
ethnographic research would breed distrust on the part of the
subjects. Only with trust and openness will people yield the
knowledge of themselves that ethnography seeks. To have
ethnography an instrument of control, a spying effort, would be to
destroy its ethnographic usefulness.

(Kirshenblatt-Gimblett 1982, p. 256)

While the researcher can probably not be held morally responsible
for the uses to which findings are put (a fact which must worry many
scientists in all walks of life), it is no doubt true that the classroom
researcher must strive to be non-judgemental, that is, neutral, with
regards to the setting that is being investigated. If this neutrality is
absent, the foundations on which ethnography is based, as a viable
enterprise, are also absent.[1]

Neutrality in CR means studying the interaction as it occurs in the
context, from the perspective of those that are being studied. This
can be done through *participant observation* or *non-participant observation*. In the former case the observer takes part in the interaction
as teacher, co-teacher, or learner, and observes either covertly (the
participant-as-observer) or overtly, with the knowledge and consent
of the other participants (the observer-as-participant). This commonly
leads to the publication of journals or diaries (Schumann and Schumann 1977; Bailey 1983) but, when combined with recording, transcription and analysis, it can be a rigorous method of classroom
interaction analysis, one which allows the researcher to be both
involved in the classroom and to take a detached, analytical stand for
the purposes of description and interpretation. In addition, as a novel
approach to participant observation, teachers and learners can use
their own recorded classroom interaction for self-monitoring, feedback, and various kinds of meta-communicative work, thus using
ethnography *as curriculum*.

The most common form of classroom observation is undoubtedly
non-participant observation. Traditionally this has been done with

the help of systematic observation instruments. Such instruments select a limited number of variables that are considered to be relevant, describe them in terms of surface features that can be easily noted by observers, and then decide on a system, e.g. a checklist, so that they can be collected in the classroom. Measurement consists of tabulation and numerical comparison of the recorded instances of variables (for an example, see Flanders' coding schedule in Box 2.1).

The non-participant ethnographer rejects such methods since they violate the two basic requirements of ethnography: a concern for the social context, or the whole picture, and the need to take the participants' perspectives as the basis for description. This means that classroom study cannot easily be conducted on the basis of one-shot, quick entry and exit observation, but requires considerable familiarity with the setting and intensive immersion in the data. The former argues for longitudinal observation, the latter for a programme of observing, recording and transcribing.

Before considering some of the possibilities for doing both participant and non-participant classroom work, it will be necessary to discuss the most common reason for doing classroom observation, the evaluative study.

Evaluative research in the classroom

Researchers and educators may have many reasons for visiting classrooms in action. One of the most common reasons is to evaluate the lesson, the teacher or (occasionally) a learner or learners. This task is often necessary within an institutional setting and may be valuable and important for observer and observed.

Some of the reasons for evaluating classrooms are:
a) management check (for renewal of contract, promotion, salary increase, etc.);
b) evaluating teachers in training (for certification, obtaining diplomas, etc.);
c) evaluating/comparing teaching methods and techniques;
d) apprenticeship (observing as part of learning the craft);
e) control by centralized agencies (e.g. government inspectors).

Evaluating a lesson is a difficult task, since there are no universally accepted criteria to judge the quality of a lesson or a teacher. It is also complex since, as the lesson unfolds in time, notes have to be made on the spot, and particular events cannot be slowed down, re-examined, or taken home and picked apart. As a result, out of the many things that happen during a lesson, a few are selected as being relevant, interesting, needing improvement, and so on. Two observers evaluating the same lesson almost invariably come up with different reports, based on different expectations, criteria of quality and pedagogical preferences.

Problems relating to classroom evaluation have led to the growth of a certain form of research, which may be called classroom evaluation research. The aim of this research is to make the evaluator's job less subjective (or 'fairer' to those being evaluated), more consistent, and more directly focused towards a certain set of criteria that are perceived to be of significance, given some specific educational setting, theory or ideology. Box 3.2 illustrates this aim clearly.

BOX 3.2   The language of teaching

No technical language exists to designate the teaching behavior in second language learning settings. (. . .) The lack of a technical language to discuss the informal teaching done in demonstration lessons and micro-teaching and the formal teaching that occurs when we judge and critique a lesson we have seen leads to a situation analogous to the one in the Japanese movie *Rashomon*, where four people give contradictory and equivocal accounts and interpretations of an event they have all witnessed. Like the characters in the movie, second language teachers and supervisors, when pressed to defend their accounts, interpretations and judgments after a lesson, highlight behaviors, exercises and communications that support their point of view, even though such items may be infrequent and even incidental to the central event.

(Fanselow 1977a, p. 18)

The crucial difference of such research and ethnography is that a notational framework, or category grid, is assembled beforehand, to ensure that all relevant information is contained in the evaluation report. *Relevance* is thus determined before the evaluator enters the classroom, rather than emerging from the classroom interaction itself.

It would be possible to conduct classroom evaluation research by using some of the methods of ethnography, including observation, the taking of field notes, the gathering of supplementary evidence in the form of lesson plans, learners' notes, interviews with teacher and learners before and after the event, and so on. However, constraints of time often prevent applications of the full array of ethnographic methodology, including especially recording and transcription. There is however another reason why an ethnographic approach has not been suggested as a practical solution to evaluation problems.

In education, as in other areas of concern in the social sciences, there has been – and is – a tendency to equate quality in research with the application of a scientific methodology modelled on the natural sciences. Thus there is a strong emphasis on experimentation, hypothesis-testing, the quantitative measurement of variables, and the generalizability of findings. Lorenz, writing about biological research, noted in 1971 that

> We are living in a time in which it has become fashionable to assess the exactitude, and with it the value, of any scientific result by the extent to which quantitative methods have taken part in producing it.
> (Lorenz 1971, p. 1)

In accordance with these scientific views attempts have been made to measure classroom performance in quantitative terms. In order to do this, certain actions or events must be isolated from the stream of classroom discourse, and assigned to a manageable set of operationally defined categories. Observed facts that are relevant in terms of the categories are coded and tabulated, and the result is a score of classroom performance of some kind, whether it be expressed as 'classroom climate' (Flanders 1970), 'communicative orientation' (Allen, Fröhlich and Spada 1984), or whatever. The results can be compared for several classrooms, correlated, and statistical tests of significance will support or reject claims that classroom A has a better climate or is more communicatively oriented than classroom B.

The procedure has obvious attractions, and is seen as a great improvement over anecdotal reports or evaluative remarks of the sort: 'Nice lesson, but watch your blackboard work.' Whether it actually adds to our store of knowledge and understanding of classroom processes, however, of *what goes on in the classroom*, is questionable. The category-coding tradition is inescapably locked into a circularity, due to the selection of categories that are deemed relevant. The criteria for their selection must come from some theory or ideology, as mentioned before. They must also be held to be clear and unambiguous, directly observable and countable, and this inevitably excludes from the sphere of operations some of the most interesting features of classroom interaction (note the interaction – in Flanders' use of the term – analyst's motto: 'If you can't see it or measure it, it's not worth talking about.'). Finally, when the time for counting arrives, it is unquestioningly assumed that more (of whatever it is that is called relevant) is necessarily better.

By way of the new numerical language into which classroom practice has been translated, evaluators aspire to 'tell it as it is', but as Stenhouse points out, 'there is no telling it as it is. There is only a creation of meaning through the use of criteria and conceptual frameworks.' (1975, p. 116–7). The limitations and dangers of the interaction analysis approach (note that in this usage interaction analysis does not mean 'the analysis of interaction'; to distinguish ethnographic work from Flanders' interaction analysis, Mehan (1979) uses the term *interactional analysis*) are also demonstrated in the case-study and triangulation approach practised by Walker and Adelman (see Box 1.2) and others (Chanan and Delamont 1975; Stubbs and Delamont 1976; Adelman 1981). Box 3.3 summarizes the procedures and problems of interaction analysis, and highlights the circularity.

BOX 3.3   Some of the problems of interaction analysis

Procedure	Problems
1. The 'good' classroom is characterized by certain features.	What is meant by 'good'? Are these features all equally relevant? Some more than others?
2. These are the features that are relevant.	What is meant by 'relevant'? Who decides? Why?
3. Translate them into categories that are clear and unambiguous.	Is the translation valid? Are all the features translatable? When you reduce ambiguity, what else do you reduce?
4. These are the classroom behaviours that fit into each category.	How well do they fit? Do some fit in more than one category, or in none at all?
5. Add them up.	Is 'more' necessarily 'better'?
6. Compare.	What does this say about lesson quality? Answer: *Back to Procedure 1*

A large number of schemes using the procedures outlined in Box 3.3 (with some, usually minor, variations) have been developed. A full survey will not be made here since there are several excellent ones available (for education in general see Simon and Boyer 1970; Dunkin and Biddle 1974; for L2 classrooms see Long 1983a; Allwright 1988; Chaudron forthcoming). Mention may be made here, however, of a recently developed observation scheme for the measurement of communicative orientation in L2 and bilingual classrooms, COLT (Communicative Orientation in Language Teaching), by Allen, Fröhlich and Spada at OISE, Toronto (1984). This is the first formal observation scheme, to my knowledge, that directly addresses communicative aspects of classroom interaction. It is further innovative in that it employs, apart from real-time coding, an analysis of recordings of all classes coded. It is my belief that, if real-time coding has any future at all in classroom research, it must be juxtaposed to detailed description and analysis of recorded data. Allen *et al.*'s work is thus of considerable interest if the ever-present temptation to put description in the service of coding can be avoided.

Classroom research and evaluation research: some basic issues

By way of summarizing the classroom evaluation approach I want to describe three major problems that prevent it from contributing in any significant way to the central goal of CR: that of understanding what goes on in classrooms. These three problems are, briefly, the *criteria for selection* of subject matter for study, the assumed *objectivity* of coding and analysis, and the failure to address the *complexity* of classroom interaction. The first problem, that of selection, has been discussed above, and I have shown how it leads to an inevitable circularity in the procedures that are followed.

The second problem, objectivity, is related to this. It is a truism that in objective tests of language proficiency the objectivity lies in the scoring, and not in the test itself. In the same way, evaluative classroom research can only lay claim to objectivity in terms of coding and subsequent quantification. This objectivity (or rather, reliability) is usually expressed as a correlational measure of inter-observer agreement (or inter-rater reliability). That is, if several observers independently code the same things in the same way consistently, objectivity is achieved. Thus, two observers may sit on opposite sides of the same classroom and code separately, using the same scheme. Upon comparing their results they may note a certain number of discrepant cases. Discussing these cases, they may decide on how to code such cases in the future, so as to achieve agreement. After a few practice runs they may thus reach a high (statistically significant) level of inter-coder agreement. While such practices (in addition to those of refining categories and behavioural definitions) no doubt increase coding consistency, in practice this may merely mean that the coders are trained to make the same (perhaps arbitrary or unwarranted) coding decisions in the same environments. It is a coder-model agreement, not a coder-observation agreement, and therefore it does not signify increased objectivity, but rather creates a mystique of objectivity.

The notion of objectivity in CR, as in any research which is observation-based, is difficult and problematic. I have already pointed out that no observation is value-free or theory-free. Even physicists observing particles under a microscope may see certain things rather than others, depending on what they are looking for. Indeed, if they had no idea what to look for, their observation would probably not be productive. This will obviously be much more true for the observation of a highly complex and intimately familiar phenomenon such as human interaction. Our observing and subsequent describing of what goes on will necessarily be selective. We must therefore be explicit – in so far as we can be – about the reasons for selection, and aware of the incompleteness of our description. Objectivity cannot be claimed at this stage; rather we must argue the relevance of our choices in terms of some perceived progress in our quest for understanding, as recommended in Chapter 1.

To prescribe what is to be seen and what is not, which is what evaluative studies, interaction analysis and most process-product studies (i.e. studies which relate aspects of learning behaviour to learning outcome; see Cazden 1985) do, merely takes the choice away from the observer.

Important though this is, the crucial issue lies elsewhere. This is the relation between that which occurs and that which is observed, and between that which is observed and that which is described, either in the form of a check on a code sheet, a categorial definition, a descriptive paragraph, or a generalized statement. That relation is one of interpretation, and its value must be assessed in terms of *truth*. Truth here does not mean absolute truth, either causal or axiomatic, but a relation of *agreement*: between observation, description and interpretation, between observer and participant, and between reporter and audience (in other words, the 'demonstration of plausibility', see Erickson 1985, p. 149). This agreement determines the *adequacy* (of argument and of evidence) and *value* (the contribution to knowledge within and outside the discipline) of the results (see Ravetz 1971 for an elaboration of these concepts).

Adherence to the principle of truth-as-agreement transforms CR into a rigorous discipline, while at the same time claiming that objectivity, in the physical-scientific sense, is irrelevant. Instead, the term *intersubjectivity* is often used to denote observer-observed relationships. This should be the focal concern of CR, rather than the pursuit of hypotheses, generalizability, and causal proof.

The third problem mentioned is the complexity of classroom interaction. This interaction consists of actions – verbal and otherwise – which are interdependent, i.e. they influence and are influenced by other actions. Pulling any one action, or a selection of them, out of this interdependence for the purposes of studying them, complicates rather than facilitates their description, just as a handshake cannot be adequately described, let alone understood, by considering the actions of the two persons involved separately. An interactive act must be studied in its context. As we have seen in Chapter 1, how wide that context should be can only be determined empirically.

To round off this discussion I shall now attempt to state, in more precise terms than has been possible so far, what the domain of CR is.

The L2 classroom can be defined as the gathering, for a given period of time, of two or more persons (one of whom generally assumes the role of instructor) for the purposes of language learning. This is the setting of classroom research, the place where the data are found. I have argued before that, for CR to be possible, this setting must be intact, and not expressly set up for the purposes of research. Next, the central question that L2 classroom research addresses can be expressed as follows:

> How to identify, describe and relate, in intersubjective terms, actions and contributions of participants in the L2 classroom, in such a way that their significance for language learning can be understood.

The search for structure and units

Any description of the L2 classroom must recognize that the interaction that occurs in it is structured, that is, it is systematic and organized. Even a chaotic classroom testifies to this basic characteristic, since we can only identify chaos in a classroom by reference to some concept of structure that we expect to be visibly and audibly observable in a classroom.

However, the concept of structure goes much deeper than a mere orientation to norms of orderly behaviour and discipline. To understand this it is necessary to reflect on what we mean when we say that the L2 classroom is a social context. Classroom *discourse* is a central part of this social context, in other words the verbal interaction shapes the context and is shaped by it. I will explain this further below, but the first and most crucial consequence is that CR

cannot meaningfully take place without a social theory which underlies observation and interpretation. If we cannot be explicit about
what we mean by such terms as structure, process, rules, control and
initiative, it is unlikely that we shall ever make the essential move from
observation and description to interpretation and understanding. The
discussion of these concepts below is kept brief, and perhaps more
abstract than many readers might wish it to be. Some readers may wish
to skip it at this stage and return to it later on. However, the issues
discussed are undoubtedly central to the study of discourse, and
hence to L2 classroom research.

Structure in social settings is difficult to conceptualize and
describe: there are many different views and definitions of it (see, e.g.
Thompson 1984, especially Chapter 4). One model that may be
helpful is Giddens's conception of social structure as consisting of
rules and *resources* (Giddens 1976). The rules are constraining factors,
the resources enabling ones. One may compare this to Stevick's
thoughtful description of the forces of *control* and *initiative* in the
classroom (Stevick 1980).

Both Stevick and Thompson point out that these forces are not
conflicting tendencies. Stevick says that initiative can only meaningfully occur in a controlled environment, and Thompson warns that
'rules ... cannot be conceptualized in isolation from the resources
which facilitate the exercise of power' (1984, p. 157). The meaning
of the term *rule* itself is far from clear-cut. One variously encounters
in descriptions of classroom behaviour terms such as regularities,
norms, routines, recipes, regulations, formulas; explanations often
employ analogies from traffic and games. For most of our work in
classrooms we probably need not go into the intricacies of sociological
specification, but rather simply employ the term *rule* as a generic
concept denoting the regularities of social behaviour.

Resources are the other side of the coin to rules. Or, if we need
to employ a visual image, the relation may be even closer than that,
perhaps rather like the famous pictures in which one sees a vase at
one moment and two faces the next, or now an old witch, now a young
girl. We can see the same setting in terms of the rules which structure
it, or in terms of the resources which enable a dynamic process to
take place, and we see a different image in each case.

Resources can be studied at different levels, literally in terms of
all those components of the classroom setting which can be drawn
upon to provide the raw material for learning, that is, accessible input,
or more globally in terms of the mechanisms which transform this input
into intake. At one level resources are teacher, materials, other

learners and the 'outside world', at another level they are interaction and cognition, together with all the strategic and cooperative work they entail.

I have suggested above that rules provide *structure* and resources *dynamism*. In terms of discourse study this link is useful, and indeed it is one that is commonly made, but we need to return to Giddens's model, which suggests that both rules and resources are part of social structure, and this means that classroom description cannot easily and truthfully separate two distinct contributing sets of phenomena. It is therefore necessary to look for a connecting pattern that underlies the classroom's social structure. To do this, I turn to Bateson's distinction between attention to *form* and *process* as the two basic modalities – alternating and complementary – of human thought (1979).

Both form and process can be seen as part of discourse structure. Stubbs describes structure as 'constraints on linear sequence' (1983, p. 85). He relates structure to *well-formedness*, particularly referring to the notion of *coherence*, and also *predictability*. To say that discourse (in our case verbal interaction) *has structure* is to say that it is well-formed, coherent and predictable. We say that discourse *has* structure, and also that it *is* a process. Another way of saying the same is that discourse is a structured process, but that may be tautologous if we define process as a sequence of actions (or better, interactions) that are intentional and purpose-oriented.

This conceptual tangle is a recurring problem source in many discourse studies. Often they focus on either form or process (mostly on form, since units and hierarchies are easier to identify when kept static), or attempt some *duality of patterning* analogous to the patterning of large numbers of morphemes onto a small set of phonemes in linguistics (see Hockett 1968). In general the problem is, in Labov's words, to relate *what is said* to *what is done* (Labov and Fanshel 1977), or the integration of propositions, speech acts, illocutions (i.e. sets of choices) on the one hand, and interactional moves, strategies, and sequencing (i.e. timing and placement) on the other.

Perhaps the best way out of this conceptual tangle is to regard form and process as two complementary sets of rules and resources. The interplay between them produces social action, in our case classroom interaction. Box 3.4 attempts to represent this view in a visual manner, emphasizing that, in the language game of the classroom, the rules allow at the same time as regulate the application of resources.

The two sources of classroom structure, *form* and *process*, are of course closely related, and when we describe the classroom we have

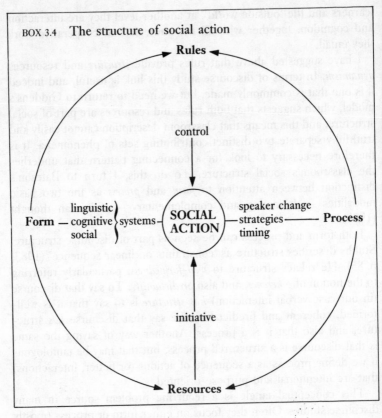

BOX 3.4   The structure of social action

Rules

control

Form — linguistic cognitive social } systems   SOCIAL ACTION   speaker change strategies timing — Process

initiative

Resources

recourse to both in an alternating fashion. Bateson (1979, p. 210) refers to this relationship as the 'zigzag ladder of dialectic between form and process'.

As suggested, rules are closely related to control (both self- and other-control), and resources to initiative (taken by self or other). These two forces can perhaps best be regarded in the following way: personal and social resources are, when they are activated, packaged by rules or, in other words, resources are *calibrated* by rules in the same way (though far more complex and multi-faceted) that the governor on a steam engine calibrates the application of steam power, or a thermostat regulates the production and distribution of heat in a home.

This examination of the social world of the classroom shows that it is a delicately balanced application of forces and sources of power, our task being to find out who and what provides the power, and who and what regulates it. Our task is also to find out what, in a particular balance of ingredients, promotes or inhibits language development.

However, if we examine any number of studies of classroom inter-action, or of discourse in general, we find that they generally fall into one of two classes: those that focus on form, and those that focus on process. In these studies, process is regarded as *that which is done*, and form as *that which results*, in other words, the *product*. Both process and product are generally referred to as *discourse* although, following a definition by Widdowson, the latter is more appropriately referred to as *text*: 'Discourse is a communicative process by means of interaction; its linguistic product is text' (1984, p. 100).

Form is in practice equated with structure, and in formal discourse studies the aim is to discover the structure of discourse, i.e. in this view, produced text. This structure consists of sequences of hier-archically related units, and research must establish what those units are and how they are related. As an example, Sinclair and Coulthard (1975) set up a hierarchy of discourse units analogous to units in sentence grammar (specifically, Halliday's rank scale grammar, see Halliday 1970). The hierarchy is one of inclusion, i.e. larger units contain smaller units, which consist of smaller units still, until elements can no longer be broken down into smaller discoursal units (at which point sentence grammar takes over with phrases, words, morphemes, etc.). Thus, Sinclair and Coulthard's hierarchy consists of lessons, which consist of transactions, which consist of exchanges, which consist of moves, which consist of acts.

A basic problem of such hierarchies is to explain how one unit or sub-unit follows another in a rule-governed way. Units do not just sit in boxes which sit in bigger boxes, and so on, they follow one another in systematic ways which cannot be explained by the hier-archy. In some cases it is possible to *predict* that a certain unit-type must follow another unit-type, e.g. that a response move must follow an initiation move, but not all sequences of actions can be explained on the basis of the hierarchical structure. The diversity of interaction is such that any unit-instance can optionally be followed by a large number of other unit-instances, either at the same level (e.g. move – move, or exchange – exchange) or at a different level (e.g. move – exchange, act – move). An example may be in order. In the following extract from Sinclair and Coulthard the third move (3 T) is coded 'elicit', and it is not followed by the mandatory unit 'response' (its absence is noted by O). It is clear however, that the teacher is closing some unit of classroom business to initiate or re-initiate some other unit (such units are transactions). Since some required initial identifying unit (called frame or boundary) that signals 'new transaction' is absent, however, the hierarchical system cannot identify the start of something new, but rather has to regard 3 T as just another initiation. The power of the formal hierarchy to show what actually happens in the interaction is therefore extremely limited.

1 P Miss the er London Bridge they're transporting that to America.
2 T Yes, they are, aren't they. They're building that somewhere else.
→ 3 T Have a word about this chap we don't seem to have finished do we?
4 P O

(Sinclair and Coulthard 1975, p. 88)

In response to the problems inherent in form-oriented models of discourse structure, several studies have attempted to systematically relate *what is said* to *what is done*. Thus Edmondson (1981) describes discourse structure in terms of a dual system of interactive moves and illocutionary acts. Mehan (1979), in his application of what he calls *constitutive ethnography*, describes separately the *structure* and the *structuring* of classroom interaction. In both cases, and I think it is fair to say in all cases that attempt a duality of patterning (see above), relating the two modes of description turns out to be problematic. The reason that all these studies run aground at one point or another on the crucial issue of relating what is said to what is done, is that they impose, from above, a classificatory framework on the data. For such a classification to be interesting it has to be reasonably detailed and comprehensive, indeed, it is commonly claimed that it must capture all that happens in the data. Leftovers are an embarrassment to such efforts, and ragbags must be kept small. In practice, the concern for classifying overtakes the concern for the overall patterns of action that occur in the setting, and reduces the sensitivity to the social world in which the actors realize their aims.

In response to these shortcomings of a form-oriented approach, we can either attempt to reduce the social complexities of the interaction by imposing experimental control of variables, or study the social context directly in terms of a theoretical framework such as the one outlined above. In the former case we run the danger of changing the context in such a way that findings are not applicable in the real world, in the latter case we may find that the social world is so complex that confident generalization and accurate prediction are impossible research goals. Classroom research is research in a field setting, and therefore it will have to tackle the context of the classroom *as it is*. As a result, it cannot be judged by standards of generalizability and prediction (or 'proof'), but rather by its power to create an understanding of how things happen the way they do, and why they may make sense to the people involved in making them happen that way. There is therefore no point in judging classroom research by criteria of internal and external validity developed for the purpose of evaluating experimental research, just as it is unrealistic to expect experimental research to shed much light on the social context in which learning takes place. By the same token, CR should not express its findings in terms of cause-effect inferences, nor should experimental research make inferences that go beyond the controlled setting in which the findings were obtained. If both types of enquiry are conducted in accordance with the dictates of their design principles, it should be possible to draw beneficial conclusions from both, thus promoting the formation of a theory of classroom learning which is neutral so far as research method is concerned.

CR can be and is conducted in different ways, as mentioned before. Whichever way it is conducted, however, it must adhere to certain principles, which flow naturally from the requirement that the object of research is the classroom as an intact field setting. My argument is that those basic principles are the same ones that underlie ethnography as a research method. In the following section I shall discuss the application of ethnographic research to L2 classrooms in a systematic way, pulling together the different strands of argument in its favour advanced so far.

Classroom interaction as process: educational ethnography

Ethnography is literally the description of culture (or of groups of people that are perceived as possessing some degree of cultural unity). It has always been a central concern of anthropology, and its methods and power to generate understanding can best be understood by reading some of the work in that area, e.g. Bateson's *Naven* (1958) and Geertz's *The interpretation of cultures* (1973).

In recent years ethnography has also become of considerable interest to sociologists, linguists and social psychologists, who see the need to study human behaviour in its social context. One of the fields in which its application is growing rapidly is education, partly due to dissatisfaction with experimental designs that rely on the quantitative processing of piecemeal or controlled data. There are a number of different conceptions about the nature and the methodological and theoretical power of ethnography, both in its mother science, anthropology, and in the widening applications in diverse fields. As an example, Box 3.5 lists a summary of views presented in Hammersley and Atkinson.

BOX 3.5

Ethnography is:
- the elicitation of cultural knowledge (Spradley 1980)
- the detailed investigation of patterns of social interaction (Gumperz 1981)
- holistic analysis of societies (Lutz 1981)
- essentially descriptive, a form of story telling (Walker 1981)
- the development and testing of theory (Glaser and Strauss 1967; Denzin 1978)
- one social research method, drawing on a wide range of sources of information (Hammersley and Atkinson 1983)
                              (Hammersley and Atkinson 1983, p. 1–2)

One might plot these conceptions on a continuum that ranges from strong to weak in terms of theoretical power and, so far as educational ethnography is concerned, it is possible to identify three major strands along the continuum:

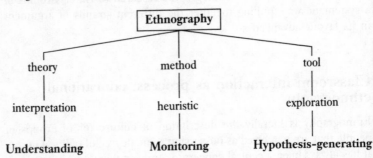

In the strong view ethnography is theory-building, and thus the core of a humanistic approach to social science. In this sense it can be traced back to naturalistic approaches to social investigations (see Erickson 1985), to phenomenology and ethnomethodology. In the weak view, currently prevalent in L2 research, ethnography is a tool consisting basically of unstructured (as opposed to systematic, i.e. using pre-determined codes) observation, used in order to identify relevant concepts, describe variables, and ultimately generate testable hypotheses. Its task would stop there, ethnographers being not unlike advance crews staking out the route and preparing the terrain for engineers and constructors to build a new highway. At the centre of the continuum we find an essentially hybrid conception of ethnography which, in janus-faced fashion, looks both ways, and aims to employ all reasonable methods of data gathering and analysis in order to investigate an educational setting or problem. Here both quantitative and qualitative techniques are combined as and when appropriate to setting, aim and tasks. This last application of ethnography, as recommended by Hymes, Mehan, Carrasco and others in the volume edited by Trueba *et al.* (1981), and illustrated in a project directed by Hymes (1981), is often called *ethnographic monitoring*. This view of ethnography would also be a natural component in the kind of *programme evaluation* recommended by Beretta (1986), and could employ various forms of *triangulation* (Box 1.3; see also Adelman 1981) and *action research* (see p. 67).

I will not here discuss the weak view, since this reduces ethnography to exploratory observation (whether participant or non-participant). Second-language classroom research, though it may offer much useful information to researchers in the experimental tradition, is best served by taking a stronger view of its potential benefits, a more encompassing view of its range of research techniques, and aiming towards a valid interpretation of the L2 classroom as a social setting in which learning can take place.

Given the range of research settings in which ethnography is employed, and the different views regarding its aims and theoretical power, it is not surprising that there are many definitions of ethnography, and as often as not they turn into lengthy discussions of what the ethnographer does (see Hammersley and Atkinson 1983 for an excellent survey). For our present discussion it is sufficient to consider Saville-Troike's formulation of the central question in the ethnography of communication, which is in fact a reformulation of Goodenough's well-known cognitive definition of culture: 'What does a speaker need to know to communicate appropriately within a particular speech community, and how does he or she learn?' (Saville-Troike 1982, p. 2; see also Goodenough 1981). This question places a special focus on communication and on learning to communicate, an emphasis which is quite appropriate to the L2 classroom.

Ethnography is guided by two central principles (see Heath 1982, where these ideas are discussed in some detail), which for the sake of convenience we may call the *emic* and the *holistic* principles. The emic principle (see Chapter 1, Note 6) requires that the researcher leave aside pre-established views, standards of measurement, models, schemes and typologies, and consider classroom phenomena 'from the functional point of view of the ordinary actor in everyday life' (Erickson 1981b, p. 20). This means that critical knowledge of the classroom derives from the study of the meaning that participants invest and develop in the social context of the classroom, as manifested through their interaction and various kinds of documentary evidence (such as interviews, conversations, lesson plans, notes, and so on).

The holistic nature of ethnographic enquiry has been stressed by many of its advocates and practitioners, among them Hymes (1964), Mehan (1979), Heath (1982) and Saville-Troike (1982). Heath expresses the requirement as follows:

> Data obtained from study of pieces of the culture should be related to existing knowledge about other components of the whole of the culture or similar pieces studied in other cultures.
>
> (Heath 1982, p. 35)

The range of methods used in ethnographic work is quite varied and depends partly on the types of data that are considered relevant, and partly also on the individual ethnographer's position along the continuum suggested above. Erickson (1981b) suggests that the two main sources of data are *asking* and *watching*. Watching refers to various techniques for observation, roughly divisible into the two types identified above, participant and non-participant observation. Asking will include questionnaires, interviews and elicitation. In addition, participants' diaries (Bailey 1983), network analysis (Milroy 1980), ethnosemantics (e.g. semantic categorization) and the study of documents (school records, lesson plans) are often part of the ethnographer's methodological baggage. In recent years, as an extension of observation, more reliance is being placed on the study of recorded events (Erickson's *microethnography* and Mehan's *constitutive ethnography*), and here the concerns of ethnography and discourse analysis (in its linguistic sense, as exemplified by Sinclair and Coulthard 1975) converge.

The status of experimental work in ethnographic research, with its concern for generalizability and cause-effect relationships, is a more contentious issue. While some of the more radical proponents of ethnography argue, as I have done earlier in this book, that generalizing and looking for causes are not the primary concerns of ethnographers (see further Bolster 1983), these goals are, in the last analysis, clearly shared by all researchers, though the proposed routes by which they can be achieved vary enormously.

In practice ethnographers employ a range of techniques which lie along a continuum from non-intervention to intervention and from unstructured to structured (see Box 3.6), and exactly at which point ethnography stops and normative science starts is unclear. For example, a range of techniques such as matched guise experiments (e.g. Lambert *et al.* 1960), story recall (Chafe 1980), elicitation of dialectal variants (Labov 1966), and many others, preselect variables, manipulate interaction, and rely heavily on quantitative analysis.

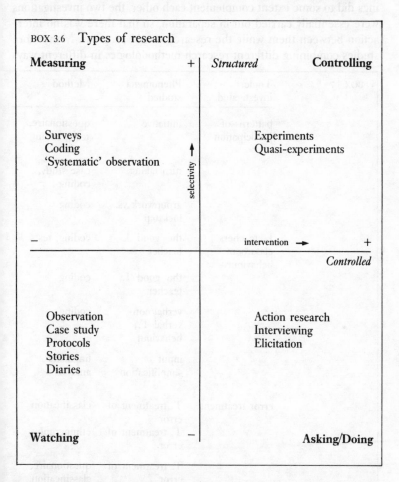

BOX 3.6   Types of research

In recent years we have seen an increasing interest in multi-disciplinary studies. It will be interesting to see if and how various research-methodological factions can reconcile their differences, work in harmony, and produce complementary findings. To my knowledge there is as yet no reported case of a successful integration of experimental and ethnographic work, though it is clearly important to explore this possibility. A recent study by Lett and Shaw (1986) takes a first step in this direction. They used ethnography and quasi-experimentation to compare Suggestopedia and the Defense Language Institute's essentially audiolingual method in teaching Russian, and juxtaposed the findings of the two research methods in an effort to show their strengths and weaknesses. Though the findings did to some extent complement each other, the two investigations were essentially carried out in separation, so that there was no interaction between them while the research was in progress. Many more studies combining different research methodologies in different ways

BOX 3.7	Topic investigated	Phenomena studied	Method
	patterns of participation	initiative	questionaire, tests, coding
		turn taking	case study, coding
		groupwork vs. lockstep	coding
	L. teachers' classroom behaviour	the 'good' L. teacher	coding, tests
		the 'good' L. teacher	coding
		verbal/non-verbal T. behaviour	coding
		input simplification	linguistic analysis
	error treatment	T. treatment of error	classification
		T. treatment of error	ethnography
		T. treatment of error	questionaire, classification
		T. treatment of error	coding, classification
	individual L-T variables	anxiety/ competitiveness	diaries

are needed to explore the possibilities of productive collaboration between researchers of various backgrounds. For the classroom teacher such combined research can be very beneficial, since it ensures that contextual variables, and the actual work that is done in the classroom, are taken into due consideration and also, if the emic and holistic principles are properly attended to, that teacher and learners are meaningful participants in the research.

The usefulness of ethnography, either independently or in combi-

Recorded data	Results	Researchers
no	classification of learners into HIG/LIG	Seliger 1977
audio	model of turn taking	Allwright 1980
audio	Embryonic Category System	Long *et al.* 1976
video	correlation	Politzer 1970
no	FLINT coding system	Moskowitz 1976
no	SCIMP coding system	Townsend & Zamora 1975
audio	input & interlanguage analysis	Gaies 1976, 1977
video	classification	Fanselow 1977b
audio	interpretation/ description	Allwright 1975
audio	quantitative & qualitative analysis	Cathcart & Olsen 1976
audio	classification & flowchart	Chaudron 1977
no	description	Bailey 1983 Schumann & Schumann 1977

(Compiled from information in Bailey 1985, p. 97)

nation with other methods, for L2 classroom research is clear. Yet, although CR is now a prominent line of research within second-language acquisition research, very little of it can be called ethnographic if we apply the standards demanded by the emic and holistic principles. This is illustrated in a survey by Bailey (1985, p. 97), who identifies four main areas of attention: patterns of participation, the speech and behaviour of teachers, the treatment of learners' errors, and individual student (or teacher) variables. What characterizes most of the studies reviewed under these headings is that they focus on specific aspects of the setting with little or no attention paid to the holistic nature of the classroom as a social context. In Box 3.7 I summarize these studies under a few salient headings.

With few exceptions (Allwright, Bailey) L2 classroom studies lead to classification models for the quantitative analysis of variables, and serve as input for comparative or experimental studies. In most cases, again, either a specific phenomenon or a prespecified model has been selected beforehand for close analysis, and the tendency is for further work to lead to ever-increasing specification and narrowing down of the phenomenon investigated. Both the holistic and the emic principles are therefore absent, and the studies illustrated lead away from, rather than towards, a description of classroom interaction processes.

The argument taken here is that, if only as a necessary balance to prevalent research practices, research is needed which closely adheres to the emic and holistic principles. The only book-length study of this kind in L2 is Ellis 1984a, which looks at L2 classroom learning as a process. For further examples it is necessary to turn to studies of first-language and bilingual classrooms, and the next section reviews some representative examples.

Ethnographic classroom studies

In this section I shall examine some recent ethnographic work in education, notably Mehan (1979) and various studies by Erickson and associates (e.g. 1981a and b, 1982). The aim is to allow the reader to judge how the emic and holistic principles of ethnography are applied, and how the research can be carried out in practice.

Mehan criticizes both quantitatively oriented surveys, coding and experimental studies, and informally reported field studies in education; the former since they fail to show how classroom work is organized, i.e. the process of interaction, or *structuring*, as he calls it; the latter for their subjectivity, lack of replicability and weak power of generalization. He proposes to integrate *structuring* (in my terms, process) and *structure* (form) into one coherent and comprehensive description. He thus proposes the approach he calls *constitutive ethnography*, which has the basic characteristics shown in Box 3.8.

BOX 3.8

1. Retrievability of the data. Video and audio-tapes provide a record of the data studied and can be used to re-examine and re-interpret the data.

2. Comprehensive data treatment. Mehan's aim is to 'construct a model that accounts for the organization of each and every instance of teacher-student interaction in the nine lessons in the corpus' (p. 20).

3. Convergence between researcher's and participants' perspectives. This requirement, relating to the perspective of truth-as-agreement described earlier in this chapter, means that the structures and actions described must be described in such a way as to reflect exactly the way that these structures and actions are perceived by the participants. One way the ethnographer generally does this is by asking the participants pertinent questions. Mehan, however, by considering only the direct data of the interaction, aims to achieve convergence by considering the consequences of actions in the course of events:

> If a researcher's description of the organization of an event is valid, the participants within that event will orient to its structural features during the course of their interaction (. . .). They will make the researcher's phenomenon visible by their actions, especially in the absence of expected forms of interaction (p. 23).

This means that the description is valid to the extent that it is able to predict features of the interaction, and that where those expected forms of interaction do not occur, this will be signalled by the participants (e.g. by means of repair, sanctions).

4. The fourth characteristic of Mehan's description is an *interactional level of analysis*. One of the goals of Mehan's constitutive ethnography is to 'locate the organizing machinery of classroom lessons in the interaction' (p. 23), in 'the words and in the actions of the participants' (*ibid.*). This requirement is an essential feature of *ethnomethodology*, as illustrated by Sacks's famous dictum: 'If it's a phenomenon it must be in the interaction.' (Sacks 1963, quoted in Humphrey 1979 and Mehan 1979). The aim is to avoid unwarranted attributions or inferences regarding participants' roles and status (see also Allwright 1980), mental states or intentions and 'the reification of unobservable, abstracted, sociological notions' (p. 24). We might add to this the reification of abstract linguistic structures and units, as expressed in many of the linguistic hierarchies and models used as tools for classifying classroom talk.

(Mehan 1979)

The four methodological policies summarized in Box 3.8 define Mehan's work as ethnography, though it is limited to *watching*, without doing any *asking*. Some researchers, notably in the more sociologically oriented tradition in Britain (a good introduction is Adelman 1981), would argue that in addition to this close observation and microethnography an element of triangulation would be beneficial, i.e. the accumulation of data from different sources, such as interviews and discussions with participants, since this would lead to a richer description. However, we must realize that the close, rigorous examination of interaction *per se*, as exemplified by Mehan (and, in different ways, by Erickson; Humphrey 1979; Edelsky 1981; and others), may reveal things about how learners and teachers get their lessons accomplished, which no amount of interviewing can reveal. In terms of second-language classrooms we can think of such perennial questions as how learners engage each other's and signal their own participation, what triggers a switch from one code to another, what separates creative language use from prespecified speech, what leads to linguistic elaboration and what leads to restriction, and so on.

Mehan's work, although conducted in an ethnically mixed English-medium elementary school, is of immediate relevance to L2 classroom research if we can see that similar L2 classroom-based studies might improve our knowledge of what goes on in L2 classrooms. Mehan's comprehensive analysis aims to show both the overall organization, or *structure* of a lesson, as well as how that organization comes about, or the *structuring* of those lessons. He does not assume, a priori, that the teacher is responsible for all this, but that whatever is said and done by no matter who may be relevant to both structure and structuring. This is important, since most L2 researchers (though see Allwright 1980) assume that it is the teacher alone who does the structuring work, and if we begin with such an assumption it is hard to see that the learners' part in this might be anything else than being passive recipients of methodological actions devised by the teacher or the system. Yet, as every teacher knows, how a lesson, or a semester, turns out depends crucially on what the learners do. What is it that they can do in the L2 classroom, and which of those things are most likely to lead to language learning? And secondly, what kinds of classroom goings-on promote the occurrence of those things?

In this context, the most interesting aspect of Mehan's work is his discussion of the structuring of classroom lessons (Chapter 3), which leads to an investigation of what makes people competent members of classroom lessons. A description of 'normal classroom circumstances' leads to the identification of turn-taking and turn-allocation procedures, including bidding for turns, floor holding and floor getting. 'Unusual circumstances', e.g. when the unwritten order of events threatens to break down, or unexpected things occur, give rise to sanctions (i.e. negative evaluations) or a range of strategies for coping, many of which are improvisational. The study of the unexpected, the breaking of rules, the breakdown of order, are of special importance in ethnographic study, since they allow the ethnographer to test presumed rules and regularities and to see if the participants' tacit rules of conduct match them. If a rule or regularity identified by the researcher is violated, and the participants appear to ignore it, the chances are that there is something wrong with the researcher's description, or at least that it is still seriously incomplete. Mehan illustrates this procedure by rigorously investigating all instances of apparently unsanctioned violations of patterns he has identified. The way in which Mehan has conducted his study of classroom interaction, more so than the details of his actual findings, is of importance to L2 classroom researchers. The task of the L2 classroom researcher, as suggested before, is first to describe in detail what goes on in the L2 classroom, and then to relate the things that are done and said to L2 learning. It is necessary to know what competent membership of the classroom involves, and to see what learners can do creatively to exploit their competent membership to increase their opportunities for learning. As an example, non-native speakers in native-language classrooms may be prevented, through not being competent members, from benefiting fully from instruction, quite apart from their linguistic abilities (see, e.g. Schinke-Llano 1983). As Mehan points out, effective participation, which in most classrooms involves taking initiative, can only occur when the learners know the rules of classroom discourse:

> Students must first find an appropriate place to introduce their interests, and having gained access to the floor, they must maintain control over it. The former involves recognizing the completion of a prior interactional sequence and the completion of previous instructional topics. The latter involves having topics picked up by others. In order to have topics incorporated into the lesson, students need to introduce new and interesting ideas, not merely comment on the prior course of events.
>
> (Mehan 1979, p. 169)

As Mehan found during the school year he investigated, learners need time to learn the classroom code of conduct:

Once the students learned to recognize the seams in classroom discourse, the raw number of students' initiation acts increased, as did the effectiveness of these acts. Soon, students' initiations were picked up by others, and finally, they influenced the course of lessons.

(Mehan 1979, p. 170)

A major procedure of ethnographic work is the detailed analysis of recorded data, or as Edelsky (1981, p. 385) puts it, 'intensive immersion in the data'. This detailed analysis, which begins with transcription, contradicts the often-made complaint by L2 researchers that recordings of L2 classrooms are too noisy and too messy for accurate transcription, and therefore that interaction between teachers and learners, and learners and learners, can only be realistically studied in simulated settings. While it is no doubt the case that large classes of 30 or more learners can be difficult to transcribe, and that in any lesson there may be sections where so much simultaneous talk is going on that accurate transcription becomes impossible, there is now sufficient evidence to show that the average L2 lesson can be profitably transcribed, including sections of group and pair work. I have found, while working in extremely noisy conditions, with large classes and very vocal children, that no more than partial transcriptions even in those circumstances could reveal classroom and interaction patterns that observation checklists, interviews and training programmes could not. Especially, such analysis, even though it may not be possible to transcribe everything that everybody says for every instant of the lesson, allows us to describe what the learners actually and actively do during the lesson, as individuals and as groups.

One of the most interesting and promising areas is that of *participation structures*, a notion first proposed by Philips (1983) in her study of education on the Warm Springs Reservation. This notion – described by Cazden (1985) as 'the rights and obligations of participants with respect to who can say what, when and to whom' – has been further developed by Erickson and associates (e.g. Shultz, Florio and Erickson 1982; Erickson 1982) in a series of classroom studies (see further p. 84 ff. and Chapter 6). Erickson and Shultz's detailed suggestions for recording and analysing data on video (see Box 3.9) provide a useful framework for the study of different classroom activities. It can be expanded to take into account not only the classroom itself, but also the stories that learners tell, conversations about the school and life in the classroom, staffroom talk among teachers, teachers' ideals as expressed in school reports, etc., as ethnographic data. Thus the ethnography of the *school* can be combined with the ethnography of *classroom interaction*.

BOX 3.9 Procedure for the analysis of videotaped data

Stage 1. Global viewing: taking sparse notes to index the tapes and note transitions between occasions of interest.

Stage 2. Choice of specific occasions of interest for more detailed analysis. Selected occasions are copied onto copy tapes. Occasions are timed, and junctures described in detail. Participants may be asked to attend a *viewing session* and give their emic views of the occasion.

Stage 3. Specification of differences in the transitions or junctures, with specific attention paid to nonverbal contextualization cues.

Stage 4. Detailed description of the participation structures between junctures.

Stage 5. Construction of a model showing the principles of social organization underlying the surface form of communication behavior in interaction.

Stage 6. Establishing the generalizability of the structures analysed.
(Summarized from: Erickson and Shultz 1981, p. 153–7)

Other approaches

Though the main thrust of this chapter, and the book in general, is towards an ethnographic approach to classroom research, it must be pointed out that this is by no means the only fruitful approach that can be taken. In particular, I wish to mention four approaches that can be profitable and revealing: *case study, diaries, experimentation* and *action research*.

Case study

The two examples of case study most relevant to classroom research are Ellis 1984a and Allwright 1980 (for other case studies, see e.g. Schumann 1978; Schmidt 1983). Ellis's work is essentially a hybrid of extensive reviews of relevant literature blended with data from three ESL learners in Great Britain, one Portuguese and two Punjabi speakers. Case studies generally need to be conducted on a longitudinal basis, and Ellis traces the grammatical and semantic development of his three learners over a period of time. In itself, this is not very different from a multitude of morpheme-acquisition studies, but Ellis does specifically address the issue of language development in the classroom. In the central chapter of his book (Chapter 5) he shows successfully how a range of activities in the classroom may promote language development parallel to naturalistic learning, and pinpoints the learner's *initiative* in interaction as being crucial to this development. Ellis's suggestions are valuable though in a large measure intuitive. They need to be further investigated and developed through detailed examination of a large body of varied L2 classroom data.

Whereas Ellis approaches classroom language learning from the psycholinguistic, developmental perspective, Allwright (1980) studies the contributions of one particular learner in an interactive sense: through a study and classification of turn taking. Both Ellis's intuitive statements about classroom interaction and Allwright's exploratory study of turn taking need to be substantiated and refined by work that systematically examines classroom data.

Diary study

I will be brief about the issue of diaries here. It is clear that, though of necessity anecdotal and subjective, diaries can provide much information about what motivates learners and teachers in a classroom. They are thus particularly valuable for insights into affective and personal factors that influence interaction and learning. Bailey's discussion of competitiveness and anxiety in learners is an excellent example of the productive use of diaries in classrooms (Bailey 1983; see also Schumann and Schumann 1977; Bailey and Ochsner 1983).

Classroom experiments

Long *et al.* conducted a study on wait time in L2 classrooms in Hawaii. By training some teachers to wait systematically before evaluating a student response, the effect on learner utterances was studied. Preliminary results of this study indicate that increasing wait time has a beneficial effect on the quality of learner responses.[2] The issue of wait time is also very relevant to the investigation of repair and correction in L2 classrooms, where it can be shown that longer wait time increases opportunities of self-repair (see Chapter 7 for a detailed discussion of repair).

Brown *et al.* (1984) conducted experiments with communication activities in Scottish schools. The aim was to find out what kinds of activities promoted development of oracy, and also to find reliable ways of assessing students' oral proficiency on the basis of interaction with peers rather than the usual oral interviews or tests.

Similar work was done by Dickson (1982), who merged sociolin-guistic and experimental methodology in an effort to study communicative contexts created by different communication games in the classroom.

Ethnography and experimentation are not of necessity incompatible or contradictory. Contextually appropriate experiments can in certain circumstances be useful and, of course, any experiment can itself be treated as ethnographic data. There are also 'natural experiments', when unforeseen things happen, and the researcher can study coping strategies (cf. Mehan's unusual classroom circumstances; see also Hammersley and Atkinson 1983, pp. 31–2). However, crucial is the 'ecological validity' of experiments: this is likely to decrease as experimental control increases. In general terms, it would be foolish to reject all experimentation out of hand: the anthropologist uses it when convenient, and so does the ethologist. It may be the only way to observe something crucial that might otherwise be unobservable. Analogous to Labov's elicitation of sociolinguistic data, classroom experiments, if conducted with respect for the classroom context, may be regarded as elicitation of interaction.

Such experiments are of course not 'true' experiments in the scientific sense, since they do not apply random allocation of learners to control and experimental groups, and since control over extraneous variables is seldom possible in a real classroom setting. Indeed, as Cohen and Manion point out, 'true experimentation in education is rarely, if ever, achieved' (1985, p. 171).

Much of the work we loosely refer to as experiments may in many cases be more adequately called *action research*, some characteristics of which are briefly discussed below.

Action research

Although action research has been prominent in the social sciences since the 1940s, it has not so far received much serious attention as a distinct style of research in language teaching. However, as suggested, many classroom experiments, as well as many programme evaluation studies, may contain elements of action research, especially since the concept is often loosely applied to projects undertaken in a work setting in order to solve existing problems.

Cohen and Manion define action research as 'small-scale intervention in the functioning of the real world and a close examination of the effects of such intervention' (1985, p. 174). They further note that action research has the following features: it is *situational*, or context-based, *collaborative* in that researchers and practitioners work together, *participatory*, since team members themselves implement the research, and *self-evaluative*, i.e. based on the ongoing evaluation of improvements achieved.

These features suggest that action research and classroom ethnography can be profitably combined, either as successive stages of research or, more interestingly, as parallel or integrated research activities. Indeed, the increasing sophistication in ethnographic methods, including the analysis of recorded data and elicitation techniques, may well be able to inspire new life and systematicity into classroom action research.

According to Sanford, action research, as originally proposed by its pioneer Kurt Lewin, consisted in 'analysis, fact-finding, conceptualization, planning, execution, more fact-finding or evaluation – and then a repetition of this whole circle of activities; indeed, a spiral of such circles' (Sanford 1981, p. 174). As an elaboration of these procedures, Box 3.10 summarizes Cohen and Manion's discussion of the different stages an action research programme might follow.

BOX 3.10   Stages in action research

Stage 1. The identification, evaluation and formulation of the problem.

Stage 2. Preliminary discussion and negotiations amongst interested parties — teachers, advisers, researchers, sponsors — culminating in a draft proposal.

Stage 3. Review of research literature and comparable studies.

Stage 4. Restatement of the problem, or formulation of a hypothesis; explicit discussion of the assumptions underlying the project.

Stage 5. Selection of research procedures, allocation of resources, choice of materials and methods, etc.

Stage 6. Choice of evaluation procedures — bearing in mind that evaluation will be continuous.

Stage 7. The implementation of the project itself, including data collection and analysis, monitoring and feedback.

Stage 8. The interpretation of the data; inferences to be drawn; overall project evaluation.

(Cohen and Manion 1985, pp. 220–21)

Conclusion

There is not one single way of doing L2 classroom research. However, it is an essential and defining characteristic that the central portion of the data derives directly from interaction in the classroom. This means that it is inevitable that *observation* will form the single most important component of classroom research. This observation can be conducted in many different ways, and again, no one way can be regarded as best or most correct. A crucial distinction is drawn between *evaluative* and *descriptive* observation, the former being often difficult to reconcile with research. Most classroom research is concerned with the establishment of formal criteria and categories for the classification of classroom events, or the development of a model of discourse structure. I have argued in this chapter that this approach, though it may shed some light on the structure of interaction, does not lead to a description of what participants in classrooms actually do. In order to describe the processes of interaction, it is necessary to follow an ethnographic approach which adheres to the *emic* and *holistic* principles.

Ethnographic research can be done in different ways and for different purposes. So long as the basic principles are not violated, a wide variety of tools and methods can be employed, in isolation or in combination. Crucial to ethnographic research is an orientation to the social context of classroom interaction, and in this sense ethnographic research is sociolinguistic research.

In L2 research statistical measurement and the search for causal links is the dominant methodological ideal. According to many social researchers such ideals are unattainable in the social sciences, but that does not mean that they are not worth pursuing nevertheless. However, there are no shortcuts to the achievement of these ideals, and they have to rest upon solid theoretical foundations. Ethnography, as it weakest justification, can claim to provide such foundations in terms of a clarification of relevant concepts and processes. But it cannot be assumed that the role of educational ethnography is merely an exploratory, ground-clearing one. Strong and respectable research traditions exist that show the theory-building potential of ethnographic study (Hammersley and Atkinson 1983; Thompson 1984; Saville-Troike 1982). The debate between *interpretive* (or *humanistic*) versus *experimental* (or *positivistic*) science has existed for centuries, and continues unabated. It is unlikely to be resolved in the near future, if ever, but it should warn the L2 researcher against unquestioningly assuming that statistical manipulation, controlled experimentation and hypothesis-testing, are necessarily scientifically more advanced or theoretically more powerful ways of doing research than descriptions based on observation. Nor are they necessarily more objective, the notion of objectivity being complex and relative.

The use of recorded data is relatively recent in ethnography, and has added a new dimension to the analysis of interaction. Indeed, it is no exaggeration to claim that this is probably the single most important factor in the (re)emergence of ethnography as a strong branch of educational research. The work of Mehan, Erickson and others shows the richness of description made possible by detailed analysis of video and audio recordings of interaction in natural settings. It is through work of this kind that the 'black box' of the classroom is finally being opened up to show how teachers and learners go about the business of learning.

Notes

1. Such neutrality is of course never entirely possible: as stated earlier (p. 38), no observation can be theory- or value-free. This paradox, inherent in all social research, can cause conflicts. However, adherence to the holistic and emic principles, and an explicit frame of reference, should guarantee openness and intersubjectivity, if not complete neutrality.
2. For an earlier study giving similar results, see Rowe 1974.

4 The subject matter of second-language classroom research

Introduction

The profession of language teaching is carried out in the classroom and that, in the last analysis, is where the success or failure of teaching is determined. Second-language classroom research, in studying the processes and circumstances of second-language development, aims to identify the phenomena that promote or hamper learning in the classroom.

It is generally accepted that second-language learning can and does occur in informal environments, i.e. without classroom instruction. In situations where both formal and informal learning is possible, the exact role of formal instruction is unclear: several studies have not shown significant correlations between proficiency and length of instruction (see Long 1983b). However, in most of these studies the actual classroom proceedings have been taken for granted, i.e. the classroom itself has not been an object for investigation. Nor has the relationship between formal and informal learning been systematically described.

As I have argued in the preceding chapters, classroom research is a necessary component of L2 research. If this necessity is granted, the question remains, what is it that we should be looking for in the classroom? The remainder of this book is devoted to this issue.

It is clear that we must have a certain approach to investigation (e.g. linguistic analysis, ethnography, coding, action research – see Chapter 3), but it is also clear that we must identify relevant phenomena for study. How do we know which phenomena are relevant? The answer to this question depends on our *assumptions* (beliefs, ideas, theories) about language learning. If, for example, we believe that language learning is largely a matter of habit formation, we will look for instances of those things psychologists tell us are essential for habit formation, such as positive reinforcements to responses and the avoidance of errors. If we believe that language

learning develops through conversation (in general, meaningful interaction), we will look for the characteristics of interaction in the
classroom.

The history of the second-language profession has at different
times emphasized different factors as being important for language
learning. In the past there has at times been a strongly deterministic
approach to language teaching in two senses: firstly the idea that an
appropriate packaging of the subject matter (in terms of syntax, functions, situations, etc.) was the key to optimal results and, secondly,
the idea that teaching, if done according to the rules, would cause
learning in the same way that the proper administration of shocks and
pellets of food causes rats to run around a maze. This deterministic
approach leads to a focus on linguistic analyses of the language used
in the classroom, to comparisons between teaching methods or techniques, and to classifications of errors and their remedies.

The present-day focus on communication shifts the emphasis away
from 'correct' ways of selecting, sequencing, grading and presenting
the language as content, and from prescribed teaching methods and
techniques, towards the activities and processes occurring in the
classroom. An extreme view would hold that teaching is ineffective,
and that language learning can only occur if the circumstances are
favourable, and then it will occur regardless of what the teacher does.
A more moderate view exhorts the teacher to ensure the quality of
activities and interaction by observing a specific set of essential principles, loosely bundled together under the name *communicative
approach*. While we may agree that this latter view is, given our
present knowledge about language acquisition, an appropriate one,
it is no doubt the case that the teacher is no longer given clear-cut
syllabus specifications, lesson plans and sequences, detailed descriptions of proper techniques at proper times, etc. In this sense, previous
methodologies such as the Direct Method, the Audiolingual Method,
the Structural Method, etc., were much more specific and gave
teachers detailed advice and instructions.

Teaching materials were able to prescribe exactly how the teaching
was to be carried out (some coursebooks even claimed to be 'teacher-
proof' or 'fool-proof'). This clarity and prescriptive precision is by
and large lacking in communicative teaching proposals, so that the
teacher has much less external guidance available for judging the
teaching. It is probably in the nature of communicative teaching and
learning to be less specific about ready-made techniques and
linguistic content, but this very fact puts much more of the burden
of choice and procedure on the teacher. These increased responsi-

BOX 4.1   Guiding the teacher: different views

Ask the pupils to detach the mask at the end of their books. Give the instructions *Open your books! Look at Lesson 51!* Explain, or indicate through mime, that the statements on the left-hand side of the page must be covered with the mask. Now play or read the dialogue as many times as is necessary for the pupils to understand it from the pictures. In order to ensure that the pupils are looking at the right pictures, count aloud immediately before each statement or group of statements is heard.

(Alexander 1968, p. 102)

Within a communicative methodology the teacher has two main roles. The first role is to facilitate the communicative processes between all participants in the classroom, and between these participants and the various activities and texts. The second role is to act as an *interdependent* participant within the learning-teaching group. . . . These roles imply a set of secondary roles for the teacher: first as an organizer of resources and as a resource himself. Second, as a guide within the classroom procedures and activities. In this role, the teacher endeavours to make clear to the learners what they need to do in order to achieve some specific activity or task, if they indicate that such guidance is necessary. This guidance role is ongoing and largely unpredictable, so the teacher needs to share it with other learners.

(Breen and Candlin 1980, p. 99)

Since oral practice exercises allow for a variety of exchanges, students must listen carefully to what their partners say before they can respond. This eliminates mechanical or artificial questions and answers and keeps the students interested and motivated.

(Castro and Kimbrough 1980, p. xi)

bilities require knowledge and understanding of classroom processes and of human interaction in general. Classroom research of a strictly descriptive kind is therefore of direct interest to the communicatively oriented teacher; it is also the one aspect of second-language acquisition research the teacher can most easily directly participate in and influence.

In this chapter I aim to place classroom research in the context of the L2 classroom, of teachers and learners, and point to some of the things L2 classroom research can do to benefit the teacher and learner directly and in the longer term. The remaining chapters will then select some aspects of the classroom reality to show how an ethnographic approach to the setting can give us a sense of what is 'really' going on.

Approaches to second-language development

There are at present two approaches to learning that dominate discussion in the L2 profession. These are the *interactive* approach to learning and the *linguistic/mental process* approach. Models based on both approaches derive to a greater or lesser extent from first-language acquisition studies and assume certain parallels between first- and second-language acquisition.

A third approach regards language development as a *social process* determined by relationships between individuals and groups. Within this general outlook two distinct models can be identified, firstly the social-psychological model which sees language development as accommodation between people and groups (the so-called 'Accommodation Theory', see Giles and St Clair 1979; Gardner 1985; Beebe forthcoming), and secondly the acculturation/nativization model which relates second-language development to processes of pidginization, decreolization and nativization or assimilation (see Andersen 1983; Ellis 1985). The different models based on the social-process-approach probably accommodate most premises of the first two approaches, but put the social context in the centre. This approach has had less impact on the L2 scene so far, though in time, with increasing information coming from studies of bilingualism and ESL students in mixed-nationality classrooms (see Cummins 1984), it is likely to have far-reaching consequences for the future of L2 research.

The interaction approach

The interaction (or social) model of language acquisition holds that language learning occurs in and through participation in speech events, that is, that talking to others, or making conversation, is essential. This view is influenced considerably by the work of Wells (1981, 1985) and a strong statement in favour of it is made by Hatch (1978):

> Our basic premise has long been that the child learns some basic set of syntactic structures, moving from a one-word phase to a two-word phase, to more complex structures, and that eventually the child is able to put these structures together in order to carry on conversations with others. The premise, if we use discourse analysis, is the converse. That is, language learning evolves *out of* learning how to carry on conversations.

(Hatch 1978, pp. 403–4)

The linguistic/mental approach

Studies of morpheme acquisition and comparison of stages of acquisition between first- and second-language development suggest that there is a natural order of development, relatively impervious to grammatical sequencing in teaching, and that this points to the creative construction of the language by the learner, or a language acquisition device which is activated when appropriate input is available and certain barriers, notably the 'affective filter', are down. A number of studies by Dulay and Burt (e.g. 1975) propose this view, and Krashen's various related hypotheses (e.g. Krashen 1985) are founded upon it. These researchers argue that, since the route of acquisition is largely predetermined, explicit instruction in grammar rules and phonological rules can have little effect. However, as, for example Ellis (1985) points out, classroom instruction, both in the form of meaningful interaction, and in the form of linguistic rules, may influence the *rate* of acquisition, even if the *route* remains unaffected (see also Dickerson 1983 on the use of phonological rules, especially p. 146).

In addition, research into universal grammar and cognitive development attempts to account for the stages of language development by distinguishing between core or unmarked rules, and periphery or marked rules. The findings of such research can help to gear the learning environment to the learner's developmental process or, at least, help avoid a superfluous or even counterproductive emphasis on certain linguistic structures at inappropriate times (for a representative sample of current studies see Hyltenstam and Pienemann 1985).

Pidginization/acculturation

Andersen (1983) points to a number of interesting parallels between second-language development and the processes pidgins go through to develop into creoles, and particularly the process of decreolization whereby a creole, through interactional and societal forces, gradually approximates to the dominant language it is based upon. This model is particularly interesting in that it systematizes variability, which may be socially motivated, in interlanguage. It is unlikely that variability in interlanguage can be adequately explained in terms of interactive and/or cognitive strategies (Ellis 1984a), or in terms of past learning history (Krashen's Monitor). Rather, social considerations may account for variability in second-language performance in the same way that they do for code switching in bilingual settings and social registers of speech in general (see Ellis 1987).

Accommodation

Accommodation theory holds that group membership and intergroup relationships are key factors in language development. These factors determine such variables as attitudes, motivation, identification and perceptions of social distance. Although accommodation theory does not attempt to explain *how* second-language development comes about, it provides much information concerning favourable and unfavourable circumstances for learning. As mentioned before, it can also account for at least part of variable interlanguage use. It has obviously more relevance for language development and language use in bilingual and multi-ethnic settings, and less for foreign-language settings where intergroup relationships and membership in target-language groups or communities are less prominent concerns. However, even in foreign-language settings individual, societal and peer group perceptions about the target language and the culture(s) it represents, can have a significant impact on the success of language learning.

BOX 4.2   A selection of second-language acquisition theories

1. Interactive focus	Discourse Model (Hatch 1978) Variable Competence Model (Ellis 1984a)
2. Linguistic/mental focus	Monitor Model (Krashen 1979, 1981, 1982) Conscious Reinforcement Model (Carroll 1981) Strategy Model (Bialystok 1978) Universal Hypothesis (Wode 1980; Pienemann and Johnston 1985) Neurofunctional Theory (Lamendella 1979)
3. Social process focus	Social Psychological Model (Lambert 1963a, 1963b, 1967, 1974) Acculturation/Nativization Model (Schumann 1978; Andersen 1983) Social Context Model (Clement 1980) Intergroup Model (Giles and Byrne 1982)

(Ellis 1985; Gardner 1985)

A consensus

It should be clear that the three approaches are not in any way incompatible, but rather focus on different aspects of the same process (for a partial grouping of the major theories and models see Box 4.2). In the classroom these aspects: the interactive, the cognitive, and the social (including societal) meet and must be combined into one developmental process. We need, of course, much more detailed information about every aspect of the process. For example, interaction in the classroom cannot be identical to interaction outside it: is that an inherent weakness, or can it be turned into a strength? A shallow dichotomy such as learning versus acquisition does scant justice to potential differences in cognitive and learning styles: how can we accommodate such differences and exploit their full potential? Relationships between learners and learners, learners and teachers, native culture and target culture, classroom and society need to be explored in depth: what might be an adequate job description for the classroom?

A consensus of classroom learning will need to put the social context of learning in centre place, in three senses:
a) learning as an interactive, hence social, activity;
b) the classroom as a social setting;
c) the place of the classroom as one aspect of social life.

The nature of the classroom

In Box 4.3 I quote several educational researchers as saying that we know very little about what goes on in classrooms. With our increasing knowledge of language acquisition processes, and the crucial role communication plays in them, it is now more necessary than ever before to focus on the classroom in different and innovative ways.

Communicative approaches to language learning have placed the classroom in the centre of attention, since it is only through a better knowledge of classroom processes that communicative principles can be applied in practice. In addition, since much of second-language research is modelled on first-language acquisition studies, where instruction supposedly plays no significant role (though see Bruner 1983; Wells 1985 for evidence of the didactic concerns of parents), the effectiveness of formal teaching is brought into question. If the keys to learning are exposure to input and meaningful interaction with

---

BOX 4.3   How much do we know?

. . . our understanding of classrooms and what goes on in them is still very limited.

(Stenhouse 1975, p. 25)

Our ignorance of what actually happens inside classrooms is spectacular.

(Stubbs 1976, p. 70)

. . . the ethnography, the sociology, the social psychology and the educational psychology of the bilingual classroom are all little more than gleams in the eyes of a few researchers.

(Fishman 1977, p. 34)

---

other speakers, we must find out what input and interaction the classroom can provide. In the first place, it is not possible to define, in linguistic or psycholinguistic terms, what appropriate input is. Krashen's descriptions of 'finely tuned' (i+1) and 'roughly tuned' input are intuitively acceptable, but perhaps deliberately vague (see, e.g. Krashen 1985). The only concrete requirement placed on input is that it must be comprehensible. Secondly, interaction comes in many shapes and fashions. Repeating after the teacher, answering a display question, acting out a dialogue, and discussing possible solutions to a task, are all examples of interaction. We must study in detail the use of language in the classroom in order to see if and how learning comes about through the different ways of interacting in the classroom.

In strictly practical terms the classroom aims to be a shortcut to language development. In a limited amount of time, measured in classroom periods, it aims to make up for the continuous and long-term exposure, and the vital need for communication that characterize the child's acquisition of the mother tongue. In pedagogical terms there is a tacit *contract* between teacher and learner, or school and learner, which governs purposes, roles and relationships, and rules for appropriate classroom conduct. In social terms the classroom is a group of people with overt and hidden aims, patterns of behaviour, standards for judging participation, efforts and solidarity, etc., similar to other social groups.

Studies of first-language classrooms have given us much insight into the classroom life of learners and their teachers. Often, in addition to detailed reports on observations, researchers have asked learners and teachers to tell stories about their experiences in classrooms, as part of the triangulated approach to investigation mentioned in Chapter 1 (p. 13). Such descriptions are often anecdotal (though increasing scientific systematicity and precision are emerging), but they do provide much needed information about the curriculum, both official and hidden, and about how classrooms turn out the way they do (see, e.g. the collection of papers in Stubbs and Delamont 1976; Adelman 1981). As yet there are few, if any, descriptions of this kind for second-language classrooms. Few researchers have examined classroom proceedings in detail, fewer still have solicited learners' views of their language learning careers. Some diary studies have provided personal accounts of individual learners' experiences, but by and large descriptive evidence about L2 learning in and out of classrooms is almost non-existent. What information we have comes largely from simulated native speaker/non-native speaker or non-native speaker/non-native speaker or conversations (see, e.g. Faerch and Kasper 1983; Varonis and Gass 1985, and many other similar studies). It may also be significant to note again (see p. 71) that Long's pertinent question: 'Does second-language instruction make a difference?' is answered by way of a review of twelve studies, not one of which looks at what 'instruction' is or means (Long 1983b). Instruction in these studies is an unqualified variable measured in terms of amount of time spent on 'being instructed'.

What to look for

If we approach CR in the same way that an ethnographer approaches the study of an unknown culture, we will not start our research by assembling a set of pre-specified phenomena, but rather assume that in principle anything that occurs may be relevant.

However, I have mentioned before that any observation, and any classroom research, is necessarily selective. It may be argued that, if we produce a complete transcription of a lesson, we may avoid this charge of selectiveness. Yet, the matter of *access* has already introduced an important element of selection: we are in *this* particular classroom and not in any other, and we may ask ourselves *why?* We may perhaps have asked a teacher who happens to be nearby, or who we know is friendly, or who has a class of only fifteen students rather than sixty-five, or who has mixed nationalities in the class rather than only Swiss students, etc. Among thousands of theoretically available classrooms we choose one, or several, for certain reasons. Those reasons may seem perfectly random, or haphazard, dictated by convenience rather than by theoretical plots, but they may nevertheless become very relevant later on.

Next, we produce a transcription. However complete, this transcription cannot possibly include everything that may be relevant. It does not include the walls, the pictures on the walls, the shuffling of feet, covert glances, smiles and grimaces, and a million other things. It may or may not include some non-verbal information, intonation, exactly measured pauses, and so on. It will not include those things that cannot be seen or heard, but only *felt*, such as sudden sensations of impatience, urgency, relaxation, frustration, and so on. What it does include are most of the words spoken, in the order that they are spoken and, preferably, by whom. But on the basis of what criteria do we decide that a word spoken is more important than a cough, or, for that matter, the colour of the ceiling? Whatever the choices, there are limits to the amount of detail that can be put in. The more detail, the less readable the transcript – it may become some abstract confusion of symbols, decipherable only by its creator – the less detail, the greater the likelihood that important information may be missed. There is no solution to this problem: the transcriber opts for some reasonable balance between accuracy and simplicity, and must be prepared to defend that balance. Yet, when the transcript is ready (if ever it is), the data have been sifted and transformed into static print. For some common techniques, conventions and guidelines, the reader is advised to consult the Appendix at the end of this book.

The next step is the analysis of the data, and this is where, traditionally, charges of selectiveness are levelled although, as we have seen, considerable selection has already taken place. We may start out with a pre-selected question which derives, e.g. from some common observation, such as that Latin-American students tend to participate more actively than East-Asian students, or some hypothesis such as that people who initiate more interaction perform better on proficiency tests (see Seliger 1983 for this particular example). In this case our course of action appears clear-cut: all we have to do is identify relevant instances of behaviour, count them, correlate them with tests if necessary, and draw our conclusions. However, problems (some of them are illustrated in Chapter 5) may emerge, and if we are not too carried away by our enthusiasm or emotional investment in our idea or hypothesis, we may notice them. For example, we may note that participation may not be uniquely manifested through verbal contributions, but also in other ways, and we may find that it is not always so easy to determine what constitutes initiation of interaction and what does not.

In general, L2 classroom research has focused on selected aspects of interaction, such as the ones mentioned above, and also questions and answers, the making of errors and their treatment, evaluatory statements by the teacher, changes in topics, and so on.

If we want to avoid selecting certain specific aspects of interaction and rather follow Sinclair and Coulthard's and Mehan's recommendations for *comprehensive analysis* (see Chapter 3), selection is no less necessary. Describing everything in a blanket fashion is obviously unfeasible and unproductive: we won't be able to see the wood for the trees. While we produce the transcription, involving as it does frequent listenings and revisions, we will become intimately familiar with the data, the people, and the things done and said. We will note repeated occurrences of actions, shifts in focus, topics, rights of participation and so on, and these regularities, shifts, rules and tacit agreements, as well as the boundaries between one kind of activity and the next will suggest patterns – non-random sequences of actions – which will form the basis of our subsequent description. Like the ethnographer walking around an exotic village, we will at first find no rhyme or reason to the sequence or unity of events, but gradually an order imposes itself. It is important that this order is one that emerges from the data rather than from what one already patently knows, and the transcription and analysis process is an aid in developing this emergent order.

The social context

I have argued that learning language occurs in the context of social interaction, both in the classroom and outside it. Of course, the second-language classroom itself is only one segment of the social world of the learner, and it is also only one – though central – component of the organized institutions that are involved in education and training. The classroom researcher must therefore study the classroom as embodying a specific set of functions and values from the point of view of the learner, and also from the point of view of social institutions at large. Ideals, expectations, and conceptions of the properties that a classroom must possess so that it can be regarded as an ordinary, good classroom, play an important role in determining what will happen in the classroom. All these influences decide that the things that are done in classrooms, and the way they are done, are not the same sorts of things as those that happen in other places. It is accepted, indeed expected, by the public at large (including most learners and teachers) that tasks and talk in the classroom look and sound different, perhaps even somewhat peculiar, if compared with everyday talk, and have a logic all their own. It is not up to the public to understand why this is: a classroom is a classroom. Whether or not this public stereotyping of classrooms is borne out in all instances, it is doubtless a significant force in the way they are set up and maintained.

Classroom research must study not only how classrooms must or should be structured in order to promote learning in optimal ways, but also why things in classrooms happen the way they do, and in this way expose complex relationships between individual participants, the classroom, and the societal forces that influence it.

Context in classroom research often means the context of inter-actional talk in the classroom (see, e.g. Erickson and Shultz 1981), and there is no doubt that this contextual view is a considerable advance over narrowly linguistic, cognitive or behavioural approaches. However, despite recommendations from many researchers (e.g. Erickson, Mehan, Hymes), the wider context remains relatively unex-amined. Dunkin and Biddle note the following:

> Possibly because most classroom research is conducted by psychologists, or because it is expensive, few studies have investigated the relationships between either school or community variables and classroom teaching (. . .) we are unaware of more than a handful of studies concerned with the impact of community variables on teaching.
>
> (Dunkin and Biddle 1974, p. 43)

Now, more than ten years later, there are signs that the picture is changing somewhat (see, e.g. the multi-level research perspective in Oosthoek and van den Eeden 1984) as far as general education, bilingual education, and studies of ESL in multi-ethnic schools (Cummins 1984) is concerned. However, the field of second-language lags far behind in this respect.

One of the main problems in contextual research of the wider variety is that it is highly complex, and requires the combination of much qualitative information with powerful statistical analyses, requiring expertise that few L2 researchers, particularly those most concerned with the issue of social context, possess. One can there-fore only agree with Erickson when he says:

> It would seem that qualitative researchers could benefit from extended consideration of such issues of technique [more elaborate statistical techniques. . .the approaches of Bayesian statistics] together with experts in statistics, perhaps in summer institutes or working conferences in which there would be adequate time to learn more about each other's expertise. That dialogue is long overdue.
>
> (Erickson 1981b, p. 34)

Cognition and social context

Pike has said (1982, p. 28) that the meanings of a word are like waves. In the same way, it can be said that the social context of learning language extends like ever-widening concentric ripples, with the individual at the centre. However, the analogy is inadequate if we consider that the ripples do not only move outward but also inward. The cognitive store and strategies also include much of the social world. That is, the social context does not begin and end at the boundaries of the individual, rather, it extends within the individual. While a person's mind cannot be said to be a complete mirror-image of the social and physical world outside, much of the work of making sense of the world in cognitive terms is social work, whether or not it involves interpersonal interaction. It is therefore likely that there are many parallels between interpersonal and intrapersonal interaction, when both are aimed at reaching an agreement or accommodation between the cognitive apparatus inside the person and the outside world, and that is most of the time when we are mentally active. When studying overt interaction between people, we are therefore not kept totally in the dark about their mental processes, and that will include such processes as learning and communication strategies. As folk wisdom has it, we know and judge people through their actions. This means that when we study language use and language learning in and through the social context of interaction, we are also in a very real and significant sense studying cognition.

This does not mean that our only clue to a learner's cognitive processes is through the interaction that learners engage in. Much useful work is being conducted through the elicitation of verbal protocols (see Mann 1982; Cavalcanti 1982), introspection by learners, diaries and psycholinguistic experiments. However, it is useful to realize that there are deep and meaningful relations between learners' cognitive processes and interactive processes.

In recent studies of learner performance a distinction is sometimes made between interactional and cognitive (or academic) performance. Most well-known is perhaps Cummins's distinction between BICS (basic interpersonal communication skills) and CALP (cognitive/ academic language proficiency). The former can be regarded as the ability to communicate successfully in everyday contexts, the latter as the ability to manipulate language in often decontextualized academic tasks. Cummins (1984) argues that LEP (Limited English Proficient) children are often assessed (and perhaps mainstreamed) on the basis of a superficial examination of BICS, where the child's CALP may not be sufficiently developed to cope with classroom demands. In such cases evaluators may erroneously conclude that, since there appears to be no language deficiency, some form of cognitive disability must be the reason that such children continue to fail in the classroom.

In my view the need for a distinction between BICS and CALP is more a reflection of inadequate classroom practices than of the actual existence of two separate types of proficiency. To substantiate this view it is useful to refer again to Erickson's distinction between ATS (Academic Task Structure) and SPS (Social Participation Structure) (see p. 64; there will also be a detailed discussion in Chapter 6, but here I want to look at the issue from a cognitive/interactive angle). Box 4.4 presents a summary of the characteristics of ATS and SPS.

BOX 4.4

ATS	SPS
1. logic of subject matter sequencing	1. social gatekeeping of access
2. information content of the various sequential steps	2. allocation of communication rights and obligations amongst participants
3. 'meta-content' cues toward steps and strategies	3. sequencing and timing of successive functional slots
4. physical materials	4. simultaneous actions of all engaged
	(Erickson 1982)

It is clear that every classroom task will present some measure of cognitive/academic complexity to the learners, and also some measure of social complexity. I assume that a communicative approach will be concerned to balance the complexity of a task with both the learners' cognitive and interactive resources, so that, if for example the cognitive resources are low (e.g. the content matter is unfamiliar) the learners' interactive resources are exploited optimally, and vice versa. This means that the design of a learning task will take into account both complexity (social and academic) and resources (internal and external to the learner). The interrelatedness of task complexity and available resources, and of social and academic aspects of classroom work, is crucial both to curriculum development and to the study of classroom processes, and CR must therefore be integrative rather than isolative in its descriptive and analytic work. Box 4.5 shows the relationships between the different elements of classroom tasks. It must be understood that certain characteristics of tasks are inherent in those tasks, in terms of content and routes to resolution, and others depend on what the learners bring to the task in terms of resources, both as individuals and as groups.

BOX 4.5

	Cognitive/Academic aspects	Social/Interactive aspects
Task	*Demands* complexity of information; rhetorical structure	level of predictability; conventionality, degree of routine
Resources	*Internal* familiarity with subject matter (background knowledge) and rhetorical structure; cognitive/linguistic skills and operations	level of socialization; social/interactive skills and strategies
	External explicitness of instructions; elaboration of sequence, steps	cooperation; negotiation

Once the interdependence of all these ingredients of tasks and activities is established and kept firmly in mind, CR can proceed to investigate a number of issues that are of prominent concern in classroom work. Some of these have been referred to already, such as:

a) control and initiative;
b) quality and kinds of participation;
c) planned and unplanned sequences of interaction;
d) feedback and evaluation, both *by* and *for* learners and teachers.

Others can readily be added, and I shall mention but a few:

a) authenticity of task and interaction;
b) comprehensibility of input;
c) perceptions and criteria of progress and success;
d) cooperation and competition in classroom work;
e) equity of rights and responsibilities.

All the above are in a sense macro-topics for research, since they are expressed in far more general terms than the issues that are usually investigated (for a comparison see the summary in Box 3.7). Many researchers prefer to investigate small, easily identifiable aspects of classroom interaction, since they are more amenable to analysis and experimentation. This brings with it inevitable problems of relevance, when the results have to be related to classroom work as a whole, and potential triviality of findings. However, such researchers may find support in Campbell's suggestion that

> for building a social science, a trivial problem which is amenable to the experimental probing of hypotheses is to be preferred to an important problem area where selection from the glut of alternative theories is impossible. With the tremendous pressures for an immediately useful social science, this has been, and will continue to be, a difficult decision to accept.
>
> (Campbell 1959, quoted in Cronbach 1982, p. 133)

Whether scientific proof of trivial details is theoretically more beneficial than an understanding of overall patterns of behaviour is an issue we cannot resolve here. It may be noted that Campbell has since substantially modified his views on this matter (see Brewer and Collins 1981; Cronbach 1982). In general, what is at stake is a distinction between scientific elegance and practical value. Since I have argued that CR should ideally be of service to the teacher, I take the view that value and relevance are more important than demands of scientific design. Moreover, ethnographic study follows different criteria of scientific conduct than Campbell's quasi-experimental approach.

Classroom, school and society

The wider context of the second-language classroom is as yet almost completely unresearched, with the exception perhaps of the social-psychological work of Giles, Gardner and Lambert, particularly in the area of attitudes to language and learning (see Gardner 1985; Beebe forthcoming). Yet it is clear that the classroom does not occur in a vacuum: before the lesson the learners come from somewhere and after the lesson they go somewhere else. What happens in those other places inevitably has important repercussions on what happens in the classroom. The relationships between the L2 classroom and other social contexts are perhaps most significant in those settings where the target language plays an important role outside the classroom, but even in foreign-language settings the L2 classroom has a certain role in society and a certain place in the learner's life.

Group and cultural relations are of prime importance, as the collection of papers in Giles and St Clair (1979) shows. However, an ethnographic study of learners in and out of class may show a number of issues which learners themselves find important, such as the desirability of native-like fluency and pronunciation, interest in colloquial and idiomatic expressions, comparisons between languages, the importance of television and rock music, and so on. Conversation among language learners frequently turns to issues of language learning and language use, and a wealth of anecdotes about in-class and out-of-class experiences is displayed. Interesting and valuable studies are waiting to be done using conversational data from language learners about language learning. These data are important since the social relevance of the classroom and of classroom learning, from the learners' point of view, is an essential component of L2 classroom research.

Conclusion

I have emphasized throughout that CR is contextual research. It begins with detailed observation, recording and transcription, leading perhaps to what Geertz refers to as 'thick description' (1973, p. 6). The researcher's task is to create an orderly account out of the mass of data, using the analytical techniques available in the social sciences. Such techniques include the analysis of social networks (Milroy 1980), conversational analysis (as a prominent application of ethnomethodology, see Atkinson and Heritage 1984), analysis of linguistic variation (Rampton 1987) and the use of rating scales to measure attitudes (Edwards 1979).

It is characteristic of most techniques used in descriptive and analytical ethnography that they involve the use of intuitive judgements and decisions. This at times displeases causally oriented researchers who feel that true scientific progress cannot rest on intuitive foundations. Yet the role of intuition in scientific progress is pervasive and crucial (see Kuhn 1962) and, as the philosopher Bergson has said, 'From intuition one can pass to analysis, but not from analysis to intuition' (Kohl 1965, p. 25).

To the question, what are appropriate topics for CR? I have in this chapter not provided an answer in terms of detailed classroom phenomena, but rather a partial list of fairly broad themes. This is inevitable as a consequence of the methodological recommendations of holistic and emic enquiry made earlier. Indeed, I feel that the only proper answer to the question is *to let the data lead the way*. To illustrate what such faith in actual data may lead to in practice, it is useful to look at an example from anthropology.

The kinds of facts and relationships the ethnographer focuses on when assembling a coherent picture – and, in this case, also an important theory – out of a collection of notes and observations, are illustrated in Bateson's epilogue to his famous New Guinea study, *Naven*, an extract from which appears in Box 4.6.

BOX 4.6

When I came to the task of fitting my observations together into a consecutive account, I was faced with a mass of the most diverse and disconnected material. I had for example a number of stories of sorcery and retribution, but not to one of them was appended a systematic study of the relevant facts of kinship, technique, emotional attitude, etc. I had collected, of course, not isolated facts, but facts in little bunches: the facts in some bunches were grouped on a chronological basis, and in other bunches they were grouped on a structural basis, and so on. No one system of organisation ran through the material, but in general my groups of facts had been put together by my informants, so that the systems of grouping were based upon native rather than scientific thought. Out of this material I had to construct a picture of the Iatmul culture. If in the circumstances I have managed to demonstrate some coherence in the culture, this achievement is the best testimony to the usefulness of the methods of analysis.

(Bateson 1958, p. 259)

Bateson stresses that his method of field work was completely unsystematic and not guided by some definite interest or theory. While, as he points out, this led to much wasteful enquiry, it strengthened the emic and holistic (contextual) qualities of the work.

The message, so far as L2 classroom research is concerned, is that it is often difficult, and probably largely counterproductive, from an ethnographic point of view, to select certain specific facts or details beforehand while at the same time aiming to be true to the participants' perspective and to the interactive and wider social context.

In the following chapters I present ethnographic analyses that derive from observation, transcription and close analysis of a central corpus of around ten hours of transcribed audio- and video-taped L2 classrooms (in different settings in Great Britain and the USA) and some transcribed pieces from other L2 classrooms. This close analysis led to the identification of several major notions or themes, and three of these form the subject matter of the next three chapters:

the notions of initiative, topic and participation structure, and repair. These themes naturally evolved out of the analysis of the data rather than out of a prior research interest. With time, or given different circumstances, other themes might have become prominent, including some of those listed on p. 85 earlier in this chapter. The fact that these themes emerged from the data rather than from a pre-established interest or framework means that their treatment looks very different from that usually found in classroom studies, and the reader will only understand this difference and its importance in the context of the research-methodological discussions in these first four chapters. The aim, in all of this, is to *make sense* of the second-language classroom.

5 In and out of turn: interaction in the second-language classroom

Introduction

There are two basic ways of studying the language produced by learners in the classroom:

1. By focusing on *what is said*, for example for the purpose of studying specific linguistic features of the learners' interlanguage and – if the study is longitudinal – their development over time. Thus, a number of studies focus on such issues as the use of negation, question formation, the emergence of *do*-support, pronominal reference, and so on (see Ellis 1985; Chaudron forthcoming, for detailed summaries). This work is of vital interest for the study of developmental stages in L2 learning and for the comparison of formal instruction with informal environments for L2 development.

2. By focusing on *what is done*, that is, on the ways in which language is used to do the kinds of work that are the *raison d'être* of the L2 classroom. This is deliberately vague, since we need to include everything from 'having a good time' to 'solving a communication problem' to 'learning pronunciation', but all this under the general umbrella of a pedagogical purpose: to learn language. Such study will examine opportunities for speaking, options and choices available to learners for using language, and the kinds of language work that are relevant to getting different classroom tasks accomplished. This work is important for the study of the cost-effectiveness of the classroom as a learning environment, for teaching training, and for classroom methodology.

A focus on *what is done* requires detailed attention to the interaction that occurs in the L2 classroom, and an examination of what is meant by such terms as initiative, participation and involvement. The investigation of these issues, through observation and analysis of transcribed data, will form the subject matter of the following chapters.

Interaction and language development in second-language classrooms

In the preceding chapters several assumptions have been made about the role of interaction in classroom second-language development. The following questions summarize some of the most important assumptions:

1. Since interaction is a defining characteristic of the L2 classroom, how can it be exploited to promote language development optimally?
2. If language learning (and learning in general, see Barnes 1975; Brown *et al.* 1984) occurs in and through meaningful interaction, what kinds of interaction can be called 'meaningful'?
3. Given the close relationships between cognitive and interactive processes (suggested in Chapter 4), how can classroom tasks systematically relate these processes; in particular, how can social interaction promote the kinds of cognitive work that are conducive to language development?
4. Interaction presupposes participation, personal involvement, and the taking of initiative in some way. In what ways are these manifested overtly through actions and, consequently, observable to teachers, researchers, and learners themselves?

When observing an L2 classroom in action it is clear that no direct link can be made between observable behaviour and language development. Learning is not generally directly and immediately observable. In the first place, it is characterized by improved performance or increased knowledge, and manifested by the learner's behaviour at some point of time (unspecified) after the learning has occurred. Secondly, the learning itself may not be produced by one specifically identifiable event, but rather by the cumulative effect of a number of events, and how these events are related is not always immediately visible (see Box 5.1). Thirdly, learning, as a process and as a result, may not be overtly signalled in ways that are observable by a researcher who does not intervene in the interaction. If we want to find out *how* and *why* learning does or does not take place in specific classroom settings, we need information from a variety of sources, one of them being classroom interaction.

Language development is a thread that runs through the social interaction learners engage in, at times visible, at times not. In unravelling this thread, CR has a function comparable to the role of ethology in biological research (see Lorenz 1971), and to all observation in the sciences in general.

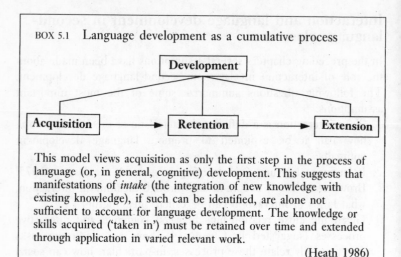

BOX 5.1   Language development as a cumulative process

This model views acquisition as only the first step in the process of language (or, in general, cognitive) development. This suggests that manifestations of *intake* (the integration of new knowledge with existing knowledge), if such can be identified, are alone not sufficient to account for language development. The knowledge or skills acquired ('taken in') must be retained over time and extended through application in varied relevant work.

(Heath 1986)

The participants in an L2 classroom are concerned with language learning. Many of the things they do are therefore done with the aim of learning in mind. Actual instances of learning may not be observable, but many of the actions and strategies (for example, processing strategies) that are oriented towards that goal certainly are. Now, part of the time there may be private and covert activities such as reading a text, doing tasks or tests, etc., during which individual learners separately work on their own and process (e.g. think about, react to, transform) some input cognitively (route B in the diagram in Box 5.2). However, normally we expect at least part of the time in a classroom to be taken up by purposeful interaction between the participants, on tasks which involve working with the target language.

When observing the behaviour of those present in the L2 classroom, one of the salient characteristics is their participation in the interaction that goes on there. As I have shown in Chapters 3 and 4, there are a number of different ways in which this participation can be studied. For example, we can look at it in *quantitative* terms, i.e. how much there is of it, in time and volume, in terms of the class as a whole, or in terms of individual participants. We can also study it *qualitatively*, i.e. in terms of the different ways in which they participate, or how intensely, spontaneously, and actively they do so. In this chapter I will use quantitative techniques in the service of interpretive (qualitative) enquiry.

The reason for focusing on participation is the assumption that it is in some way directly related to learning, or at least to opportunities

BOX 5.2   The role of interaction

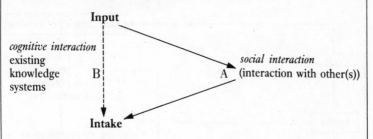

The diagram suggests that interaction mediates between input and intake. Most important and central is the interaction with others in meaningful activities, but as a complement, and perhaps partial replacement, the learner's cognitive apparatus may also interact directly with the available input or sections thereof.

for learning. This assumption is clear in Seliger's (1983) distinction between HIG (high input generators) and LIG (low input generators). It is furthermore obvious that participation presupposes attention, and it is of course a basic tenet of the psychology of learning that attention is a prerequisite for learning (see further the conclusion to this chapter).

However, one of the problems that CR faces is that attention, and indeed participation, need not necessarily be overt at all times. Participation may consist in 'eavesdropping', thinking about what is going on, internal repetition, etc.

In focusing on overt participation, CR may be tacitly assuming that this is what is most likely to lead to learning, and this may be an unwarranted assumption. However, despite these limitations it is useful to describe active participation in the classroom, since it is a prerequisite for interaction and hence communication, as the hierarchy in Box 5.3 shows.

The two bottom elements in this inclusive hierarchy may not always be directly observable to the classroom researcher (though see Haysom 1985, particularly Chapter 5, for some interesting suggestions). However, we may assume that they are prerequisites, i.e. must be present if the elements higher up in the hierarchy are to occur. Any investigation, descriptive or otherwise, may approach the area from two directions: from the top down, or from the bottom up. In the present and subsequent chapters I shall attempt to illustrate both bottom-up and top-down procedures, and show how they can be

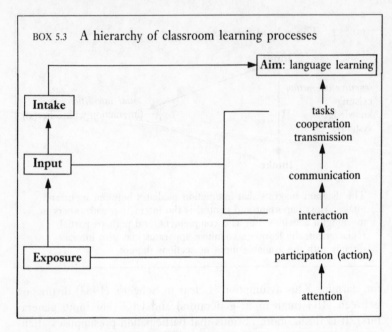

BOX 5.3   A hierarchy of classroom learning processes

related in a coherent framework. To start with, we shall examine the issue of turn taking, which will give us some idea of the orderliness of interaction, the rights and duties of participants, and their expression of initiative.

What is turn taking?

Interaction in the classroom is not random. In particular, the matter of who speaks and when is governed by regularities of some kind, whether we call them rules, regulations, routines, or conventions (see Chapter 3). This non-randomness is probably characteristic of all interaction anywhere, but at times there appear to be more constraints than at other times. For instance, the two extracts in Box 5.4 illustrate two different degrees of restriction. Both these examples come from L2 classrooms, and serve to alert us to the fact that many different kinds of activities can go on there.

Everyday conversation between friends is less restricted in terms of who speaks when than a cross-examination in a courtroom. Turn taking studies the systematic nature of speaker change in different settings. In doing so it addresses a basic problem of discourse analysis, formulated by Labov (in Labov and Fanshel 1977) as the question of 'how one utterance follows another in a rational, rule-

---

BOX 5.4   Constraints on turn taking: two examples

a) *less constraints*:

```
 1  E   can you fo- can you follow any conversation? any people?
 2  A   sometime yes but ah ... many times I can't
 3  E                    ᴸhm::
 4  E   and what about you?
 5  D   the same but depend of (who) the conversation no?
 6  A   yah
 7  D   or the point because sometimes is point very very easy, but
        the:: depend of the theme
 8  E   [si:m]
 9  D   theme
10  E   [si:m]
11  A   the topic
12  E   [si:m] ah! [si:m] ah yes [si:m]              yeah yes=
13  A                 ᴸ((chuckle)) ((unint)) topicᒕ
    E   =yes [si:m] tee- aitch- ((spells)) ... theme ... theme
14  D                                             ᴸyes
15  A                                                  ᴸyeah
16  D   yeah theme
17  A   okay ... next thing
```

b) *more constraints*:

```
 1  T   how many people are talking. Elly? ... how many people
 2  L7                                    ᴸ((unint))
 3  L7  two people
 4  T   yes that's right two people. and what are these two people
        talking about. Marcia.
 5  L4  ((unint)) people ask the way
 6  T   uhuh
```

---

governed manner'. There is of course more to this question than the exchange of turns *per se*, but it is worth looking at the different aspects separately before attempting to integrate them. One of the problems the observer faces is that the regularities of turn taking are rarely overtly stated, but rather, are tacit norms that are followed by the participants. However, when things do not work as they 'should', we can hear people in the classroom refer to the norms. Thus we may hear utterances such as:

'It's my turn now.'
'You're next.'
'I've already said that.'
'Hands up if you know the answer.'
'I can't hear you if you shout out.'
'Only the boys are answering. Where are the girls?'
'In English please.'

In general, the kinds of things that are said and done when the tacitly assumed order is violated, that is, the *sanctions* that are issued (see Humphrey 1979 for a detailed study of teachers' turn-taking sanctions in kindergarten and primary classrooms), can give the investigator valuable information as to what that order is, what the underlying rules, norms and routines are.

The taking of turns is of course common to many human activities that involve more than one person. We may queue up for our turn at the dentist's, the checkout, a ride on the roller-coaster, and so on. Turn-taking problems are dealt with in different ways. We may be issued a number when entering a popular restaurant, and we tell children not to 'interrupt' when adults are talking. Turn taking can also be problematic in traffic, as can be painfully obvious at Mexican '*glorietas*' or roundabouts, when two lanes of the '*Autobahn*' suddenly become one due to construction work, or when, as a stranger, one arrives at a 'four-way stop' in the USA. Sometimes the rules are specified and spelled out, at other times we have to make them up as we go along. Games are one type of human activity that depends heavily on rules for turns: in chess the order is unproblematic and predetermined, but there may be restrictions on length. In soccer the players fight for their turns at the ball (though following well-defined rules), in volleyball they can only hold on to their turn (the serve) by scoring points. In conversation it is up to each of us to take a turn when we want to, but at times we don't find the 'proper' thing to say at the right time, at other times someone won't let us get a word in edgewise (see Yngve 1970).

In sum, the articulation of contributions or turns in any interaction is governed by certain procedures. These may be predetermined in the form of strict rules, or they may evolve as norms or routines in the interaction itself. The procedures basically address the following issues:

1. the 'proper' size or length of a turn;
2. identification of the end of a turn;
3. the sequence of turns, or 'who's next'.

In addition there is the issue of the appropriate content of a turn, or what counts as a 'fitting' contribution, i.e., what do we do with a turn-slot once we have obtained it? This, however, is an issue that is in a sense separate from the other questions, and may best be treated as such. In making this distinction between turn-taking mechanisms and what is done with and in turns, I follow common practice in conversational analysis. As Goffman puts it:

a turn ... refers to an opportunity to hold the floor, not what is said while holding it.

(Goffman 1981, p. 23)

In general conversation turn taking is governed by competition and initiative; participants watch for opportunities to take the floor and, once they obtain it, try to hold on to it even though there may be others who want it. This means that whenever people are keen to talk there is a tendency on the part of the hearers to minimize the size of a turn, coupled with a tendency on the part of the current speaker to maximize it. At the same time, there is a constraint, or even stigma, against interrupting, i.e. cutting short an unfinished unit. What counts as a unit is not a clearcut matter, since it is in itself a nego- tiable entity. Phrases, clauses, sentences, tone units, and ritual utter- ances (hello, thank you, right you are, etc.) have been proposed as possible turns, turn units or unitary building blocks for turns, but it is clear that a turn is a social action, not just a linguistic one. Sacks *et al.*, speak of *turn-constructional units* – TCU's – which we plan and execute so as to do our share of the talk (1974, p. 12; see also Scheg- loff 1981). During a conversation hearers watch for possible completion points as opportunities to take the floor, while speakers may indicate, at the beginning, that their turn is going to be a long one, consisting of several building blocks or TCU's that must not be interrupted. Indicators of the end of a unit may be a downward intonation curve, items such as question tags, the completion of syntactic units (e.g. the end of a verb phrase), signs that the speaker is running out of breath, the direction of eye gaze, gestures and posture, and possibly many others (see Duncan 1973; Goodwin 1977; Erickson 1979), typically several of them co-occurring in the form of a 'bundle' of contextual cues (Gumperz 1982). Speakers may try to prevent the 'bundling' of such cues by spreading them out at different places in the unit (e.g. delay breathing until after the first constituent of the next (sub-)unit, speeding up delivery across junctures, etc.) and thus minimize the chances of take-over. Part of the game is for the speaker to make any putative take-over look like an interruption, hence sanctionable, and for the hearer to make any interruption look like a valid take-over. The game is thus delicately balanced, and requires complex skills, not least among them linguistic skills. Sacks *et al.* have described the basic systematics of turn taking in conver- sations (1974), showing the complexities as well as the skills involved. In practice, however, things may be even more fluid and more complex than Sacks *et al.* suggest, as Erickson's analysis of dinner-table

---

BOX 5.5   Turn signals

a)   auditor   1. back channel – 'go on'
              2. claiming turn – 'I want to talk'
              3. unmarked – 'no response'
b)   speaker   1. turn signal – 'end of turn'
              2. turn-claim suppression – 'let me finish'
              3. within-turn signal – 'there's more to come'
                                                    (Duncan 1973)

---

conversation illustrates (1981a). Some possible reasons for this are that much of Sacks *et al.*'s data consisted of telephone data, that it was primarily dyadic, and that it did not include a visual record (e.g. videotape). Erickson shows that, at least at Italian-American dinner tables, overlapping and simultaneous talk are permitted and common, suggesting a heavy reliance upon rhythmic integration. Such conversation is, if anything, more difficult to perform than the more straightforward variety analysed by Sacks *et al.*

The second-language classroom is neither an Italian-American dinner table nor a telephone conversation, and we may therefore expect a different turn-taking system to operate. Some of the features of the classroom that we may expect to have a bearing on the shaping of the interaction are as follows:

1. The requirement for centralized attention, or the 'one-floor' law. On the whole, the rule is: one speaker at a time, rather than: many at once (Mehan 1979). The classroom is characteristically reluctant to allow overlapping or simultaneous talk.

2. At least one of the participants arrives at the event with preformed notions as to what is to be said and done during the event (see Schegloff 1981). This is most notably firmly expected of teachers, who therefore may be seen to enact a cognitive plan which, by virtue of the authority vested in them, the other participants are constrained to accept. The things that in actual practice happen to the plan are of course of particular interest to the classroom researcher.

3. At particular points during the event, the entire event (lesson) or sub-parts of it (tasks, activities, etc.) are prefaced or 'framed' (see Goffman 1974), so that their ideal performance or sequence is determined in advance. These prefaces also typically entail instructions to the learners about permissable ways to participate.

Even where prefaces or frames are minimal or absent, we can observe specific patterns of participation, indicating that there are well-established routines that are so well known that they no longer need prefacing. Instances where the rules are made up during the event, where the interaction is assembled impromptu, as it were, are rare in whole-class activities.

BOX 5.6 Setting it up

T I'm going to break you up .. into .. three- groups- of four .. all right? each group will have a tape recorder ... if I can find another one ... I want you to go *out* of the classroom ... each person in the group needs to find somebody ... and ask them the directions to the post office in Saffron Walden ..... now. *try* to use .. different ways of asking directions ... not the same way each time ... and you can re*co:rd* ... your voice .. when you ask for directions, and when the other person gives you directions ... ... and after ... I think I'll give you *fif-teen* minutes .. so you need to be quite quick. after fifteen minutes .. if you can come back here .. and *listen* ... to .. your recordings ... using your map of Saffron Walden ... which you should have in your file .. it's a more detailed map ....

---

4. Since the purpose of the gathering is language learning, the concerns that usually occupy participants, e.g. attention to topic, making small talk, asking favours, etc. are, officially at least, of secondary importance. Equally or more important are verbal contributions that provide fuel for learning (input), that illustrate linguistic skill, or that repair linguistic problems.

Bearing these points in mind, we can therefore expect there to be significant differences between the classroom and many other interactive settings in terms of the way participation is organized. The peculiar problem of the L2 classroom is that this means that the classroom, by its very nature, may not provide the contextual and interactional ingredients that make language use a skilful and relevant enterprise in natural settings. It may be comparable to learning to swim on dry ground or, less dramatically, to skiing on an artificial ski slope. How teachers can deal with this inherent problem, how serious a limitation it is, and what can be done about it, are questions that can only be answered by sustained and detailed description of what goes on in actual classrooms, and comparing this with the actual demands of language use in different situations.

What is a turn? or: When is a turn?

Intuitively, the status of the turn as a unit seems clear and unambiguous. When someone asks us about a verbal interaction that is going on: Who has the turn now?, we can usually point to the right person without hesitation, or at least we can say: 'A and B are fighting for it.' We might say that a turn-at-talking occurs whenever one person speaks, for as long as this person speaks, and until someone else speaks. We could use Harris's definition of utterance:

> A stretch of talk, by one person, before and after which there is silence on the part of that person.
>
> (Harris 1951, p. 14)

However, in the rough and tumble of verbal interaction there will be moments, as in football, when several players are trying to gain control over the ball, or the floor, and for a while we are not sure who is going to emerge victorious. The borderlines are blurred, turns may overlap, we may encounter false starts, restarts, half-finished or cut-off turns, and so on. Harris's definition appears therefore to be too clean-cut to be usable, and at the same time too unrevealing in its limited scope. In the following extract, for example, Harris's definition leads us to observe that there are three turns, by R, O and M respectively – and nothing more than that. Yet, if we were to ask O and M what happened, they would be likely to say that they didn't get the (or a) turn, and that R 'got the floor'.

EXTRACT 5.1

1 R but I re- I re-I remember I remember honestly honestly =
2 O ⌈nye::-
3 M ⌊other thing is-
  R =I remember eh this JMB for me is- no really I don't know
    what happen ((cont.))

R obtains his victory by repetition, speeding up delivery (until the token 'eh' in the second line of his turn, when his rate of speech drops down to a more relaxed pace), and increasing loudness. O and M give up their attempt to take the floor, yielding to R. In practice, then, there are problems with a simple, straightforward definition of *turn* as a unit. Goffman's more detailed 'definition' of his unit *move* (though not identical to *turn*, which he does not employ as a unit) brings to light some of the problems, as well as some of the potential richness, of turn-taking analysis:

I refer to any full stretch of talk or of its substitutes which has a distinctive unitary bearing on some set or other of the circumstances in which participants find themselves (some 'game' or other in the peculiar sense employed by Wittgenstein), such as a communication system, ritual constraints, economic negotiating, character contests, or 'teaching cycles' (Bellack) or whatever.

(Goffman 1981, p. 24)

This definition, or perhaps rather, this description, raises a number of questions, some of which will be discussed in this and the following chapters.

When we try to define turn or utterance (regarding these, for the sake of convenience, as equivalent terms), we find that we run into all sorts of problems that we do not have when we define such linguistic units as word, sentence, paragraph, story. Discourse analysts working in a linguistic model have, unsurprisingly, found it extremely difficult, if not impossible, to fit the turn *as a unit* into their framework, or any framework that relies on precisely bounded discrete units. Thus, in their review of Sinclair and Coulthard's work, Coulthard and Brazil note the following:

Sinclair *et al.* (1972) report that it was their attempt to fit utterance into their rank scale which made them realize that it was not in fact a structural unit.

(Coulthard and Brazil 1981, p. 86)

Other linguistic descriptions face similar problems (see, e.g. Edmondson 1981, p. 42; Chafe 1979). A discussion of the propositions or the temporal sequence of talk does not account for the organization of talk, even when this is regarded as a story rather than a conversation. For example, anyone who has witnessed the telling of folk tales in traditional settings will have been struck by the essentially interactive nature of the telling. The distinction between content and sequence, or vertical–horizontal (the terms are taken from Labov and Fanshel 1977) parallels such sets of terms as structural — sequential (Sinclair and Coulthard 1975), hierarchy–flow (Chafe 1979), and is closely related to the paradigmatic–syntagmatic distinction in structural linguistics (de Saussure 1959). I briefly referred to this 'duality of patterning' in Chapter 3 (p. 49), and we can see once again that it makes a description in terms of one single framework, or one single set of units, extremely difficult. According to Levinson (see Box 5.7) it has led to two distinct and possibly incompatible approaches or 'schools' of discourse study. It appears that we tend to either think in the 'vertical' or in the 'horizontal' mode, and that an accommodation between the two modes is not easy to obtain.

BOX 5.7

Which is the correct manner in which to proceed? The issue is a
live one: DA theorists can accuse CA practitioners of being
inexplicit, or worse, plain muddled, about the theories and
conceptual categories they are actually employing in analysis (see e.g.
Labov and Fanshel 1977, p. 25; Coulthard and Brazil 1979); CA
practitioners can retort that DA theorists are so busy with premature
formalization that they pay scant attention to the nature of the data.
The main strength of the DA approach is that it promises to
integrate linguistic findings about intra-sentential organization with
discourse study; while the strength of the CA position is that the
procedures employed have already proved themselves capable of
yielding by far the most substantial insights that have yet been
gained into the organization of conversation.

(Levinson 1983, p. 287)

Note: DA = Discourse Analysis
CA = Conversational Analysis

The fact that the turn cannot be defined in the same way that
linguistic units are defined means that linguistically oriented models
cannot deal adequately with the issue of speaker change. This does
not mean, of course, that turn taking has no bearing on the structure
of interactive discourse; rather, it means that linguistic descriptions
of discourse are partial descriptions. In the same way, a description
of turn-taking patterns in any interaction is a partial description, but
it is one that cannot be overlooked if we want to find out how interaction is organized and managed. If we assume that the structure of
discourse and the organization of interaction are related (if not
synonymous), and this is the crux of the argument outlined in Chapter
3 (pp. 47–53) and continued here, a single set of units and relationships will not suffice. Moreover, we shall need to move from the
concept of dual patterning towards a view of interaction as *multiple
patterning*. In this view, turn taking plays a central part.

To return to the title of this sub-section, the question, 'What is
a turn?' can probably not be answered in terms that are much more
specific than Goffman's description of *move*. 'When is a turn?' might
be a more relevant question, since this leads us to a description of
what a turn will 'turn out to be', what characterizes the skills involved
in speaker change. The view taken here can be succinctly expressed by a few brief quotes from Goodwin:

> [A] definition of the turn as a static unit with fixed boundaries does
> not accurately describe its structure. Rather, the turn has to be
> conceptualized as a time-bound process.

[T]he delineation of the turn is not properly an analytic tool for the study of conversation but rather part of the phenomenon being investigated and as such should be approached empirically.

It [. . .] does not seem possible to first define the turn and then work out how it is to be exchanged. Rather, intrinsic structural elements of the unit being exchanged, its boundaries, seem implicated in the process of exchange itself.

(Goodwin 1977, pp. 41–42)

Floors and prominence

Turn-taking mechanisms are generally designed to solve the dual problems of *transition* and *distribution*. The former addresses issues such as turn length, avoidance of overlap, and minimization of inter-turn pauses. The latter deals with who the next speaker will be. One of the prerequisites for a turn to count as a turn is *prominence*, i.e. it must be attended to by the other participants, or at least one or more of the other participants. How this attention is expressed is a matter for investigation, but for a turn to be a turn, it must have a *floor*. When more than two people are involved we can distinguish between the 'main' floor if the attention of all those present is sought and obtained, and a subsidiary or 'sub-floor' if the turn is aimed at or attended to by only part of the entire audience (see further Edelsky 1981). If it is not attended to by any of the participants, the turn has failed, or misfired (cf. Edelsky's definition of *turn* as an 'on-record speaking'). Turns can thus be more or less prominent, along a continuum of prominence, but at the same time some degree of prominence, or attention by others, is necessary. To illustrate this, consider the following extract:

```
EXTRACT  5.2
       1  T    'n what did- did you- yes- did you sing English songs or were
                   you singing-
       2  LL   //yes//oh yes//yes//
 →     3  L                        ᵗnou ja:::, singing*
       4  T    which- which
       5  LL          ᵗ//ehhehehe//
       6  T    which songs were you singing
       7  L9   o:h-
 →     8  L      ᵗwe TRY to sing
       9  L      ᵗGrandfather's Clock
      10  T    what's that?
      11  LL   ///Grandfather's Clock///
```

* Tr: ah well,
singing --i.e., if you want to
call it singing.

In this extract, in 3L, a learner tries to introduce a joke to the effect that the noises produced might not warrant the term 'singing'. This may be responded to by one or two learners (5LL), i.e. gaining a sub-floor, but not by the teacher and not by the rest of the class. In 8L the same learner again tries to introduce the joke, now phrased entirely in English. This time it remains unnoticed or is ignored by the entire group, perhaps because it is uttered simultaneously with 9L, whose voice is louder or more distinctive. 8L therefore achieves no prominence at all, and to all intents and purposes it must be regarded as failed, or misplaced.

Thus, participants may intend prominence, and not achieve it, the achievement of prominence itself being an important turn-taking, and in more general terms, social skill. Conversely, prominence may be granted to a turn that was not intended for it. For example, in an L2 classroom learners regularly direct utterances to one or more neighbouring learners, e.g. to clarify a point without disrupting the official teacher-learner business in progress. In addition we find utterances or actions that are more or less involuntary (coughs, movements, sighs, facial expressions, etc.) and which may or may not get attended to by other participants (see Box 5.8), as well as wholly private turns that appear to function as rehearsals, or 'trial runs' for production. Of course, the ostensible privateness and non-prominence of these turns may be exploited by participants to perform actions which for one reason or another they do not wish to perform by means of full-prominence turns, but whose prominence is nevertheless surreptitiously intended. It is hard to assess through an interactional analysis when this is the case (since we have no direct access to a speaker's intentions), but there is no doubt that it occurs and that participants orient to it.

BOX 5.8

TEACHER What kind of a person do you think he is? Do you – what are you laughing at?
PUPIL   Nothing.
TEACHER Pardon?
PUPIL   Nothing.
TEACHER You're laughing at nothing, nothing at all?
PUPIL   No.
         It's funny really 'cos they don't think as though they were there they might not like it. And it sounds rather a pompous attitude.

(Sinclair and Coulthard 1975, p. 30)

To sum up, prominence is a psycho-social notion, involving intention by actor and attention by recipients. In conversation or in classrooms prominence is an interactionally negotiated good (in the positive or negative sense, that is, we may seek it or avoid it), and as such it is a prime concern and target of the turn-taking mechanism. The weight or impact of a particular turn in an interactive setting cannot be determined on the basis of linguistic features or content alone, but must take into account factors of transition, distribution and initiative. Prominence is a *result* of successful turn taking.

Turn taking in the second-language classroom: towards a classification

Competent turn taking is a complex skill. It involves monitoring the ongoing construction of a current turn while at the same time assessing one's opportunities to take the floor and, if possible, actively planning what to do once the floor is obtained. It includes using culturally appropriate ways to compete successfully with other would-be speakers, interpreting their intentions through their actions, a fine sense of rhythm and timing, and, once speakership is obtained, the ability to say what one wants to say effectively.

In multi-party settings, including L2 classrooms, turn transition and distribution problems can occur that may cause communication problems, more so than in dyadic conversation, simply because there are more potential participants. In such settings some form of *allocation* of turns is often set up as a way of dealing with potential transition and distribution problems. In some cases, particularly in more formal settings, including many L2 classrooms, rules of turn distribution emerge or are instituted, so that the matter of *who* speaks *when* (as well as perhaps, about *what*) is predetermined. On such occasions transition ceases to be problematic, and consequently ceases to be governed by negotiation, competition, or personal initiative. The participants are no longer concerned with resolving transition and distribution problems, but rather with observing rules. At the same time this means that, because of the turn-taking rules, participants are restricted in their power and initiative to change and influence the discourse (for example by changing topic). So far as the L2 classroom is concerned, this state of affairs can lead to at least three possible consequences which can be empirically investigated:

1. The ways in which classroom activities are conducted are determined by the forces (usually the teacher, but also tacit norms of classroom conduct) that govern allocation of turns. That is, control

over proceedings, including topics and types of activities, co-occurs and coincides with control over turn taking. This being the case, a study of turn taking is vital to a study of discourse topic, instructional 'logic', sequential structuring, etc.

2. In a situation of rigid turn control learners will not be able to explore the ways in which speaker change is effected through turn taking in the target language, which means that they will not be practising vital skills involved in interacting in the target language. Even if underlying turn-taking rules are universal, which is by no means clear (see, e.g. Philips 1983), the ways in which they are realized socially, contextually, linguistically and behaviourally are manifestly very different in different languages and cultures.

3. As Sacks *et al.* point out, the conversational turn-taking organization provides 'an intrinsic motivation for listening'. They continue:

> In its turn-allocational techniques, the turn-taking system for conversation builds in an intrinsic motivation for listening to all utterances in a conversation, independent of other possible motivations, such as interest and politeness. In the variety of techniques for arriving at a next speaker, and in their ordered character, it obliges any willing or potentially intending speaker to listen to, and analyze, each utterance across its delivery.
>
> (Sacks *et al.* 1974, p. 43)

This is an important observation as far as the L2 classroom is concerned, for two reasons. Firstly, it is commonly assumed that the chances of learning language are greatly improved if the learners pay close attention to the language they hear around them: attention and comprehension are essential if language exposure is to be tranformed into usable input. Secondly, conversational turn taking forces participants to be actively involved, and to plan and structure their contributions in contextually appropriate and acceptable ways.

If, as is frequently the case in L2 classrooms, turn transition and turn distribution follow highly predictable paths and routines, it is likely that much of this intrinsic motivation is lost, and we can expect a corresponding lack of attention to some aspects of the talk in the setting. The talk itself may be stripped of much of its interactional complexity, both in terms of that which is available as input, and of that which is generated as a result of that input.

In order to find out the seriousness of these suggestions, and the viability of classroom proceedings as vehicles for language learning and acquisition, a turn-taking study is essential. In the following, I shall first provide a detailed analysis and classification of the L2

classroom turn-taking system, next take a look at participants' opportunities for creative contributions (in terms of turn construction,
initiative, and self-investment or, in one phrase, active participation);
and finally make a brief comparison with conversational turn taking.

A classification of turn taking in the second-language classroom

The value of a classification – any classification – depends on what
can be done with it, i.e. how useful it is for subsequent work. It is
not and cannot be an end in itself. It is a static enumeration of items
that are in some way related. The classification shows the relationships between the items and attempts to make each and every one of
them discrete and mutually exclusive. It is thus an exercise in the
clarification of concepts, and it provides the analyst with a toolbox
of useful terminology. In every classification, however, there will be
items which, like the duck-billed platypus, do not let themselves be
classified discretely.

Usually a classification is designed to do coding and quantitative
work. However, my aim here is different. I want to examine, in more
detail than is customary in classroom studies, the different actions
learners and teachers engage in, and the options for speaking that
are available to them. Though this exercise involves much discussion
of minute details and distinctions, it is essential for the next step of
the analysis of participation, when we will focus directly on the notion
of initiative, or *choice of action*. This is of course central in an investigation of L2 classroom communication, and the detailed description
paves the way for an understanding of how and when initiative is
possible, and how it can be identified. While reading through the
description of the various turn-taking categories the reader must
therefore bear in mind the purpose of the exercise and continuously
ask what *communicating in an L2 classroom* means.

In the foregoing, we have discussed turn taking in terms of four
basic ingredients or underlying principles:
1. transition: particularly, turn progression and turn size;
2. distribution: particularly, speaker selection, allocation;
3. prominence: the status of a turn as attended-to action;
4. initiative: voluntary (i.e. actor-originated) participation in the
   goings on.
These principles are shown in the form of a continuing cycle in Box
5.9.

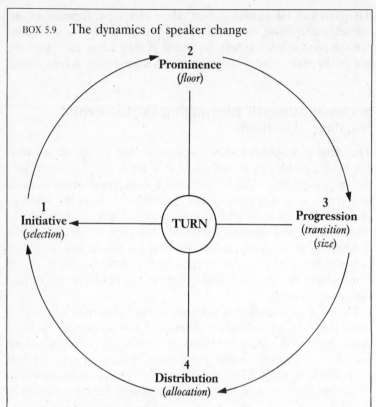

BOX 5.9   The dynamics of speaker change

At the start of a new turn:
1. Initiative is used by the would-be next speaker, or else the next speaker has been selected through turn allocation.
2. Prominence is obtained, either by virtue of 1, or through loudness, non-verbal behaviour, or other attention-getting factors.
3. The turn is proceeding now, 1 and 2 having been achieved. Its rough length is staked out, if necessary by projecting the various chunks, turn claims are countered by turn-claim suppression signals; the focus is on orderly progression, working towards orderly transition.
4. The turn is coming to an end and, if appropriate, content and/or speaker of next turn are indicated.

Transition and distribution are by and large directly observable, and hence most easily translated into classification criteria. Prominence and initiative relate to intentions and perceptions of participants, not directly observable, but rather intuitively rated on the basis of observed actions. The classification will thus not be able to capture the latter two principles directly, but it enables their subsequent description and evaluation. At some point the notions of activity and topic orientation will also become relevant, but their detailed description will be left until Chapter 6.

The classification employs as primary distinctions the following:

a) *Prospective*: the way the turn is linked (through turn-taking devices) to (the) subsequent turn(s). Most notably, the turn influences the subsequent turn(s) by constraining content, or by delimiting next speakership.

b) *Retrospective*: the way the turn is linked (through turn-taking devices) to (the) preceding turn(s). In other words, the turn may exhibit varying kinds and degrees of influence from (a) preceding turn(s), e.g. it may be allocated, or it may be self-selected.

c) *Concurrent*: a turn that is taken during a current turn which is related to that turn in a servicing sense. In this category fall such brief turns as e.g. back channels or listening responses ('uhuh', 'yes').

d) *Neutral*: a turn which is indeterminate as to a), b) or c), and which is not implicative of prospective or retrospective relations to its surrounding turns.

I will now go through the classification in detail to explain the more specific distinctions in sequence from top to bottom. It will be useful to consult the chart on page 110 while reading the description.

Prospective

1 *Allocating*: the work of specifying a speaker for the next turn or turns. This work is done in three basic ways, and in combinations of them:

a) nominating, i.e. verbally selecting a next speaker by giving a name, description or pronoun ('you there');
b) signalling, e.g. pointing with finger, chin, arm, postural orientation;
c) eye gaze.

This category is often called *specific solicit* or *personal solicit* (e.g. Allwright 1980). A clear example of turn allocation follows. The technique used here is nominating:

EXTRACT 5.3

1 T   okay so . . Willy did you ask somebody in the church
2 L10 yes

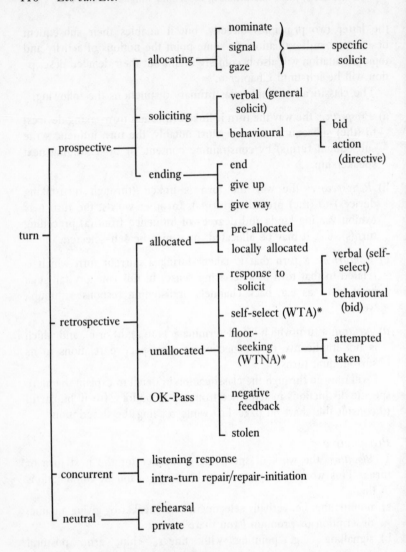

*WTA = When Turn Available
WTNA = When Turn Not Available

2 *Soliciting:* the work of specifying the content or substance of the next turn (allocation of content or activity, cf. Heap 1979) without specifying the next speaker. This action can be further specified in terms of the type of activity requested: a verbal action (e.g. an answer to a question), a bid for a turn (e.g. 'Hands up if you know the answer.'), or a non-verbal action (in which case the solicit is usually

called a directive (see Sinclair and Coulthard 1975). This is not a very important distinction, since a non-verbal action can be accompanied by, and in many cases is appropriately accompanied by, a verbal action, as turns 2–4 in Extract 5.4 illustrate. Below are two different examples of general solicits:

EXTRACT 5.4

```
1 T    shall we get our grammar books out?
2 L2   grammar books
3 L1   grammar books
4 LL   grammar books
```

EXTRACT 5.5

```
1 T    uhuh so how does he do his job?
2 L    he's good=
3 L    he's good
```

Note that when a general solicit is made, all or any of the participants can choose to answer. There is thus initiative on the part of the students involved, and potentially several participants may take a turn simultaneously. This may violate a 'one-at-a-time' rule, if such a rule is in operation. To counteract possible problems of intelligibility a bidding procedure may be instituted, i.e. several participants make turn offers vocally ('Miss! Miss!') or gesturally (raise hands), and subsequently one of the offerers is selected as next speaker (see, e.g. Griffin and Humphrey 1978; Humphrey 1979).

3 *Ending:* ending a turn without implications for content or speakership of subsequent turn(s). A turn can be simply ended because it has completed its designed course, as in the following example (turns 1 and 3), recorded during a general hubbub before the lesson proper has started:

EXTRACT 5.6

```
((Learners coming into the room, bustling about; finding their seats))
→ 1 L  ya es hora ((tr.: it's time already))
  2 L  ((unint))
→ 3 L  somebody smoke here
  4 L  who is the owner of this pen?
```

Any intentions to influence subsequent content, speaker or activity are not marked, and absence or presence of related next turns do not seem to matter. In other words, the speaker does not assume responsibility for whatever comes next, if anything. A relevant next turn is not implicated. Thus, in the following extract, 2L is not required or requested by 1T:

EXTRACT 5.7

```
   1 T    anyway we better get through this . . .
                ((checking handout)) . .
                tempus fugit . . time flies . . .
→  2 L    you forgot the second part of that
   3 T    what?
   4 L    when you're having fun
   5 T/LL  ((laughter))
```

In many cases such turns are similar to talking to oneself, to ritual accompaniments of actions, or to fillers of silence. If they are taken up in one way or another, as in the extract above, they may change their sequential status, but they do not thereby become allocating or soliciting if they are not so marked.

4 *Giving up*, or *trailing*, occurs when a speaker cannot or will not bring the turn to its projected or projectable conclusion, perhaps due to planning problems, or for a host of other possible reasons. Often this leads, after a pause, to completion by a hearer, but it may also remain unfinished. This must be distinguished from stopping in mid-stream to induce completion by (an)other participant(s), a technique often employed by teachers and in such a case more correctly classified as allocating or soliciting. Below I first give an example of trailing (note that 4T remains unfinished), and next an example of completion invitation.

EXTRACT 5.8

```
   1 T    oh! for Waltzing Mathilda
   2 L2   yes . . the *olds me*lody . . . the *old* melody
   3 T                        ⌐uhuh
→  4 T    oh the original Australian- . . .
   5 L7   yes
   6 T    yes . . ya . which is very different isn't it
```

EXTRACT 5.9

```
→  1 T    very efficient and . . and-
   2 L    patient
   3 L5   patient
   4 T    and patient that's right
```

5 *Giving way* is said to occur when a speaker stops short before the projected completion of his/her turn in order to give way to competition, i.e. when another speaker has 'interrupted' (this is a somewhat dangerous notion, since what is interruption to one person can be appropriate turn taking to another), or as a result of simultaneous starts.

EXTRACT 5.10

   1 T   I'm going to tell you what was happening . in this block of
            flats: last night- . .
→ 2 L8 not a fire?
   3 LL ehhehehehe
   4 T   not a fire? . . . no not a fire

EXTRACT 5.11

   1 T okay so *what* were the children doing? . . . hm?
   2 L the children were looking
→ 3 T   ᶜthey were *watch*ing television

Retrospective

6 A turn is *allocated* when its speaker has been specifically given the
right or obligation to speak in a previous (not necessarily contiguous)
turn (local allocation) or speakership has been determined by means
of some pre-allocation rule (which may be set up specifically at the
start of an activity or event: 'We'll go round the table clockwise', or
which is part of the basic rule-set of a specific activity, e.g. of a ritual
kind). Note that with pre-allocation nomination (etc.) can be used as
a reminder of pre-allocated sequence ('John, I think it's your turn
now.'). Certain activity types may employ a mixture or blend of pre-
allocation and local allocation. The blend may be part of the characteristics defining a particular activity type.

In Extract 5.3, 2 L10 is an example of a locally allocated turn. In
the following extract pre-allocation (though in a sense 'spontaneous',
since no one tells the students they have to follow a clockwise order)
occurs, when students introduce themselves around the table:

EXTRACT 5.12

   1 T   . . . if you can just introduce yourselves . to him
   2 L12 I'm Mien
   3 L11 My name is Carla
   4 L10 My name is Willy
          ((etc.))

7 A turn is *unallocated* when speakership has not been specified,
either by local or pre-allocational means. Specific instances are
responses to solicits (verbal or behavioural, i.e. the execution of a
requested action, or a bid for a turn). These turns are evidence of
self-selection, but content or activity have been specified by the (or
a) previous turn. Bidding procedures need detailed study, since there
are various possible allocational trajectories which involve bidding.

Often in classes of adults a solicit is followed by some indication on the part of participants that they wish to answer (e.g. by raising a hand), and the speaker then chooses from among the bidders. This bidding of course also replaces interruption during long turns (or lectures), when a hearer wishes to make a comment.

As I mentioned under 2, a general solicit can lead to a number of simultaneous unallocated turns, when several learners self-select at the same time. This may result in unintelligibility, and this may be resolved by changing to specific allocation. An example follows:

EXTRACT 5.13

```
        1 T    good. allright. now I'm asking the questions what is the
                question that I've been asking you . . .
                what's the- what . . .
    → 2 LL    ((unint – – – – ))
        3 T    yes Willy can you tell me
        4 L10  what was- doing Jenny?
```

8 A next sub-category of unallocated turn is the *self-select* (WTA). This occurs when the preceding speaker has ended or given up a turn. The term *discourse maintenance* is sometimes used to refer to this kind of turn taking (see 4).

9 Floor-seeking, or self-selecting (WTNA) occurs when a participant begins a turn (other than a concurrent or neutral turn, see below) during another speaker's turn. It is important to exclude from this sub-category turns which overlap slightly with preceding turns, i.e. where a next speaker starts to speak before a prior speaker has quite finished, but where it is already clear that prior speaker is about to finish. This issue relates to perceptions of TCU's, which are to some extent negotiable entities.

We often call such floor-seeking *interruption*, though this tends to be a subjective notion. Often, as in the example below, jokes and comments are thrown into the interaction; far from disrupting the interaction, such self-selection adds to the naturalness of the discourse, quite apart from alleviating the predictability and potential dullness which can endanger classroom practice.

EXTRACT 5.14

```
        1 T    what are your hobbies
        2 L6   my hobbies is ah:
    → 3 L2                    ⌐parties hehe
        4 LL   (party hehe)
        5 L6   no I ride horse
```

10 Intra-turn *negative feedback* is closely related to floor-seeking, since a negative signal during another's turn has the potential effect of cutting that turn short. This does not necessarily happen, but signallers must be aware that it may happen, hence they are faced with the possibility of taking the floor. Negative feedback actions may have a cumulative effect: if one of them occurs in isolation the speaker may continue; however, if a series of them occurs during one extended turn, there is an increasing likelihood of that turn being prematurely ended (an exception may be negative signals, such as ritual booing, heckling, etc., during political speeches). Negative feedback signals are thus not concurrent turns. Although they are in a sense subsidiary to the current turn, they do not service it.

11 A turn is *stolen* when it occupies a slot which was designated for a turn specifically allotted to another speaker. This must be distinguished from prompting or helping, and from taking over when a nominated learner indicates that he/she cannot or will not do the allocated turn. A clear example of stealing is the following:

EXTRACT 5.15

```
   1  L8    teacher what kind which one ... is it possible-
→  2  L6    what kind and which one, the same.
   3  LL/T  ((unint))
```

The following is an example of prompting or helping:

EXTRACT 5.16

```
1  T    uhuh, good. which way ... ((addressed to L11))
2  L1   excuse me-
3  L11            ⌈excuse me which way is the- theatre please?
```

12 Finally in the retrospective category, an *OK-pass* (the term is taken from Weiner and Goodenough 1977) can be either allocated or unallocated, i.e. freely made. These turns are made upon the conclusion of a previous turn and do not seek the floor, but merely acknowledge, express approval, understanding, etc. If they are allocated, they tend to follow such items as: 'All right?', 'OK?', 'Do you agree?', and question tags. The tokens that realize these turns are by and large identical to those that realize listening responses and, indeed, the two categories are in practice difficult to keep apart (see below). The crucial difference is that the utterer of an OK-pass always has the option to produce a 'full' or substantive turn.

Concurrent

13 *Listening responses* and *intra-turn repair/repair-initiation* occur during a turn and are related to the current turn in a subservient capacity. Listening responses are also called back-channels (Yngve 1970; Duncan 1973), but the term listening responses, introduced by Erickson (1979) is preferred here. In some accounts of turn taking, listening responses (and related utterances, including brief requests for clarification – here referred to as intra-turn repair) are not regarded as turns (e.g. Oreström 1983), but rather as turn lubricators. However, the view taken here is that this is an unnecessary, perhaps arbitrary restriction of the term *turn*, a concept which, as we have seen, cannot be precisely defined. Restricting it to some classes of utterances while excluding others would imply claiming some measure of definability. For the sake of simplicity we would rather take turn to mean any utterance that bears on the discourse, whether verbal, non-verbal, even non-vocal (head nods, etc.), in line with the suggestions made earlier in this chapter. Listening responses fulfil an important function in verbal interaction, in conversation as well as in lectures, debates, interviews, etc. (see Erickson 1979; Schegloff 1981). They are typically demonstrations of approval, attention, encouragement, understanding. Their character is supportive or neutral as regards the turn in hand, and in that sense they may facilitate that turn's development ('lubricate' it), and may boost its duration and smoothness.

BOX 5.10   The importance of 'uh-huhs'

In (doctor-patient) interviews, doctors interrupted patients after 18 seconds on average. Only 23 per cent of patients said they were able to complete their opening statement, Beckman said.
'The old clinical adage is "if you let the person tell you what's wrong, they will". People have forgotten that,' Beckman said. 'We found that three "uh-huhs" can get (doctors) a tremendous amount of information if (they) can just be quiet a little longer.'

(Waterloo Courier, Thursday, May 15, 1986, page A6 — reporting on a study conducted by H. B. Beckman *et al.* of Wayne State Medical School.)

In many cases, especially during extended turns consisting of several TCU's (such as stories, jokes, instructions, etc.), listening responses can be seen to be elicited, called for or expected by the speaker. That is, a speaker may create specific slots in an extended turn to allow for or invite listening responses. They therefore do not occur at random. Even so, especially in a non-dyadic setting such as the L2 classroom, we must regard them as being produced voluntarily, i.e. every listener decides freely in each instance whether or not to produce a listening response. Absence of appropriate listening responses, whether invited or not, usually has a severely disrupting influence on the current turn. They are perhaps more culturally specific than most other turn-taking devices, thus warranting special attention in studies of cross-cultural communication. For example, Erickson (1979) shows how absence of culturally recognizable listening responses leads to hyper-explanation in white-black counselling interviews.

Some examples of listening responses in the L2 classroom follow.

EXTRACT 5.17

1 T so can you tell me the way to the cinema please?
2 L6 e:rm . . . go e:r along this street   till the: traffic=
3 T   ᶜuhuh
   L6 =light . . .

EXTRACT 5.18

1 T you should know dropped because when the coach took you to
       London the coach . . *dropped* you=ᶜja:
2 L
       =at the National Gallery=
3 L9   ᶜye:s
   T =when the coach took you to Cambridge the coach dropped you
      at Emanuel Street . . .=
4 LL =//oh yes//ja/((unint – – – –))
   T =a'right?

In Extract 5.18, 3L9 and 4LL could be regarded as OK-passes, since they occur at points which could be interpreted as ends of turns. This shows the difficulty of deciding at times between a listening response and an OK-pass, especially when the speaker uses questioning tokens such as 'a'right?', 'okay?', etc. in intra-turn position. A test to decide between a listening response and an OK-pass is to insert, instead of the brief token, a hypothetical full turn and to evaluate whether or not the prior turn has been cut short. This apparently minor issue may be important to L2 learners who may not be able to distinguish between interrupting and appropriate contributions. Actual recordings and transcripts of previous talk can be used in class so that learners can discuss and analyse appropriate turn taking.

Teachers frequently insert questioning tokens, both within turns to elicit listening responses, and at the end of turns to elicit OK-

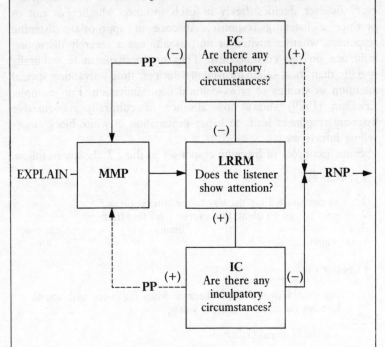

BOX 5.11   Social and cognitive model of making a point.

Key:

MMP   = Moment of Making a Point

EC   = 'Exculpatory' Circumstances
           (Previous performance, social identities, unimportance of
           point, point made only partially)

LRRM   = Listening Response Relevant Moment

IC   = 'Inculpatory' Circumstances
           (Previous performance, social identities, culturally
           inappropriate listening re-responses, listener should
           have shown understanding as well as attention)

PP   = Persist at Point
           (Talk down, give reasons, ask point-relevant questions)

——   = Frequent 'unmarked' paths

- - -   = Infrequent 'marked' paths

RNP   = Raise New Point

(Erickson 1979, p. 112)

passes or responding turns, and the following extract is an example:

EXTRACT 5.19

1 T that's- sorry ((knocks st. over)) we'll leave it off there's- you're
getting enough composition (I think) e:rm ... tomorro:w well we're
not gonna have time tomorrow we'll go over the eh Apollo Eight
thing ... okay? I haven't finished grading those autobiographies
that you wrote okay? I will have them for you tomorrow okay? what
I did on those autobiographies was to grade them the way that I
will grade the Michigan test ... okay? ... so when you get them
back you'll see what a Michigan test grade would look like. and
we'll talk about those tomorrow also. all right?
2 L all right.
3 T no questions?
4 L no questions
5 L6 no for the moment.

If we interpret 1T as one extended turn rather than as five different
ones, all of them separated by OK-passes, we may regard the
teacher's use of 'okay?' and other such items within turns as listening-
response initiators. The teacher is asking, in effect: 'Can I go on?'

A final point to make is that a study of listening responses will
obviously need fairly detailed visual information and can therefore not
be conducted without video-taping.

The sub-category of *intra-turn repair/repair-initiation* includes brief
requests for clarification, replacements of errors, and also instances
of prompting and helping. Like listening responses they are subservient to the turn in progress, but unlike them they alter that turn.
However, unlike negative feedback they cannot be regarded as
(potential) attempts to take over the floor, to cut the speaker short,
or to obstruct the turn in progress.

The distinction between intra-turn repair and inter-turn repair,
like the distinction between listening responses and OK-passes, is
a fluid and flexible one: often a brief repair utterance causes a turn
to be modified so that the second part may be regarded as another
turn. For example, two transcriptions of the following extract are
possible, the first counting the teacher's contribution as one turn, the
second as two turns.

Whether one or the other interpretation is chosen must be largely
a matter of convention, and for present purposes all one can recommend to the transcriber is to be consistent (see further, Appendix).

EXTRACT 5.20

1 T ok. do I have eh- all your grammar homew- I mean the composition
homework   composition homework
2 L   ⌈what?

EXTRACT 5.20

1　T　ok. do I have eh- all your grammar homew- I mean the composition homework
2　L　what?
3　T　composition homework

The above is an instance of repair-*initiation*, more specifically, other-initiation, i.e. repair initiated by a participant other than the speaker of current turn. A further example of intra-turn repair-initiation follows:

EXTRACT 5.21

1　L1　they are watch televi- television
2　T　okay, now, yesterday at eight o'clock
3　L1　they are　　　they watches　　　watched they were . . .watching
→ 4-5-6　T　ᶜthey-　　　　ᶜthey:::-　　　ᶜthey (-)

As the above example shows, intra-turn repair is often used by the teacher to guide the learner in the formulation of a turn. Guidance and evaluation are thus commonly conducted in intra-turn position, and this may be a significant pedagogical feature of L2 discourse (a detailed description of the functions of repair will be given in Chapter 7). The following two extracts offer further examples of intra-turn repair:

EXTRACT 5.22

1　　L2　I was listening　　　　listening
→ 2-3　L1　　　　　　　ᶜin the ra-³　　　ᶜto the radio in (bed)
4　　L2　oh ja
5　　L1　while you having a bath
6　　L2　and you and you was having　　　　　　　a bath
→ 7　　L1　　　　　　　　　　ᶜyou were-were *ha*ving³

EXTRACT 5.23

1　T　o::h okay. Ruben how about number five . . .
2　L7　five oh
3　T　　ᶜnumber . . .　　　I'm sorry . . four okay yeah
4　LL　　　ᶜ/four/four/³

Neutral

14　Finally, the two neutral sub-categories are *rehearsal* and *private* turns. These may comment on other (concurrent or preceding) turns, or use items in them for personal trial purposes. Also, comments may be addressed to another (usually neighbouring) learner or a small subset of learners, relating to the main business of the moment or to other business, usually delivered in a soft voice (these are termed side comments by Edelsky – 1981, p. 403). When things are discussed in such sequences which are not part of the official business of the classroom at the moment, a phenomenon similar to schism (see Sacks *et al.* 1974, p. 19) occurs. Some examples of different kinds of neutral turns follow:

EXTRACT 5.24

```
    1   T   ... but th- for these we just use- shorten it to
                w'z not was  but w'z  a'right?
→ 2–3 LL              ⌜w'z    ⌜w'z
```

EXTRACT 5.25

```
    1   T   okay. I'm going to add a bit more to this ...
                ((drawing on board))
→   2  L1   till, wat is till eigenlijk? ((tr: till what does till actually
                                     mean?))
→   3  L-L4 tot/tot
→   4  L1   oh
```

EXTRACT 5.26

```
    1   T   now this one is a little more complicated ...=
    2  L9                                   ⌜Saffron Walden
        T   =this is Saffron Walden  on- on the right-hand side
→   3  L1?                          ⌜ta ta ta ta ta h:::::⌝((looking at map))
```

EXTRACT 5.27

```
    1  L7   last year we have walked
    2   T   yes well the thing is that we're not sure about the weather
→   3  L10  kwart voor twee?          ((tr: quarter to two?
→   4  L9   kwart voor twee ja           quarter to two yes))
```

Using the classification

The classification described above is intended to be complete and comprehensive, i.e. it should be possible to code every turn in a stretch of classroom talk in terms of the categories presented. It is perfectly possible, should we wish to do so, to iron out fuzzy edges and resolve ambiguous instances in a programme of coder training, and thus to achieve a high degree of inter-rater reliability.

However, as I suggested earlier, my aim has been to provide an exploratory description of L2 classroom interaction which can pave the way for a more focused study of active participation and, particularly, the notion of initiative. The turn-taking categories identified in the classifying process give clues to the kinds of interactive work that different turn-taking actions imply. Using the classification as input it will now be possible to address directly the issue of how participation is manifested in the classroom, in other words the fourth question posed in the introduction to this chapter, and through this begin to examine the other issues raised there. Summarizing them again in a different way, we are thus moving towards an investigation of two basic issues:

1. the relation between interaction and intake;
2. the place of interaction in instruction.

The procedure which will be illustrated below aims to allow the study of a range of questions concerning the role of participation in L2 classroom learning, for example:

1. Does active participation correlate with improved performance on tests?
2. Does task-type x lead to more active participation than task-type y?
3. Do learners of type a participate more actively than learners of type b, in a given set of classroom circumstances?

Such questions are amenable to classroom research conducted by classroom teachers in their own regular classrooms, perhaps as part of a programme of action research, and are therefore of immediate practical relevance. The analysis which follows now illustrates how quantitative work of a very straightforward kind can be used without sacrificing the centrality of the social context.

Participation in the second-language classroom: an exercise in quantification

I have suggested earlier that a turn-taking analysis can use both qualitative and quantitative information. More specifically, quantitative information on turn-taking behaviour may supplement interpretive work, such as case study, comparison of activity types, and so on. In this way researchers such as Allwright (1980) and Seliger (1983) have employed different forms of 'crude' quantification in order to compare learners' patterns of participation. Crucial in such quantification is the identification of the learner's *initiative*, for example whether a particular contribution was initiated by the learner or made in response to a teacher's specific allocation. However, important though this feature is, it is not a sufficient measure of participation.

The classification in the previous section allows us to identify not only whether a turn was allocated or self-selected, but also if that same turn subsequently allocates a next turn or a next activity (or task). We may argue that the latter form of initiative is not an option available to learners in a classroom (see the quotes from McHoul 1978 on pp. 136–7), but we do not know this until we have analysed relevant data in detail. We cannot a priori rule out that learners actually do more than we routinely give them credit for. Thus, at least potentially (and definitely, if we consider group work and concurrent talk, and I see no reason not to), initiative is expressed in two ways: through retrospective and through prospective actions, that is, by acting on prior talk and by influencing future talk. But this is not all. At times topics may be changed, a denial may be made, a certain piece of information may be questioned, etc. It seems clear that, over and above issues of selection and allocation, topic control and management are important manifestations of initiative. Again, it may be argued that topic is the exclusive territory of the teacher, but it needs to be shown that this is indeed so.

Fourthly, a turn-taking action can reflect an attempt, successful or not, to set up, alter, or close a series of sequentially related turns, or in other words, to influence the kind of activity that is being conducted. We thus have four basic ways in which initiative, or personal involvement in the interaction, is expressed:

1. retrospective actions (self-selection);
2. prospective actions (allocation);
3. topic management;
4. activity management.

I suggest that this is sufficient for a close analysis of active participation on the basis of turn taking. Though it does not explicitly address the crucial notion of prominence, this is to a large extent the result of the four initiative-bearing features identified.

We have seen what it is in the interaction that marks a participant's active involvement, and the next step is to find a way to score every contribution in terms of the criteria identified. This can be done in two ways: firstly, we can prepare a 'schedule' containing columns for the four criteria and rows for the participants, and do a real-time coding. Secondly, we can record the lesson or a series of lessons, produce transcriptions, and conduct a detailed analysis, relieved from the pressures of time. The second approach is obviously rather time-consuming, but the first approach is superficial, since concurrent and private turns (listening responses, private comments, and the like), as well as simultaneous talk, will be difficult to code, and a single turn may not be codable for more than one of the four criteria.

Below, I suggest a series of questions intended to permit a detailed coding for active participation, based on micro-analysis of recorded and transcribed data (i.e. not real-time). Particularly important questions, from the point of view of initiative, are asterisked, and I shall focus on these subsequently while discussing the kinds of work the coding instructions can do. It may be useful to compare the micro-ethnographic approach illustrated here with the real-time coding approach chosen by Seliger (see Box 5.12).

BOX 5.12   Coding language interaction

a. Which student spoke? Did he/she address another student, the teacher, or the whole group?
b. Did the student initiate the interaction (shown by +) or was he or she responding (shown by /)?
c. Was the student using English or his or her L1 in the interaction? (Shown by (+) for initiated interaction but in L1 and (/) for responding but in L1.)

The number of these interactions was tabulated for each student in the observed class at the end of each observation session. At the conclusion of the four hours of observation, the students were ranked according to the total number of interactions and the type of interactions in L2. Three of the highest interactors (HIG) and three of the lowest interactors (LIG) were selected for further study.

(Seliger 1983, pp. 254–5)

A. Topic

1. Is the turn or turn-part on-stream (continuing, contributory, convergent)?
2. Is the turn or turn-part parallel to on-stream discourse (i.e. private, involuntary, the result of schism)?
*3. Is the turn or turn-part off-stream (discontinuing, divergent, marked-for-change); does it introduce something new? Or does it deny/dispute a proposition or request of a prior turn?

Note: For the notion of topic and topic change employed here, see the extract in Box 5.13 from Keenan and Schieffelin.

B. Self-selection

*1. Does selection to speak originate from this speaker?
2. Does selection to speak originate from a previous speaker, or from a pre-allocation rule?
3. Indeterminate.

BOX 5.13 Defining discourse topic

discourse

continuous		discontinuous	
collaborating discourse topic	incorporating discourse topic	re-introducing discourse topic	introducing discourse topic

[Discourse topic] is a proposition (or set of propositions) expressing a concern (or set of concerns) the speaker is addressing. It should be stressed that each declarative or interrogative utterance in a discourse has a specific discourse topic. It may be the case that the same discourse topic is sustained over a sequence of two or more utterances. We have described these as topic collaborating sequences (. . .). On the other hand, the discourse topic may change from utterance to utterance, sometimes drawing on the previous utterance (incorporating topic) and sometimes not (introducing topic, re-introducing topic).

(Keenan and Schieffelin 1975, pp. 342–3)

C. Allocation
*1. a) Is it part of the work of this turn or turn-part that it selects from among those present one specific next speaker?
   b) Does it specify next activity or content?
   c) Does it continue the work mentioned under a) and/or b), done by this speaker in a previous turn?
 2. Does the turn or turn-part not specifically select next speaker or specify next activity/content?
 3. Indeterminate.

D. Sequence, Activity
 1. Is the turn or turn-part part of a sequence of turns (but excluding listening responses and neutral turns)? If yes, is it:
   *a) first part (whether or not other parts in fact follow);
    b) subsequent part (continuing part, or repetition of first part);
   *c) closing part (if the sequence is more than two turns long)?
*2. Is the turn or turn-part independent of sequence, but not a listening response, OK-pass, or neutral turn?
   Note: if a turn or turn-part is simultaneously closing part and first part, code **.

It is suggested that affirmative responses to the asterisked questions indicate some degree of initiative on the part of the speaker. Any turn or turn-part (or turn-constructional unit, or turn consisting of several such units) may thus be given one or more stars. I think that it is important, and a significant advantage of this procedure, that only clear cases need to be coded, so that ambiguities and unclear turns in a transcript can be ignored, at least for this particular purpose (for other purposes it may of course be of interest to focus precisely on such unclear turns).

In order to assess its feasibility, I have tested this procedure on several stretches of transcribed data, including both teacher-led activities and group work, and have found that it works very well, although no attempt has thus far been made to test it for inter-coder reliability. A coding exercise such as this is best regarded as one facet in a multi-method analysis of classroom interaction, aimed at understanding the language work that is involved.

TABLE 5.1

	Total turns	%TT	* ∅	*	**	***	****
	A	B	C	D	E	F	G
T	99	31.23	16	10	36	28	9
L1	10	3.15	1	4	2	3	—
L2	20	6.31	1	4	4	10	1
L3	20	6.31	6	4	4	6	—
L4	1	0.32	—	—	1	—	—
L5	6	1.89	—	6	—	—	—
L6	31	9.78	10	4	7	9	1
L7	2	0.63	—	2	—	—	—
L8	4	1.26	—	1	—	3	—
L9	1	0.32	—	—	1	—	—
L10	6	1.89	5	—	—	1	—
XL	61	19.24	12	22	15	10	2
LL	56	17.67	38	16	2	—	—
Total	317	100	89	73	72	70	13

XL: Unidentified learner
LL: Several learners simultaneously (including laughter)

The procedure of starring turns in the way suggested allows for quantitative work of two kinds: a) a crude quantification of total stars per participant, which can be shown as a percentage of total stars for a stretch of classroom discourse, or divided for each participant by the number of his/her turns that have one or more stars, to give a rough level of participation. Table 5.1 illustrates this type of quantification and shows how it can be used to conduct rank order correlations between participation and various measures of performance.

The explanation of the columns is as follows:

A: total turns taken by each participant

B: percentage of the total number of turns in the extract

C to G: number of turns allocated no stars, one, two, three or four stars respectively

H: total number of turns starred

I: total number of stars obtained

J: participation level (PL): I divided by H, or star-average of starred turns

K: participation index (PI): the square of J multiplied by B, which

Total starred turns	Total stars	Part. level (PL)	Part. index (PI)	PI rank order	PI rank order
H	I	J	K	L	M
83	202	2.43	184.26	1	—
9	17	1.89	11.25	6	5
19	46	2.42	36.95	3	2
14	30	2.14	28.90	4	3
1	2	2	1.28	9.5	8.5
6	6	1	1.89	8	7
21	49	2.33	53.09	2	1
2	2	1	0.63	11	10
4	10	2.5	7.88	7	6
1	2	2	1.28	9.5	8.5
1	3	3	17.01	5	4
49	90	1.84	65.10	—	—
18	20	1.11	21.77	—	—
228	479	2.1	—	—	—

takes into account star-average, but also share of total turn taking
L: rank order, including the teacher
M: rank order, excluding the teacher

The quantification as outlined so far provides a measure of the *amount* of active participation of learners during certain lessons or parts of lessons. However, the list of criteria allows us to go beyond this and identify also various different *kinds* of participation. We are thus not yet exploiting its full potential. A more interesting and revealing procedure therefore is a tabulation of starred turns per question area A–B–C–D. This shows if there is a pattern for certain participants (or for certain lessons or activities) to employ initiative in the areas of topic work, self-selection, allocation, and sequencing of discourse.

In order to illustrate the potential of this procedure I reproduce below the summarized result of a brief stretch of talk from a group discussion about problems of learning English as a second language (the entire discussion lasted for about two hours). In this discussion the teacher has just one turn, in which he asks student A to get the discussion going (all students have written a draft essay on the subject). The summary shows that A does more topic work than the other participants (column A), as well as doing more allocation of speaker and activity (column C) by controlling the 'agenda', and he also starts more sequences (column D). However, student E, being a highly vocal person and eager participant, challenges A's 'gate-keeping' role early on in the extract, and throughout plays a very active part, without in fact being able to take over as discussion leader. His high number of overall turns is partly due to a relatively high number of listening responses (included in column B). Student D acts in some ways as a balancing influence, though asserting his views successfully and with confidence. Student C participates little, and his sense of insecurity in the group, as a relative outsider (a lone Colombian amongst Venezuelans) is illustrated by the fact that he does not allocate next speaker or activity. This coding, though based on a relatively brief stretch of talk, shows how different learners participate differently in group work, and captures a sense of what goes on in the discussion. It suggests that this procedure is particularly well suited for the analysis of group work and group relations, and that it is very learner-friendly, as opposed to most other coding systems which are largely teacher-oriented.

In conclusion I quote two extracts from this discussion in order to illustrate the coding and give a sense of the type of interaction this represents.

TABLE 5.2 Pilot coding VENS 2:

	turns	TT%	A	B	C	D	Total
T	1	0.59	1	1	1	1	4
A	51	30	18	43	16	35	112
C	14	8.24	7	7	—	9	23
D	38	22.35	10	27	9	23	69
E	66	38.82	12	63	13	24	112
Totals	170	100	48	141	38	92	319

EXTRACT 5.28

```
A B C D
  *  *  *    21    A   I did in this m: order       yea?
     3*       22–24  E          ⌈m      ⌈yes   ⌈all right
  *  *  *    25    A   what do you think?
  *        *  26    D   the same but eh: I think that the main
                              problem     in the future is that eh: we
        *      27    A           ⌈uhuh
                    D   have eh: m:: our English well my
                              English or our English is very shortage
                              .. in knowledge no? as a language ..
                              ehm: I think that ... in the main
                              problem is for writing .... (4) ..
  *  *  *  *  28    A   maybe for you
        *      29    D   yehes
```

EXTRACT 5.29

```
A B C D
*  *  *  *    67    A   and ... understanding people who do
                              you think?
*        *    68    C   [e'sta] ((= understand)) people I think
                              .. yes m: no I don't have problem
*  *  *  *    69    A   no?
                    70    C   no ...
*            *    71    A   fine
*  *  *  *    72    D         ⌈depend of the people?
```

Some comments on the coding

1 Listening responses

Listening responses receive one star (*B) since selection to speak originates from their producer (see e.g. 22–4). Since coding is conducted on the basis of a transcript, and since non-verbal listening responses do not show up in a transcript (at least not in this method of transcription), this favours those LL who tend to produce vocal listening responses over those who tend to produce non-vocal ones. It also possibly favours those LL who happen to sit close to the microphone, or who have distinctive voices, since many listening responses are uttered more softly than full turns. Allocation of speaker can be difficult also if a number of LL produce listening responses simultaneously.

The bias that these difficulties create need not worry us unduly if the coding is used to pave the way for close analysis of particular turns or sequences, and for case study. For certain kinds of comparative work (e.g. correlations) based on a quantification of turns using this model, it might be advisable to amend question B to exclude listening responses from the category of self-selected turns. In that case listening responses would receive no star, although they might still be counted as turns. The alternative would be to code all listening responses, including non-vocal ones, which would be laborious though not impossible (given a reasonable video recording).

2 Topic change

The distinction between on-stream and off-stream discourse is not at all times a clear-cut one. Like so many other distinctions, this is in reality a gradient, or continuum. Discoursal elements are more or less on- or off-stream, and they may be regarded as on-stream by one person but as off-stream by the next. The two extracts in Box 5.14 indicate some of the problems in identifying topicality; for a more detailed discussion, see Chapter 6.

BOX 5.14   Identifying topic

Part of the process of analysing discourse in terms of 'topic' is an attempt to make explicit the basis for our intuitive ability to recognise why what is said is appropriate in a particular discourse fragment.

(Brown and Yule 1983a, p. 78)

It seems that the relevance of an utterance is largely a matter of its fitting in with the whole of some discourse context, such that its pertinence both to an immediately prior utterance and to the conversation-to-date is apparent.

(McLaughlin 1984, p. 37)

This means that to conduct the coding we have to rely on our intuitions as to what constitutes 'something new' (etc.) and what does not. Rather than being a drawback, this is in effect a significant virtue of the analytical model, since it allows it to be used as an integral part of an ethnography of interaction. Participants also rely on their intuitions, and hence may not always agree. It is extremely unlikely that any coding approach or classification will be able to eliminate the reliance on intuitive judgements. Rather, one of our tasks is to investigate the principles and procedures underlying the making of intuitive judgements. It is less dangerous to build intuitive judging (compare, e.g. the grading of essays) into the coding process, than to conduct such research with the implicit or explicit pretense that it relies on nothing but clear evidence. If we regard the coding as a heuristic instrument to support the focusing on specific issues of interest, we can gain considerable advantage from a close examination of the role of intuitive judgements in interpretation.

Attempts to eliminate such judgements may be unhelpful and counterproductive as well as being impracticable. As a small example, in a teacher-led stretch of 271 turns, 22 topic changes were identified by means of an application of question A. Seventeen of these were the responsibility of the teacher, and of the remaining five, four were denials or disputings of prior turns, specifically:

no (2x)
that's wrong
I've already said that

There was thus only one learner turn that was coded as off-stream, and the pertinent extract is quoted below (see turn 38L9):

EXTRACT 5.30

A	B	C	D			
*	*	*	*	37	T	now you don't need to write it down . . ((laughing)) no need to write it down . so. that's one way . to ask for directions . are there any other ways .
→ *	*			38	L9	yes (this)- polite way
	*			39	L	⌜yes
*	*	*	*	40	T	it's a polite way uhuh . but are there any other ways that you know

38L9 is the first reference, in this lesson, to politeness as an attribute of TL utterances. It is furthermore not directly relevant to 37T since this merely asks for more 'ways'. In 40T the teacher's 'but' shows that she does not regard L9's comment as being germane to her purposes, and she reinstates her initiation.

3 Allocation and sequencing

Allocation and sequence are in a sense mutually implicative. In particular, allocation of next speaker or next activity implies the start (or continuation) of a sequence that will be at least two turns long: minimally including current utterance and next utterance. When the allocating utterance is the first part of a sequence (rather than a continuation), it is given two stars (for C and D), and this may be regarded as an undue duplication of coding. This duplication could be ironed out by amending D to code a star for the first part only if the sequence turns out to be more than two turns long, i.e. is more than a straightforward adjacency pair. This could be done, provided one edits out inserted (e.g. clarification) sequences, but it might in some cases imply assignment of intentionality (i.e. the speaker's intention to start a sequence of more than two turns in length) on a *post hoc* basis. This can be dangerous since we cannot assume that, whenever an interaction happens in some way, its originator intended it to happen that way (this would constitute reasoning backwards; see Griffin and Humphrey 1978 for a detailed discussion of 'retrospective definition').

In the pilot codings I have given additional weighting to all allocating utterances, since they are important initiative-bearing instances. Differential weighting could, within the system, easily be designed for utterances which, apart from allocating the next turn, allocate (or project) an entire series of turns, such as the following:

EXTRACT 5.31

A	B	C	D		
*	*	*	*	T	okay let's just go through these if I say- bus station I want you just to go through each one, all right? first one- bus station . . use- excuse me

Turn taking in conversation and in the second-language classroom

The turn-taking patterns of the second-language classroom, as illustrated so far, show some differences from the turn-taking system of general conversation. It is clear, however, that speaker change in classrooms is not all of one kind, but can vary significantly from one activity to the next. As I shall argue, the same can be said for speaker change outside the classroom. This means that a comparison of interaction inside and outside the classroom cannot simply be based on the comparison of one single rule-set with another single rule-set. However, a common assumption among conversational analysts is that there is a normal unmarked system of interaction which can be referred to as *general conversation*. Speier thus defines conversation as

> those cases of talking where there is a state of conversational participation open to all parties, where there are shared rights of communication.

(1973, p. 72)

It is further assumed that the rule-set for this general conversation is the basic one which children learn as part of their natural socialization and language development, and that other, more specific rule-sets are derived from it. These assumptions are by no means proven, but they can be regarded as a reasonable starting point for an investigation of the relationships between interaction and learning. More specifically, I advance the possibility that those activities (or speech events, or speech exchange systems (SES), see below) which allow participants to express initiative in the four areas (A–D) outlined in the previous section, are most likely to lead to the acquisition of skills in speaker change, interactional competence, and therefore to language development. In order to appreciate the importance of this argument, several points must be borne in mind:

1. It is part of a person's communicative competence to operate effectively and fluently the turn-taking systems of the language.
2. Unless substantial evidence to the contrary can be obtained, we may assume that the turn-taking system for conversation is basic, and that other turn-taking systems are derived from it, modulating it through the operation of various contextual constraints.
3. Turn taking is intricately woven into the texture of discourse, requiring the manipulation and interpretation of linguistic and prosodic systems.
4. A significant source of motivation and attention is lost when turn taking is predetermined rather than interactionally managed by the participants.
5. Children learn their first language in and through interaction. Indeed, some researchers (see Hatch 1978; Wells 1985, especially Chapter 10) suggest that conversation (in the sense of verbal interaction) is a prerequisite for language acquisition. Points 1–4 may give a partial rationale for this view.

It is clear that these suggestions provide us with a brief to study in close detail both conversational and classroom interaction, and to compare them. To date, most classroom discourse studies have been unable to address turn taking systematically (exceptions include Humphrey 1979; Mehan 1979; McHoul 1978).

Most if not all studies of conversational turn taking build upon the classic study on the subject by Sacks, Schegloff and Jefferson, which I have referred to before (Sacks *et al.* 1974). The basic systematics suggested there has so far withstood the test of time (though see Erickson 1981a for a partially diverging view, based upon the rhythmic integration of talk), and the rules proposed by Sacks *et al.* are generally accepted as the basic unmarked set underlying the turn-taking process. It is often assumed that this basic rule-set presupposes complete equality of speaking rights, which in practice rarely, if ever, occurs, but the rules in actual fact allow for a wide range of dominant and subordinate roles in terms of allocation, self-selection, topic management, and so on.

Referring to turn taking in different interactional settings, Sacks *et al.* use the term *speech exchange system* (SES) to indicate that rules vary according to the structure of an event, and that turn taking is part of the structure of an event, or activity type, in Levinson's terms (1979). Following Ervin-Tripp (1972), every instance of interaction can be described in terms of constraints deriving from the charac-teristics of *setting, participants* and *topic*. Sacks *et al.* thus regard conversation as one type of SES among others, e.g. 'ceremonies, debates, meetings, press conferences, seminars, therapy sessions, interviews, trials, and so on' (1974, p. 45). General conversation, in Sacks *et al.*'s interpretation of the term, is relatively unconstrained in terms of setting, participants and topic. The rule-set developed to describe turn taking in conversation therefore does not need to take contextual information into account, and in that sense it can be regarded as not context-specific. Many other SES are more constrained, and they tend to be described in terms of the factors that constrain them. As a result, the conversational turn-taking system does not apply, but rather is transformed in context-specific ways. According to Sacks *et al.*:

[I]t appears likely that conversation should be considered the basic form of speech-exchange system, with other systems on the array representing a variety of transformations on conversation's turn-taking system to achieve other types of turn-taking systems.

(Sacks *et al.* 1974, p. 47)

The array referred to is a suggested continuum from unconstrained SES to progressively more constrained SES, with conversation at the unconstrained pole and ceremony at the constrained pole. Such a linear array might look like this:

− (less constrained)	(more constrained) +

conversation discussion classroom interview debate ceremony

It is tempting further to specify the array by including the features formality and allocation, as follows:

− less formal	more formal +

local allocation   pre-allocation

However, to do so would be to assume that the features:

    contextual constraints
    formality
    allocation

always co-vary. I am not sure that such an assumption is warranted a priori, and it may be advisable to treat these parameters as empirical issues to be investigated through further analysis.

If conversation is basic and central, one might argue that the basic conversational rule-set can be preserved in a study of any SES as an underlying resource which, though ordinarily transformed in context-specific ways, may be employed by participants when for one reason or another the constraints are relaxed. The conversational rule-set thus remains relevant in two ways:

a) it may serve as a basis for developing and applying context-specific constraints;
b) it may surface at times when constraints are relaxed or weakened.

The basic rule-set then becomes a kind of 'rock bottom', overlaid, transformed or superseded in various ways by characteristic context-specific rules, but always available as a resource and at times manifested overtly. Such a rule set will be theoretically very powerful: it serves the participants as a shared resource for developing and negotiating their interactive work, and the analyst as a tight framework for the analysis of interactional processes. Following on from the above I suggest that many (if not all) SES are not characterized by a single static set of rules which applies at all times for all instances of that SES, but that they are 'hybrid' events with various types of verbal activities going on at different times. As a striking example, consider the informal sketch of a traditional ritual in the Peruvian highlands: the annual payment to mother earth or *pachamama*, in Box 5.15.

BOX 5.15   **An Andean ritual**

This ritual is conducted by a specialist in these matters, call him the master of ceremonies. It follows a sequence of steps and actions, rigidly defined and accompanied by set phrases, incantations, and prayers. From time to time ritual responses, in chorus, are required. At other times, individual responses from all the participants, but in a certain unwritten order, determined on the spot in invisible ways, are appropriate. Certain things must form part of these responses, other things may be added. These latter must be appropriate, but also ingenious. They are publicly praised, commented on, and even jokes may be cracked about them and their producer. At various points in the ritual, which may last for a number of hours, conversations may be inserted, about the weather, somebody's uncle, a visiting gringo, etc. Other kinds of talk are also permitted, at the proper moments: about the skills of the master, the shape and quality of the coca leaves, the quality and price of the wine, the generosity or stinginess of some participant, etc. Looking at such an event globally, we see a solemnity which waxes and wanes, tension and relaxation following one another in rhythmic waves. At all times, however, one is aware of a collective sense of propriety, delicately balanced, with all participants keenly focusing on producing the elements that make the occasion a fitting instance of its kind. The event must be efficient in procuring the *pachamama*'s benevolence; at the same time it should be entertaining and good fun.

What kinds of knowledge are involved in the construction of a successful speech event of this kind? I do not wish to produce an ethnographic analysis of the event illustrated above, but rather point to a possible analogy with the L2 classroom, in terms of event structuring. The analogy serves in the first place to caution us against setting up a single rule system, or a static rule set. Secondly, even if we do not want to go so far as to claim that the classroom is a distinct *culture*, with all the ethnic characteristics and underlying cultural templates, an ethnographic approach to classroom interaction is necessary if we want to uncover its dynamics. It is worth bearing these considerations in mind when comparing, as McHoul has done, Sacks *et al.*'s turn-taking systematics for general conversation with a rule-set for classroom talk.

McHoul's study (1978) is one of the most explicit comparisons of classroom turn taking and conversational turn taking. He asked himself the question:

> In what ways are the rules of turn-taking management for natural conversation to be modified to account for the organization of turns at talk in the classroom?
>
> (McHoul 1978, p. 186)

From the classroom data at his disposal McHoul derives the summary rule that 'only teachers can direct speakership in any creative way' (1978, p. 188). This rule is based on two observations:

a) learners cannot decide who the next speaker will be, since the next speaker (after a learner's turn) will automatically be the teacher;

b) whenever a learner is speaking, this learner is speaking because the teacher has allocated the turn to the learner.

Taking a similar view, Sinclair and Brazil (1982) suggest that characteristic situations are those 'where the teacher takes the controlling role and conducts a fairly ritual conversation with the pupils', and that pupils 'have only very restricted opportunities to participate in the language of the classroom'. These are disturbing comments, even though they appear to be rather overstated. They derive from analytical models which bias every observation in such a way that it conforms to the rules stated. My own view, based on experience and inspection of data, is that, at least in the overwhelming majority of L2 classrooms, there is far more flexibility in terms of learner participation. Moreover, I have no doubt that a micro-ethnographic analysis of the same data that McHoul and Sinclair and Brazil base their categorical statements on would reveal ways in which learners employ initiative to shape their own and each other's interaction. Indeed, an important function of ethnographic analysis is to bring out differences between learners, between tasks, and between different classroom circumstances, and to show how these differences come about.

In L2 classrooms, learners frequently self-select in various ways and for various purposes, as the following extract shows:

EXTRACT 5.32

1 T   whose cup is that?
2 L   yours
3 T   mine
4 L2 it's wrong eh who:: whose is that cup?
5 T   whose is that cup? no no that's ok. but it would be more common
      to say whose cup is that
6 L2 it's very ... but it's good

It is interesting to note that, when a learner's turn is exclusively allocated by the teacher, next speaker will always automatically be prior speaker (i.e. the teacher), so that we cannot speak of student-selects-teacher. However, if a student has self-selected, as in 4L2, it makes more sense to speak of student-selects-teacher, since the lockstep, as it were, is broken.

Overwhelmingly, of course, self-selecting students do in fact select teacher, rather than another participant, as next speaker. However, in the next extract a learner specifically addresses, in a non-schismic way, another learner, and the teacher joins in (i.e. there is no repair or sanction):

EXTRACT 5.33

```
1 T    what are you
2 L2   I'm a professor
3 T    ok
4 L6   you're professor ah ((laughs))
5 L    ((unint))
6 T    so be careful
```

Although it is relatively rare for a learner to select another learner as next speaker, a learner's turn, especially when self-selected, can and does often address the entire audience, or sub-sets of the entire audience (e.g. a small group of learners in the vicinity, the other learners minus the teacher, etc.), often in order to obtain a response (e.g. laughter, commentary, explanation) from one of the addressees or the entire group of addressees. A turn's addressee is not necessarily always selected as next speaker by virtue of being addressee (i.e. addressing is not the same as allocating), but in most cases addressing at least makes a next-speaker self-selection relevant for the addressed party. Moreover, there are many possibilities for turns to be directed at several audiences at once, perhaps with a differentiated perlocutionary function, e.g. to reply to a specific solicit and simultaneously to invoke laughter from the rest of the participants. In the next extract, 4L2 can be regarded as directed to three audiences simultaneously (L6, the teacher, the class), but without allocating a next turn:

EXTRACT 5.34

```
1 T    Marty called you cuckoo?
2 L6   no: the w- the sentences that we can . . . (we making)
3 T                                            ⌈oh the sentences were
       cuckoo that happens sometimes
4 L2   and S6 . . . she's cuckoo too=
5 L6            ⌈yeah
6 LL   =((laughter - unint. comments))
```

On the basis of these considerations we must conclude that rigid specifications of rules such as those proposed by McHoul and by Sinclair and Brazil are not adequate for the L2 classroom. It may well be that they characterize a specific type of L1 secondary class, or a specific activity type in classrooms in general, but it cannot be assumed that they constitute the 'normal' state of affairs in L2 classrooms, and that more conversational ways of speaking are departures from it.

Interestingly, Sinclair and Coulthard's question of 'how the five-year-old who speaks when he wants to, becomes the ten-year-old who waits to be nominated' (1975, p. 113) suggests that, in the initial days of schooling at least, McHoul's rule-set is the marked form so far as the children are concerned.

Considering L2 classroom data I would argue, and Sacks *et al.*'s remarks are consistent with this, that it is most likely that the unmarked – marked, or ordinary – specifically-established continuum is matched by an unconstrained – constrained continuum for turn taking, so that the rule-set McHoul advocates, being highly constrained through specific speaker selection and diminished permutability of speakership options, is more derived and more marked than a rule-set which allows for undirected (i.e. not specifically speaker-allocating) talk and for self-selection. Work in early child-parent interaction further supports this position (see e.g. Trevarthen 1974, 1979). Longitudinal studies, conducted in different school grades, may show how particular turn-taking patterns become established over time, and how preferred rule-sets may vary from classroom to classroom. An interesting study in this respect is Humphrey (1979), which focuses on turn-taking sanctions in primary classrooms.

What makes the classroom different?

In order to arrive at a 'rock-bottom' systematics we must turn to a consideration of what, minimally, makes classroom discourse different from everyday conversation. I take it that these minimal considerations will include pedagogical orientation and a relationship of instructor – instructed, or competent – not-yet-competent between teacher/tutor(s) and learner(s). In most L2 classrooms the number of participants is a further relevant factor.

Flowing from these considerations is the requirement, for some parts of classroom activities, of centralized or centrally focused attention. This leads to the formulation of a basic rule:

1. In L2 classrooms, whenever centralized attention is required:
   a) one speaker speaks at any one time;
   b) many can speak at once only if they say (roughly) the same thing, or at least if (a proportion of) the simultaneous talk remains intelligible.
2. If not a) or b), repair work will be undertaken.

This rule is not so different from that underlying general conversation, since intelligibility is a requirement of most verbal interaction. What is different is that different techniques are needed to achieve the desired outcome. It is, for example, assumed that intelligibility of contributions is enhanced through some form of centralized control of turns.

Underlying the rule is another, more basic rule: when centralized attention is required, participants' contributions must conform to the pedagogical orientation (the purpose of the interaction) that warrants the centralized attention, and these contributions must ostensibly be intelligible to all participants. This leads to 1a) and 1b), since overlapping or simultaneous speech is generally not conducive to intelligibility.

Intelligibility as a property of classroom talk is a flexible entity. In any transcript of classroom interaction there will be some utterances, often during simultaneous talk, and also during schismic talk (when several distinct conversations are going on) and private rehearsal, which will remain unintelligible. I suggest that, to a lesser extent perhaps, a proportion of talk will also be unintelligible to the participants themselves, who therefore will need to cope with a certain measure of unintelligibility. How much unintelligibility, and hence how much simultaneous talk, private talk and schismic talk, is tolerated, will vary from classroom to classroom, from activity to activity, and from participant to participant. Intelligibility is thus visible as a feature of turns at classroom talk, and if the level of intelligibility falls below a certain perceived tolerance threshold, repair work will be undertaken. The following extracts all provide examples of simultaneous talk, and a variety of ways of dealing with them.

EXTRACT 5.35

```
1 T    what- what were the words that he used to describe the person
2 L9  ┌he's very tall
3 L   └dark haired
4 T    okay dark haired
```

Here there are two simultaneous turns: 2L9 and 3L, and the teacher picks up 3L, ignoring (for the moment) 2L9. L9, in the following nine turns after this extract, persists in offering 'very tall' as a candidate response; this is eventually echoed by other LL, and is then finally picked up and repaired by the teacher (the desired response being 'fairly tall'). The simultaneity of 2L9 and 3L is here not an issue, intelligibility is not problematic, and no repair or sanction follows as a result of the simultaneity.

EXTRACT 5.36

1	T	now. can anybody tell me the difference between something like . . . . . . wiry, dark . . strong . . . and- something like quietly, clearly and fast
2	L	fast?
3	T	what's the difference in meaning . . the difference in the way we've used them in sentences
4	L	((unint – – –))
5	L9	((unint –)) (wiry)
6	LL	((unint – – –))
7	L	⌜wiry
8	L	difference in ((unint))=
→ 9	T	=just the difference between them . . . let's try it this way . . . can you just give me a sentence with wiry . . Elly?

In this extract the teacher begins by asking an undirected question (1T), repeating it in a different form in 3T. The answer turns out to be problematic, with overlapping talk, unintelligible attempts, and repetitions of some of the teacher's words. In 9T the teacher decides to switch to a different tactic explicitly ('let's try it this way'), and a next speaker is nominated. Intuitively, one feels that no violation of turn-taking rules has occurred, no sanction is implied, and repair is directed towards resolving the inability of the learners to answer the question.

Though schismic talk during whole-class activities is often regarded as disruptive, it can fulfil an important function for learners who wish to resolve individual problems in an interactive way without disrupting the central proceedings. It can act as a safety valve, and if it occurs frequently it may indicate that learners need more time to resolve problems through peer interaction.

In the next extract, schismic talk occurs during preparations for an activity which has been previously explained by the teacher (it involves two learners going out of the class and coming back in after a while to conduct a guessing game). During these preparations, a lot of simultaneous talk goes on, all of a schismic though task-related nature. The end of the extract signals the beginning of the activity or game, and the switch is entirely executed by the learners themselves:

EXTRACT 5.37

```
1 LL  ((comments throughout the extract, up to 8L))
2 L9  zeg ( - ) dat wij wij toch steeds weer vragen stellen
3 L10      ⌐has he=
    L9  =fout   door te gaan- has he
4 L10      ⌐ja
5 L10  maar does=
6 L   =s:::::::t=
7 L   =s:::::::t
8    ((door))
9 T  ((to entering LL)) so (one of you) one at the time just ask
     somebody to do something
              ((tr: 2L9: say ( - ) that we we
              always keep asking questions= wrong
              by going- has he
              5L10: but does))
```

Sometimes the teacher allows learners to comment freely for a while before continuing, and in her continuation does not attend to the actual comments made, whether they were intelligible or not:

EXTRACT 5.38

```
1 T   Brigitte Bardot
2 LL              ⌐yea::h/hehh
3 L1  how do you say
4 T   [brimadʒit – brimadʒit] Bardot
5 L9              [brimadʒit]
6 L                    ⌐Brigitte Bardot
7 L                         ⌐((unint))
8 L   she is (veranderd)
9 L         ⌐in 'r goeie jaren dan
10 L            ⌐she is veranderd
11 L                ((unint - - ))
12 T                    ⌐so. Brigitte was
     phoning her boyfriend
              ((tr: 8L she has changed
              9L in her good years then
              10L she has changed))
```

Explicit turn-taking sanctions are rare in adult L2 classes, although there are likely to be occasions where simultaneous and overlapping talk, private utterances and schismic talk occur. These can be routinely dealt with in a variety of ways, some of which are described above.

There is often a considerable degree of tolerance for unintelligibility at certain points in the discourse, and a return to one-speaker-at-a-time at the end of brief episodes of many-at-once requires no overt concerted effort. However, such a relatively relaxed, easy-going state of affairs may be more characteristic of fairly small groups of adults than of all L2 classes *per se*.

Given the frequent occurrence in this particular type of data of undirected teacher utterances and learner self-selections (coupled with the absence of bidding procedures), I feel that Sacks *et al.*'s rule-set can safely be postulated unmodified as an underlying resource, and that various constraints (e.g. predominance of next-speaker-selection by teacher, and consequent absence of learner-self-selection) can be derived from this rule-set for different activity types (to be discussed in the next chapter).

A particularly important constraint will be the bias mentioned in Sacks *et al.* for general conversation: 'for speaker just prior to current speaker to be selected as next speaker' (1974, p. 18). When the teacher makes an undirected solicit, or selects a next speaker, it is common for speakership to revert to the teacher after the learner's turn. This need not be accounted for by the turn-taking rules: the sequential organization into exchanges and extended sequences will naturally favour this occurrence.

Conclusion

In his detailed study of first-language development, Wells looks at the features of speech adults address to children in terms of the intentions that guide the adults' communication. He proposes four broad types of intention:

1. to secure and maintain inter-subjectivity of attention;
2. to express one's own meaning intentions in a form that one's partner will find easy to understand;
3. to ensure that one has correctly understood the meaning intentions of one's partner;
4. to provide positive responses in order to sustain the partner's desire to continue the present interaction and to engage in further interactions in the future.

(Wells 1985, p. 398)

Noting that parents often have quite deliberate didactic intentions (for example, of teaching vocabulary, frequently through using display questions), Wells adds a fifth intention:

5. to instruct one's partner so that he or she may become a more skilled performer.

(Wells 1985, p. 399)

It is reasonable to expect, particularly in a communicative approach, that teachers in L2 classrooms will have similar intentions, though they may be realized in different ways.

If the implementation of such intentions leads to types of interaction conducive to language development, we need to see how L2 classroom interaction allows for such implementation. In this chapter I have, quite deliberately, focused on the mechanisms of interaction rather than its content, and particularly explored the notions of participation and initiative. I have examined these notions through the mechanisms of speaker change, since it is through the taking of turns, the holding on to them and the allocation of further turns that initiative becomes manifest.

In the rigidly controlled classroom settings described by McHoul (1978) and Sinclair and Brazil (1982) it is unlikely that interaction optimally promotes language development. In those cases it is, of course, not designed to do so, but similar control can also at times occur in L2 classrooms, and its purposes and effects need to be examined.

In this chapter I have not aimed to prove that active participation in second-language classrooms is beneficial, but rather to show how interaction can be analysed in actual classroom settings. The importance of participation and initiative has been *assumed*, on the basis of recommendations from communicative teaching theory, and evidence from first-language studies. It is important that teachers are conscious of the participation that their teaching techniques allow and encourage, and find ways to monitor it in their own classrooms.

6 Topic and activity: the structure of participation

Introduction

Any time that social interaction is going on, this interaction can be interrupted by the question: 'What are you doing?' and a substantive answer can be obtained. Participants may reply that they are 'just chatting', 'having a meeting', 'cooking', 'fixing the bicycle', and so on. A further question, in the order of 'What about?', 'What?', 'What's wrong with it?' and so on will yield replies such as 'about dentists', 'our next picnic', 'sweet and sour pork', and 'the chain is too loose'. Every interaction can be characterized in these two basic ways: what *kind of activity* it is, i.e. what it involves *doing*, and what it is *about*, i.e. its *topic*.

These two aspects of interaction do not always carry equal weight: sometimes what is talked about does not matter much so long as the talk progresses satisfactorily for that kind of activity. At other times the topic is of supreme importance, i.e. something must be transmitted, resolved, fixed, learned, etc., regardless of how it is done. In daily life we may pass on information or seek to obtain it, exchange ritual talk to establish or maintain social relationships, participate in tasks to get something accomplished, and so on. We also play interactional games where the object may be to tease others, show our cleverness, gain points, or invite laughter. Sometimes it is not quite clear whether a game is being played or not, as when Alice meets Humpty Dumpty sitting on a wall (see Box 6.1). Her aim is to make polite conversation, but for Humpty Dumpty, Alice's question is a riddle.

In their daily interactions people will take pains to ensure that they are 'on topic', and that they are in the same kind of activity as the other interactants. Confusions and misunderstandings about these two issues can lead to much trouble and even embarrassment. The problem of being on the same wavelength in both senses is compounded by the fact that rarely, if ever, are explicit guidelines provided about what counts as being the same or different, since this

---

BOX 6.1

'Why do you sit out here all alone?' said Alice, not wishing to begin an argument.
'Why, because there's nobody with me!' cried Humpty Dumpty. 'Did you think I didn't know the answer to *that*? Ask another.'
'Don't you think you'd be safer down on the ground?' Alice went on, not with any idea of making another riddle, but simply in her good-natured anxiety for the queer creature. 'That wall is so *very* narrow!'
'What tremendously easy riddles you ask!' Humpty Dumpty growled out.

(Lewis Carroll: *Through the Looking-Glass*)

---

is generally governed by tacit social and cultural rules and routines. These rules and routines are culturally very specific, and lead to problems for foreign learners both in the classroom and outside it. For example, the foreign learner may take at face value such comments as:

You're from Nigeria! I'd *love* to learn more about your country.
Do come and see us some time!
What an interesting dish. You *must* give me the recipe!

Such conversational remarks may of course be mere pawns in a conversational game and not intended as genuine requests. In the classroom, as in conversation, it is not always made overtly clear when a linguistic game is in progress, such as repeating lines of a model dialogue, important information is presented which is to be remembered, or contributions about some topic welcomed from volunteering students. Learners thus spend a lot of time trying to determine what may constitute an appropriate response or a valid contribution to whatever it is that appears to be going on at any particular time.

Topic

The term *topic* has a long history in linguistics, both in sentence grammar and in discourse analysis. However, so far it has not been possible adequately to define topic in linguistic terms, either as a syntactic category, or as a unit of discourse. It is not even entirely clear if sentence grammarians and discourse analysts are essentially referring to the same phenomenon when they talk about topic, or if there are two separate notions (for some recent discussions, see Brown and Yule 1983a; Givon 1983). The lack of definition that surrounds attempts to examine topic rigorously does not prevent investigators from deriving much useful work while using the construct: we thus read about topic continuity and discontinuity, cohesion and coherence in discourse, topic initiation and topic change, and so on. We can say that topic is at present used as a hypothetical construct with fuzzy components and possibly a lot of surplus meaning. This is nothing new in science of course: in psychology hypothetical constructs such as personality, motivation and intelligence have survived and thrived through many years of non-definition, and in our own area of second-language acquisition notions such as proficiency and communicative competence are equally vague, yet useful. In Chapter 5 I have myself used *topic* in such an essentially unanalysed way, when attempting to identify instances of initiative in interaction.

The notion of topic is clearly useful to analysts of discourse, and in the absence of operational definitions it is regarded as a 'pre-theoretical notion of what is being talked about' (Brown and Yule 1983a, p. 71), or 'a vernacular term, roughly referring to "what is talked about" through some series of turns at talk' (Schegloff 1979, p. 270fn.). From the point of view of an ethnographic analysis of L2 classroom talk, such an intuitive working definition can be regarded as entirely appropriate: it allows us to take an *emic* view of the issue, i.e. to focus on what the participants mean by the topic of some interaction.

There are basically two ways of looking at topic that are relevant to second-language classroom research: topic as a *unit of analysis* and topic as part of the *discourse process*. In the first sense, a lesson can be divided into topics in the same way that a conversation can be divided into topics. Thus for example, the topics of a lesson might be: the homework, a dialogue about asking the way, a presentation of *Wh*-questions, pair work using a map of the city, a role play *At the airport*, instructions for further homework, and a song called *Can't miss it*. Yet, the criteria for dividing the lesson up into topics may not be unproblematically clear: someone might, in all justification, say that the whole lesson was only one topic: asking the way. Indeed, the question: 'What is a topic?' is really not very different from the famous unanswerable question: 'How long is a piece of string?' The reader may remember that we had similar problems in Chapter 5 with the question: 'What is a turn?', and I suggested that a more appropriate question might be: '*When* is a turn?' By analogy, we may be advised to ask *when*, rather than *what*, a topic is.

It is easy, and therefore tempting, to regard topics as items existing in the social world quite independent from what people do, stored in big bags in our collective and private memories. When we need topics for interaction we grab into the bag and take them out one after the other, according to the dictates of personal fancy, societal etiquette, or pedagogical relevance. When we have done with them we replace them in the bag until further notice. I take it that such a simplistic notion will be rejected by most, yet, if we regard topic as a discourse unit, we essentially assume that it is a discrete, tangible notion. I suggest that this is not a useful way to discuss the issue where an analysis of interaction is concerned. After the event, when discourse has become *text*, it can be profitable to regard topics as sets of related propositions, or macro-propositions in van Dijk's sense (e.g. 1977), or as classes of 'mentionables' in certain speech events in ethnomethodological terminology, but basically a topic is not a topic until it is talked about. In a classroom ethnography, topic is therefore a sustained focusing of attention, *through* the talk and *across* a stretch of talk, on some single issue or set of closely related issues. Now, what is regarded as a single issue or set of related issues is not up to the analyst to decide: generally the participants themselves will decide this, and the analyst will find markers in the discourse that signal when participants initiate, change and close topics, and also when they disagree about the relatedness of some contribution. Rather than talk about 'topics', we will therefore talk about topic *orientation*, and the interactive mechanisms that serve this orientation. This is important: an analysis of topic into component parts such as propositions or speech acts does not reveal the organization of inter-action. Rather, interaction is partly organized *for the purpose of* raising issues to topical status, maintaining them, changing direction, etc. The point is made clearly by Levinson:

> (. . .) topical coherence cannot be thought of as residing in some independently calculable procedure for ascertaining (for example) shared reference across utterances. Rather, topical coherence is something *constructed* across turns by the collaboration of participants. What needs then to be studied is how potential topics are introduced and collaboratively ratified, how they are marked as 'new', 'touched off', 'misplaced' and so on, how they are avoided or competed over and how they are collaboratively closed down.
>
> (Levinson 1983, p. 315)

In the L2 classroom orientation to topic is not always equally important or salient. At times attention is focused primarily on how things are done and the way they are said, rather than what is talked about. The following extract is an example of strong topic orientation, in this particular case the transmission of information about a specific place and a planned visit to it:

EXTRACT 6.1

1	T	Audley End House which is just down .. *down* the road it's not very far- not very far away but=
2	L	^rvery nice
	T	=it's s- yes it's a stately- stately home=
3	L9	^r((unint)) huis
	T	=beautiful big house and beautiful inside lots of pictures and furniture and everything
4	L9	^ruhuh
5	LL	((unint comments))
6	T	^ra:nd eh:m ... also it has lovely gardens=
7	L	^ruhum
	T	=if the weather is good ... it's a lovely place=
8	LL	^ryes/nice/((unint))
	T	=to go
9	L	m: – at two o'clock?
10	T	e:r it will be at quarter to two .. leaving at one forty-five ... and there'll be a minibus to take you down there and to bring=
11	L	^ra::h
	T	=you back
12	LL	^rahah
13	L7	last year we have walked

We can note that the learners' contributions in this extract are not elicited by the teacher. They largely consist of brief comments and listening responses (e.g. 2L, 4L9), one request for further information (9L), and a topical contribution (L7). This last contribution shows how topic is an interactionally negotiated issue. 13L7 is clearly relevant to the topic, yet introduces something new: last year's visit. In doing so L7 simultaneously suggests that walking might be an alternative to going by bus. This in turn makes the issue of *the weather* relevant, as the subsequent response from the teacher shows (see Extract 5.27 on p. 121).

Activity

Orientation to topic can be described as orientation to what the talk is *about*. As mentioned above, a second orientation concerns what is being *done* and *how* it is done. We shall call this *activity* orientation. It may be useful, though we shall come back to this, to point out straight away that this is not an either-or distinction: both orientations may and usually will be simultaneously visible in a stretch of talk, although one tends to be more prominent than the other at any one time. This is the key to the description of larger sequences in a lesson, and to participation structures, as will be discussed later on in this chapter.

Activity orientation manifests itself through a focus of attention on saying things in a particular, previously agreed way (e.g. using full sentences, repeating particular questions or structures, imitating an intonation pattern, etc.), and/or taking turns in a particular sequence, playing roles, taking part in a game. In the extract from *Through the Looking-Glass* quoted in the introduction to this chapter, Alice focuses on topic, whereas Humpty Dumpty focuses on activity. The two orientations are in that example not compatible, and this illustrates that, if interaction is to be successful, participants must agree on the orientation of that interaction. In activity-oriented interaction, that agreement involves knowing the rules for the activity. In general conversation the activity rules are tacit and largely determined by social conventions. They are acquired through the process of socialization, and can also be found in books on etiquette. They involve Grice's cooperative principle (Grice 1975), Leech's maxim of tact (Leech 1977), Edmondson's Hearer-Support maxim (Edmondson 1981), features of positive and negative politeness (Brown and Levinson 1978), and so on. This orientation to activity in conversation must always be present, but generally as an underlying resource, as part of a cooperative contract between participants, surfacing only when some aspect of the contract is violated, and even then often in covert ways. In conversation, the participants' public work is mostly concerned with topic construction and management.

In the L2 classroom activity orientation manifests itself in a number of different ways, which can best be compared with rituals or games. The activity rules are not the tacit ones that govern conversation, but often specifically established ones that have to be stated, until some activity becomes well known and well tried and turns into a classroom routine. The following extract shows clear orientation to activity, and it is prefaced by specific procedural information:

EXTRACT 6.2

1 T   okay let's just go through these if I say- bus station I want you
         just to go through each one, all right? first one- bus station . .
         use- excuse me
2 L12   e:r

```
 3  L12  excuse me e:r which way: e:r . . . is the way to the=
 4  T                                    ⌈uhuh
    L12  =bus station
 5  T    which way is the bus station
 6  L12  which way is the bus station
 7  T    okay can you say it again . . . excuse me
 8  L12  excuse me . . which way is the bus station?
 9  T    good okay . . theatre . . . just use one of these. yes?
10  L1   e:r excuse me e::r where is the theatre?
11  T    good. cinema.
```

The notion of activity orientation illustrated in this extract is one that appears to be peculiar to L2 classroom discourse, and is related to drills and exercises that are advocated in language teaching textbooks. Note that the way things are said is specified, and also that when learners speak and about what is determined in advance by the teacher. This is different from Extract 6.1, where learners contribute on a voluntary basis. What appears to be common to activity-oriented sequences in the L2 classroom is that they require learners to *perform* verbally in some way. This leads to a kind of interaction which is very different from most out-of-class interaction (though settings such as courtrooms and political debates may make similar requirements).

Topic-activity interplay

Topic and activity orientation are related in complex ways in all verbal interaction, but perhaps mostly so in conversation. For example, the activity of 'small talk' limits severely the range of issues that can be used for topics, and this will vary considerably across cultures and social groups. In such conversation, the issue of topicality or topic treatment is governed by rules which are activity-specific. These rules form a loose kind of *frame* (see Box 6.2) within which participants operate and are able – within certain constraints – to show their individuality and creativity. Some people are prone to joking, others are more seriously-minded, some like to use themselves as topics, others delight in talking about others, and so on. All conversationalists will find a certain amount of leeway to do what they think they are best at, but at the same time they conform to the basic unstated rules. These may include that topic change must occur smoothly but regularly (don't be a bore, don't be rude) and that everyone must have a chance to participate in the talk (don't interrupt, don't monopolize, don't be too quiet). The guidelines may be difficult to follow so that things regularly go wrong, necessitating repair work of different kinds.

BOX 6.2   Frames

I assume that definitions of a situation are built up in accordance
with principles of organization which govern events – at least social
ones – and our subjective involvement in them; frame is the word I
use to refer to such of these basic elements as I am able to identify.
That is my definition of frame.

(Goffman 1974, pp. 10–11)

When one encounters a new situation (or makes a substantial
change in one's view of the present problem) one selects from
memory a structure called a *Frame*. This is a remembered framework
to be adapted to fit reality by changing details as necessary.

(Minsky 1975, p. 212)

The basic structure of a frame contains labelled *slots* which can be
filled with expressions, *fillers* (which may also be other frames). (. . .)
Formulated in this way, a frame is characteristically a fixed
representation of knowledge about the world.

(Brown and Yule 1983a, p. 237)

In the L2 classroom things appear to be simplified somewhat if we
regard topic and activity as being under the teacher's management and
control. While this is no doubt true in general, and facilitated by the
teacher's official status as turn keeper and allocator, at times there
is considerable room for the learners to manifest initiative.

When the talk is topic-oriented learners appear to have the right
to self-select as speakers, and also have the freedom to produce
listening responses of different kinds. The range of things they are
free to say may still be limited, but minimally they may express agreement, request clarification or elaboration, and perhaps add additional
information. Do learners also have the right to introduce new issues
as candidates for next topic in these situations? In the data I have
examined there is little evidence of this, but I expect that this will
vary from teacher to teacher, and class to class. Often in strongly
topic-oriented sequences the discourse is preplanned, i.e. it has been
decided beforehand that certain information must be transmitted, and
perhaps a limited amount of time has been set aside for this. In such
cases it is likely that there is concern for economy of transmission,
so that there is pressure to avoid changes in focus. The situation is
different when time has been allotted to 'conversation', i.e. the official
business of some segment of a lesson may be to encourage the learners
to talk about things that they themselves volunteer to bring up. I have
no examples of such activities, but it is no doubt of interest to analyse
them in detail to see what learners can do and say at such times (see

Extract 6.4 for a brief sequence of talk that approaches such unplanned interaction).

Apart from such 'official' topic-orientation, there are examples in many lessons of what might be called *topicalization*, when learners take up something the teacher or another learner says and (attempt to) make it into next topic. This may result in a side topic that is inserted into the main business of an activity (which may be activity-oriented, e.g. the production of questions with 'which'). The extract below is an example of such topicalization. At the time, the teacher might have been asked if this topicalization was invited (by the choice of 'baby' as an example), or if it occurred totally unexpectedly; as it is, we shall never know, but it may well be that side topics are interactively produced in order to leaven otherwise dull or heavy-going activity sequences.

EXTRACT 6.3

```
((L2 is male, L6 is female; throughout the lesson they
engage in much mutual joking))
 1  L2   'which' – a person or things
 2  T    yes .. yea which dog is yours ... okay? which baby=
 3  LL      ᶜyes/ya
    T    =is yours ... okay?
 4  L              ᶜm:
 5  L2   I don't have baby
 6  LL   ((loud laughter))
 7  T    are you sure?
 8  LL   ((loud laughter))
 9  L6   I don't know
10  LL   ((laughter))
11  L2   o:::h ((mock consternation))
```

As we have seen, orientation to activity is often manifested by opening statements pertaining to rules to be followed (see Extract 6.2) and, in the execution of the activity, by the regular invocation of rules such as the 'unique response rule', and frequently by specific allocation or pre-allocation of various kinds.

Orientation to topic, on the other hand, is characterized by the exchange of information between participants and, when the sequence is preplanned, the aim is to impart this information as efficiently as possible. Repair work is oriented to requesting clarifications, suggesting additions, etc. Questions asked by the 'knower' are predominantly undirected, and are often requests for confirmation. Listening responses are frequent, and self-selection is common. During activity-oriented talk, however, self-selection (apart from self-selection by the conductor of the activity – in most cases the teacher) is rare, and when it occurs it occurs during a *switch* in the interaction, e.g. between one drill item and the next, between an evaluation and next initiation, or between one dyad and the next. Private rehearsal turns are more common than listening responses.

As a result, turn-taking rules during topic-oriented talk are much closer to those of general conversation than the turn-taking rules of activity-oriented talk. During the former the teacher generally addresses the entire audience, does not select next speaker, and consequently any talk from the audience is generally self-selected talk. During the latter, specific allocation is predominant, and this frequently stays in force over a number of turns until, that is, it is cancelled out by another allocation or by some form of closing marker.

However, sequences of talk are not always rigidly uniform internally in turn-taking terms. As Extract 6.3 shows, the process of topicalization may lead to topic sequences inserted into activity-oriented sequences. In addition, the teacher will often insert comments of a topical nature (that have arisen from previous talk) which may also lead to brief stretches of open-floor talk, with undirected questions, comments and questions from learners, listening responses, etc. An activity-oriented sequence may thus be interspersed with brief sequences of topic talk, and the boundaries between activity talk and topic talk in these instances are often fluid.

If we regard interaction in this light, with topic talk and activity talk intermingling throughout a lesson, it becomes inappropriate to speak of 'phases' or larger units in a lesson as simply topic or task units. The dynamics of interaction are too flexible to be treatable in this way. This does not mean that larger units cannot be isolated or that the lesson has no internal structure. We can see openings and closings to a lesson, but in terms of the structuring of the discourse segmentation of the form 'opening-middle-closing' is relatively trivial. What is more interesting is the switching from topic-orientation to activity-orientation and vice versa, and the switching from topic to topic and activity to activity. Thus, boundaries between stretches of talk that have a unitary character, and the talk immediately preceding and following those boundaries, become of primary initerest. Although boundary markers can help to identify unitary sequences they do not give information about the internal structuring and coherence of such sequences. Such information must derive from the sequences themselves, in the form of patterns of participation. This point is important since, if the location of units is based only on the identification of boundary markers, we will end up with a description which intuitively does not fit the data (see the section on boundaries below).

There is thus no doubt that, if structural units are to be located, their location must be based on the internal structure of these units as evidenced by surface features in these units, and not on the identification of boundaries.

Without ignoring the occurrence of boundaries, my analysis of sequences and episodes below will therefore focus on their internal coherence rather than on superficial markers of change. The discussion so far of topic- and activity-orientation provides one avenue of enquiry into lesson coherence. I shall consistently relate this to our earlier discussion of turn taking and initiative, and thus arrive at the identification of specific participant structures in the L2 classroom.

Interaction types

At different times during L2 classroom interaction a differential emphasis on activity-orientation and on topic-orientation can be in evidence. These two types of orientation are neither mutually dependent nor mutually exclusive, though they interrelate and interact in complex ways to provide organizational structure. We can therefore not divide the lesson up into topics and tasks as distinct units, rather every sequence must be examined for its relative focus on topic and activity, in terms of 'more' or 'less'.

This combined orientation is expressed in Diagram 6.1, where '+' stands for more, and '−' stands for less. This diagram yields four spaces of differential orientation, or four *interaction types*, which can be glossed as follows:

1. Less topic-orientation, less activity-orientation.
   Gloss: 'Talk about anything you want in any way you want to, observing the usual social rules.'
   Examples: small talk, general conversation over a cup of coffee, etc.
2. More topic-orientation, less activity-orientation.
   Gloss: 'There is some information that needs to be transmitted, or some issue that needs to be sorted out.'
   Examples: announcements, instructions, explanations, lectures.
3. More topic-orientation, more activity-orientation.
   Gloss: 'Some information needs to be transmitted, and this transmission needs to proceed along specific lines, following certain rules.'
   Examples: elicitation (teacher-learner 'recitation'), interviews, reports, summaries, discussions, debates, jokes, stories.

DIAGRAM 6.1

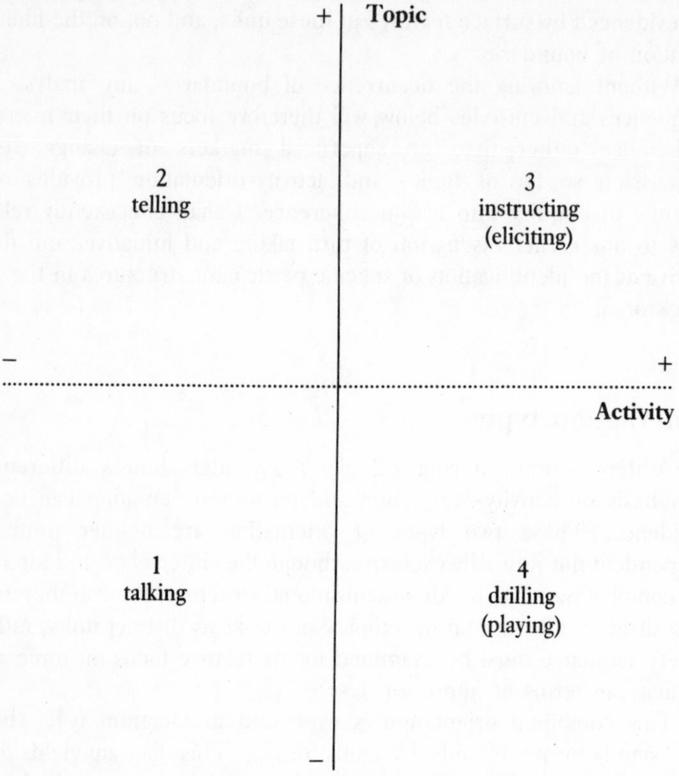

4. Less topic-orientation, more activity-orientation.

   Gloss: 'Things of a certain kind must be said following specific rules. Follow the rules and you'll be all right.'

   Examples: repetition and substitution drills, pair work, role taking, games.

Before proceeding, it must be emphasized that these are not four watertight types: one cannot construct discrete units out of two intersecting continua. However, the lack of clear borderlines does not detract from the usefulness of the four interaction types if it can be shown, as I aim to do, that they imply distinct organizational and interactional patterns in the classroom. To put the argument in the strongest possible terms: every one of these four types leads to different rights and duties of the participants, and consequently to different kinds of contributions to the interaction. If these unitary types can be identified in a relatively unarbitrary fashion in a classroom lesson, and if they can be consistently related to certain patterns of participation, we have a simple but powerful tool to analyse sections of a lesson in terms of the kinds of input they provide, and the quality of language practice (communication) they encourage the learner to participate in.

Below I shall give clear examples of each of the four interaction types, together with some comments to point out their main characteristics.

Interaction type 1

EXTRACT 6.4

```
 1 T    okay ... right. you had a- singsong last night didn't you?
 2 L1   yes
 3 T    was it good?
 4 LL   //yes//oh yes/
 5 T    was it just- just the e:rm Teleac or were there other students
 6 L    only the Teleac group
 7 T    only the Teleac group
 8 L9                  ⌈e:h- ja
 9 L1                      ⌈and later in the evening eh the: hoe heten
        die ((unint))              ((tr: what are they called))
10 L        ⌈(Arabians)
11 L    Saudi Arabians
```

This extract occurs at the beginning of a lesson and illustrates the so-called 'warming up' which is often done to get things going. Although the teacher introduces the topic, the learners can say what they want to if they want to. They do not change topic in this case, but no doubt in many such warming-up sessions they can, provided it is done appropriately. It is clear that learners collaboratively contribute to the conversation, since the last four turns are taken by four learners consecutively. They interestingly contain a repair sequence conducted entirely by the learners themselves: it is initiated in 9L1 and completed in 10L and 11L. There is no allocation of turns, i.e. learner turns are self-selected. Not all turns have to be addressed to the teacher, viz. 9L1 which is addressed to other learners, and 10L and 11L which are addressed to L1. Naturally, this type of interaction, where there is little express focus on either topic or activity, is as close as we may be able to get to ordinary conversation in the classroom.

Interaction type 2

EXTRACT 6.5

```
1  L7  and one bus . is going back at six o'clock?
2  T   yes . well we still need to find out this bec'z we need to
       find out how many people sign up for tickets and if there
       are:    enough people not going to the theatre then one=
3  L       ⌜((unint))
   T   =bus or coach will come back here a bit earlier but it depends
       on the numbers . . . really
4  L9                       ⌜yes
```

Here the teacher is providing information about a forthcoming trip
to London. It is important that the learners understand and grasp this
information, and the focus is on getting that job done. The learners
ask for clarification and further information when necessary, and
produce listening responses to indicate their understanding. Most of
the talk is teacher talk, but there is no allocation of turns.

Interaction type 3

EXTRACT 6.6

```
1  T   any other ways?
2  L5  uh can you help me?
3  T   yes. good okay
4  L5          ⌜please can you help me?
5  T   can you help me- uhuh ((writes on board))
6  L4  may I ask you?
7  L5  dat heb ik net gezegd ((tr: I've just said that))
8  T                    ⌜you've just said that yes
```

This is an example of elicitation: the focus is on information of a
specific kind, and while the sequence is in progress a list of ways of
asking the way is written on the blackboard. The information must
be provided in specific ways: specifically, the teacher asks for it, and
the learners propose candidates for the blackboard list. As 7L5
shows, the unique-response rule is in operation here, since every
candidate can only be proposed once. We can clearly note here, then,
a dual focus on topic and on activity.

Interaction type 4

EXTRACT 6.7

```
1  T   good. David have you got any questions for somebody . . .   . . .
2  L8  Felix . . . Felix
3  L                    ⌜why ((softly))
```

```
 4 T   Felix
 5 L8  why did you ... why did you decide to come here
 6 T   why did you decide to come here
 7 L   oh
 8 L   no?
 9 L1  my parents eh: sent me here
10 T   okay
```

Looking at this extract, we must first of all note that, even during teacher-learner dyads, other learners are doing things which may or may not be directly related to the exchanges in question. These extraneous turns serve to remind the analyst that the teacher-learner dyad (which turns into a triad) is performed in the presence of a participating audience.

The characteristic that turns this interaction into a type 4 one is its explicit ritual structure. The teacher appoints a learner to ask a question of another learner, who then responds to the question. It is not important what the question is about, so long as it is a proper question, and likewise the answer is not assessed for its information value, but rather for its successful linguistic completion. The teacher's evaluations in 6T and 10T show a focus on utterance form rather than message. One has a feeling that L8 might just as well have asked 'When did you last change your socks?' or 'Can you count to ten?' Of course, such interactions may at any time be changed into interaction types 1 or 2, if a particularly interesting or humorous remark is made.

The above are relatively clear cases of different interaction types generated by a differential orientation to topic and activity. Not surprisingly, there are many instances of sequences of interaction which do not fit so neatly into the pattern suggested. For example, in the extract below a type 3 activity is changed into a type 2 activity since it appears that the type 3 orientation does not yield the desired results. Prior to 4T the teacher elicits ways of asking the way from the learners, i.e. gets information from the learners in a specific way (see Extract 6.6, which occurs earlier on in the same activity). When no more information is forthcoming from the learners the teacher switches from *eliciting* information to *telling* information (4T and 12T). Note that in 4T the teacher has to all appearances made this switch, but that L7 in the next turn continues to offer a candidate 'way' in accordance with the previous activity type. It requires some effort for the learners to switch from one activity type to another, since it implies other rules for participation.

EXTRACT 6.8

```
  1  T    ((cont)) if you said would you tell me the way to the bus
          station     they can just say yes or no . .=
  2  L         ᶜjaha
     T    =so it's the same problem. any other ways . . .   . . .
          ((unint)) . . .
  3  LL   ((unint – – – – – – – – – – – – – –))
→ 4  T    how about – which way . . which way is the bus station
  5  L7   do you know (the way)
  6  LL            ᶜ((unint – – – – – – – – –))
  7  T    which way – all right? so you can say- excuse me . .=
  8  L              ᶜo::::h
     T    =can you help me? which way is the bus station please?
  9  L    jaha::
 10  T    which way
 11  L    (which way) . . .   . . . ((teacher writing on board))
 12  T    uh:m which way . . . how about just- *whe:re i:s* the bus station
```

At times an activity may not produce the desired results or cease to
be effective after some time, and the teacher must effect a change.
One option is to drop the issue at hand and go on to something else,
another is to transform the activity type chosen into another one
without dropping the issue. In the above case the teacher changes
from type 3 to type 2, or from eliciting to telling. Another example
can be found in Chapter 5, in Extract 5.36 (p. 141), where a type
3 interaction is changed into a type 4 interaction. The switch there
occurs in 9T: prior to it the teacher has been eliciting items in a
personal description, this proves ineffective (again, considerable
confusion precedes the switch), and the teacher resolves the problem
by changing to allocating sentences with specific words in them. The
decision to switch is marked explicitly by the words 'let's try it this
way'.

Finally, learners may at times also attempt to change a specific
interaction type into another one, particularly instances of 2, 3 and
4 into type 1 if, as is not unreasonable, they prefer just talking to
other, more regimented activities. In the following extract a type 4
interaction is thus changed into a type 1 interaction by means of using
an allocated question to introduce an interesting topic.

EXTRACT 6.9

```
  1  T    okay do *you* have any questions about using these words? okay?
  2  L    okay
  3  L6   yeah
  4  T    what
```

5	L6	how many- girlfriends do you have here? ((to L2))
6	L2	o::h
7	T	how many *girl*friends does he have here?
8	L6	yes
9	L	((unint))
10	L2	are you very interesting? ((meaning: interes*ted*))
11	LL	((unint))
12	T	that's his business. he's not telling you
13	LL	((modest laughter))
14	L6	I cry
15	T	you cry
16	LL	((loud laughter))
17	T	are you jealous?
18	L6	ya

In the last extract below we see another example of topicalization: the learners pick up a remark by the teacher, made to exemplify a linguistic issue that is being explained (interaction type 2) and use it to start a conversation (interaction type 1). As happens a number of times in different lessons, learners thus negotiate time out of the 'official business' of the lesson to engage in some lighthearted conversation. This game can of course only succeed if the teacher goes along with it. In 13T below the teacher attempts to return to the lesson activity in hand, but then almost immediately re-opens the inserted conversation in 15T. The asparagus episode in fact continues for another fifteen turns after the close of this extract.

EXTRACT 6.10

1	T	angry- sort of yeah you don't like something you *don't* like something and you don't like it *very much* you *hate* it
2	L3	you::
3	T	ᵗhate something if you don't like it very much. for example I hate asparagus
4	L2	I love it hehe I love asparagus
5	L	ᵗ(like everything)ᵣ
6	T	ᵣI hate asparagus
7	L3	asparagus
8	L6	asparagus?
9	T	asparagus
10	L6	I like it
11	L2	you I like it too yeah
12	L	I don't like it yu:a:h
→ 13	T	anyway that's the meaning for hate okay?
14	LL	((laughter, comments))
→ 15	T	just remember that. if you ever invite me to your house don't give me asparagus

16 L2   oh-
17 L6   ᶜif I do the first time
18 L1   yes is good idea
19 T   first time ((laughs))
20 L1   make him asparagus
21 L6   in the party I make him asparagus

Lesson structure

There can be little doubt in anyone's mind that a lesson is structured, i.e. that it is not a random succession of (speech) actions. However, attempts to identify a common underlying structure to all lessons have so far failed. As I suggested earlier, structural statements of the type opening-middle (or main body)-closing do not amount to much, since the same statements can be made about practically any speech event. Moreover, unless the separate sections can be precisely defined in terms of their functions or exponents, the structure is vacuous, since in that case the elements can only be described in terms of their placement: the opening is that which comes first, or, in other words, that which comes first is that which comes first. This kind of description does not get us very far at all.

Lessons can start, proceed and end in all imaginable ways. Some lessons begin with a song, others with an oral or written quiz, others yet with physical exercises. They can end in these same or in many other ways, and what occurs in the middle is just as varied.

Yet, whenever we transcribe and analyse lessons we get the strong feeling that they all have a sense of rhythm to them, or some form of cyclical progression. It is hard to pinpoint this rhythm in exact terms, and impossible to give predictive rules on the basis of small sets of data, but it is quite likely that further research will show regular and consistent cyclical rhythms in L2 lessons. So far as I can tell, the centre of gravity, or the base line of the lesson, invariably consists of sequences of type 4 interaction. Much of the rest of the lesson fits around these sequences, either leading up to them or trailing them. This does not mean that other business does not also occur, but the type 4 interaction is invariably the focal point. I suggest that, more as a result of natural patterns of interaction in groups, and sound classroom practices, than of methodological fashions, this cyclical rhythm is in actual fact rather general (or 'typical'), and if this turns out to be the case, an analysis of lesson structuring must focus on what these activities do and how they work, and how they are prepared and followed up by activities of other kinds. In general it can be said that they are preceded by procedural information, telling the students what they have to do and the rules they have to follow, and these introductory sequences are instances of interaction type 2. They are also preceded by elicitation sequences, where the information that is to be used in the activity is gathered and in some way systematized, and this leads to sequences of interaction type 3. Instances of interaction type 1 are in my data rather incidental, designed to do introductory warm-ups, or to temporarily break out of more strenuous type 4 activities, but this does not diminish their importance.

As an example, an analysis of one language lesson in terms of interaction types yielded the following pattern (brief inserted sequences are superscripted above the major sequences, the underlined sequences consist of pair or group work):

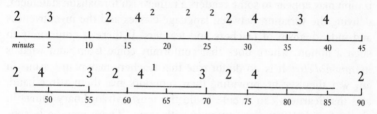

Type 4 interaction thus forms the core of the lesson, and since it is the interaction type that is the furthest removed from natural conversation, one may raise doubts as to its value in terms of realistic language practice. However, this slot is in many classes used for pair work and group work, and this of course opens up opportunities for the use of interaction types 1, 2 and 3 within that same slot, depending on the type of task that is set. The cyclical rhythm of the classroom can thus break out of this gravitation towards a ritual type 4 interaction by transforming it, through group work, into other types of interaction. Group work can thus be useful to provide variety in interaction and participation patterns within the framework of a 'typical' lesson.

The recommendation that group work is beneficial is of course nothing new. Its advantages over lockstep, or teacher-fronted procedures in general, have in fact been stressed so much at times that teachers may feel that they are doing something wrong whenever they stand in front of the class talking to all the learners. I think that that is a serious misconception, and would argue for a principled integration of teacher-fronted and group work (see Peters 1983, especially pp. 109–113, for the role of memorization, pattern practice, substitution drills, and so on, both in classrooms and in naturalistic environments). It may be conceded for a number of reasons that the type 4 slot is the centre of gravity of the lesson, so that what is done to occupy it is of the utmost importance. However, that does not mean that it can profitably be the *only* slot in a lesson. The other slots, filled by teacher-fronted activities, may be of equal importance, partly since they allow the type 4 slot to be exploited maximally, and partly since the classroom is a social group which needs to build its own social context, learners and teacher together. In addition, an examination of what learners do during these teacher-led sequences will reveal that they are important sources of input for the learners, as well as opportunities to practise necessary skills and strategies of communication.

My suggestion of a basic cyclical rhythm underlying lesson organization may appear to some readers a rather rash formalistic statement, denying the variation between language classes and the inventiveness and individualism of teachers and learners. If there is conformity to such a notion, where does that conformity come from, and what is its *raison d'être*? It is no doubt true that teachers may plan lessons in any way they see fit, providing their superiors give them a free hand, and that learners can decide to do the most extraordinary things in class, provided they can get away with them. There may be lessons that are filled from beginning to end with a teacher's talk and the learners' scratching of pens on paper, others that are filled with the sound of many voices talking all at once, none of them intelligible. If organizational statements have to account for all and every lesson, even the strangest ones, I doubt that anything meaningful can ever be said on this issue. However, there are certain common-sense notions and expectations as to what counts as a 'proper' lesson, and I have said that there is an implicit social and pedagogical contract between teachers and learners, and between school and society, which tends to lead to a lesson being accomplished in some recognizable basic way. In a similar sense we can accept the validity of such conversational notions as turn-taking rules, cooperative principles, tact and politeness, regardless of the number of times they are violated in conversations we happen to participate in.

Although the idea of lesson organization as rhythmic and cyclical remains at present not fully specified, it leads to a conception of *unmarkedness* or *wellformedness* for a specific speech event. If we proceed with such a notion we must assume that it is a socially motivated wellformedness, and not one measured by criteria of pedagogy or subject matter sequencing. It is thus not directly related to lesson planning or notions of 'good' or 'bad' teaching.

An L2 lesson, like any other lesson, is a mixture of planned and unplanned discourse. The ratio of planned to unplanned elements is variable, depending as it does on the extent of prior planning as well as on the things that actually happen during the execution of the plan. Overwhelmingly – too often perhaps – the planning is done exclusively by the teacher, who is thus the only one at the beginning of the lesson who knows what is going to happen during that lesson. The learners just have to wait and see and follow the directions given to them, or rely on whatever information the teacher may give them beforehand (through handouts, introductory overviews, etc.). This practice is one of the ways in which the teacher's power, control and superior status are manifested and maintained in traditional classrooms. One of the aims of a communicative approach is to give learners at least part of the responsibility for the planning of activities, and the teacher can then become more of a consultant rather than being a master of ceremonies.

BOX 6.3   On planned and unplanned discourse

We can talk about planning, then, on a number of levels. Discourses may vary in the degree to which they are planned. Discourses in which the form of every social act is worked out in advance are the most planned. Discourses in which only certain acts are attended to in advance are somewhat less planned. And discourses in which acts are thought out in the course of their production are even less planned, and so on. Discourses vary not only in the extent to which they are planned but also in the extent to which they are *plannable*. For example, truly spontaneous conversation is, by definition, relatively unplannable well in advance. Unlike other forms of discourse, in spontaneous conversation it is difficult to predict the form in which entire sequences will be expressed. The content may be even less predictable. Rather, what will be said, the form in which it will be said, and who will say it can be anticipated for limited sequences only (e.g., certain adjacency pairs for certain speaker-hearer relationships). In terms of conversational analysis (Sacks, Schegloff and Jefferson 1974), spontaneous conversation is 'locally managed'. It tends to be designed on a turn-by-turn basis. Other forms of discourse are more plannable. For example, ritualized speech events tend to have more predictable sequential ordering of social acts and more predictable message content. Communicators can anticipate more what will be said and what their verbal contribution should be.

(Ochs 1979, pp. 57–8)

L2 classroom lessons are thus 'hybrid' events of the type described in Chapter 5 (p. 135). They are partly planned in advance, and partly constructed on the spot. In their plannedness they may show elements of several organizational sources and resources, notably *cognitive*, *institutional*, *methodological* and *ritual*. Specific mixtures of these ingredients of predetermination will lead to different expectations and different orientations in the classroom. When construction has to be done locally, i.e., during the lesson itself, the same set of resources may be drawn upon, but one essential other resource becomes of prime importance: the *social context*. Experienced teachers will in their planning of course take the social context into account as well as other resources, i.e. they will be able to predict the role that social interaction may play in the projected lesson procedures. However, the social context is essentially a *local* resource, whereas other resources can be both local and *nonlocal*.

Lesson organization thus relies to varying degrees upon these different types of resources, and some examples of their influence are suggested below:

Cognitive: the selection of suitable content matter and its logical breakdown into hierarchical or sequential components.

Institutional/cultural: the amalgam of cultural and institutional demands and expectations in terms of such issues as general standards, comparable procedures and quality control. This includes evaluation of progress and of programmes.

Methodological: the ideologies and beliefs of all involved as to what constitute sound teaching and learning methods.

Ritual: the reliance on tried and tested routines and practices in the classroom that constitutes much of the teacher's professional baggage and gives the lesson much of its characteristic identity.

Social context: the dynamics of a gathering of learners and their teacher, patterns of participation and initiative, issues of control, support, challenge, the use of storytelling, rapping and joking, degrees of formality and informality, and so on.

It is no doubt possible to add to this list of resources, e.g. by considering the learners' personal (neurological, affective, etc.) characteristics, vocational demands, and so on. Seen in this light it is clear that there is much substance to the often-made remark that classroom discourse is complex, that learning in the classroom is a 'multidimensional phenomenon' (Long 1983a). When describing the organization of a lesson the analyst may have to draw upon all the resources that the participants themselves also draw upon. When we identify regular patterns, it is important to resist the temptation to describe these patterns exclusively in one set of terms, such as linguistic, topical (i.e. propositional), functional (i.e. illocutionary) or pedagogical terms. The dangers are clear: we may for example be led by our particular scheme for analysis to believe that it is characteristic for classrooms that learners 'behave largely as one many-headed participant, avoiding cross-conversations, and acknowledging the authority of the teacher in their verbal behaviour' (Sinclair and Brazil 1982, p. 3). As a consequence we end up with summary comments and descriptions such as those mentioned in Chapter 5 (p. 137). No doubt these observations are accurate for large portions of many classrooms, but if they are built into the fabric of an analytical scheme or model (as they are in Sinclair and Brazil 1982 and McHoul 1978) they do not allow us to notice that learners do employ creative initiative, even at times during the most regimented of activities and drills. Moreover, we need a framework for analysing lessons which incorporates group and pair work since, at least in L2 classrooms, they are now an integral part of virtually all recommended methods.

In summary, I advocate an analytical approach which is a dialectic between the *holistic*, which looks at the broad sweep of patterns and rhythms of events, and places those events in the wider social world of the participants (e.g. the sociology of education tradition), and the *localistic*, which looks at the minutest details of interaction and attempts to pinpoint what the people involved actually do. This is the essence of ethnographic research, and to many researchers it may seem like the long way around, especially to those who believe that there are shortcuts to understanding.

In the next section I shall use the evidence of interaction types and the suggestion of cyclical rhythms to describe the participation patterns that occur in L2 classrooms.

Participation structures

The concept of participation structure was first proposed by Philips (1972) who called it *participant structure*, to refer to structural arrangements of interaction within the framework of teacher-controlled interaction. The term was changed to *participation structure* by Erickson to capture its dynamic nature, and I shall follow Erickson's example, though the point is one of detail. Cazden (1985) describes participation structures as 'the rights and obligations of participants with respect to who can say what, when, and to whom' (p. 19).

Philips used the concept to illustrate the differences in classroom participation between (American) Indian and non-Indian children. She noted that at times Indian children participated freely, at other times not at all. She found that, when verbal participation implied 'performing in front of others', either voluntarily or on command, Indian children frequently refused to do so. However, during group activities in which students controlled and directed the interaction themselves, they became fully involved and interacted a great deal with each other. Comparing the classroom behaviour of Indian and non-Indian children, Philips draws the following conclusions:

> First of all, they show relatively less willingness to perform or participate verbally when they must speak alone in front of other students. Secondly, they are relatively less eager to speak when the point at which speech occurs is dictated by the teacher, as it is during sessions when the teacher is working with the whole class or a small group. They also show considerable reluctance to be placed in the 'leadership' play roles that require them to assume the same type of dictation of the acts of their peers. Parallel to these negative responses are the positive ones of a relatively greater willingness to participate in group activities that do not create a distinction between individual performer and audience, and a relatively greater use of opportunities in which the point at which the student speaks or acts is determined by himself, rather than by the teacher or a 'leader'.
>
> (Philips 1972, p. 380)

The crucial characteristics appear to be self-determination and speaker-audience relationships. While it would be foolish to compare L2 learners to Indian school children, these are also characteristics that are important in L2 classroom lessons, though perhaps for different reasons.

Philips identifies four participation structures which can be briefly summarized as follows:
1. teacher–whole class, with chorus or individual responses, either allocated or undirected, possibly with bidding for turns;
2. teacher–group, with individual allocated responses, while rest of class works on other tasks (e.g. reading groups);
3. teacher–individual learner, while rest of class works individually;
4. group by itself, possibly with 'chairperson', teacher supervising at a distance (group projects).

While this division may work for primary native-language classrooms, it is not specific enough for the second-language classroom, particularly in terms of self-selection and control, and perhaps too specific in its division of teacher–class and teacher–group (1 and 2) as two separate structures. Also, type 3 is a dyad without audience, and as such does not need to be included in a basic format of classroom interaction structure.

In their comparison of talk at a dinner table and a maths lesson,

Shultz, Florio and Erickson (1982) also propose four participation structures, but they turn out to be quite different from Philips's set. Shultz *et al.* distinguish participation structures along three dimensions:

a) number of people talking at one time, either one or more than one;
b) participants' roles, either equivalent or primary and secondary participants;
c) the number of conversational floors, either one, or more than one.

According to Shultz *et al.* the same participation structures that occur at a dinner table also occur during the maths lesson, but with different frequencies and in different sequences. Notably, more than one person talking at once, and more than one conversational floor, are only allowed at the beginning (preparation) and end (wrap-up) of the lesson. In between, the dominant structure is one person at a time, differential participants' roles, and only one floor. Within that condition Shultz *et al.* do not distinguish, and this makes their analysis, though detailed and insightful, insufficiently specific for the L2 classroom.

In another paper Erickson (1982) focuses more narrowly on classroom discourse, another maths lesson, but this time in a bilingual classroom. In this paper a distinction is made between *academic task structure*, or 'a patterned set of constraints provided by the logic of sequencing in the subject-matter content of the lesson', and *social participation structure*, 'a patterned set of constraints on the allocation of interactional rights and obligations of various members of the interacting group' (1982, p. 154; the reader is advised to briefly consult Chapter 3, p. 64, and Chapter 4, pp. 84–5, where this distinction is introduced in the context of a different discussion). Erickson's concept of two sets of *constraints* can be complemented with the different kinds of *resources* I mentioned above, so that the first four resources (cognitive, institutional/cultural, methodological and ritual) contribute to academic task structure (better perhaps, structur*ing*), and the fifth resource, social context, to social participation structure. We may bear in mind the complementary nature of constraints and resources (rules and resources in Giddens's terminology) referred to in Chapter 3 (especially p. 50).

Academic task structure is 'moderately specified' (p. 164), somewhat less so than a Roman Mass, but more so than an ordinary conversation. The social participation structure of the lesson can be somewhat like an ordinary conversation at times, but, in Erickson's comparison, resembles more the evangelical sermon with audience participation. The two sets of constraints/resources, loosely specified as they are, with both local and nonlocal organizational aspects, 'provide a theme around which variations can be constructed' (p. 165), and this provides opportunity for *improvisation* ('strategically adaptive action' — p. 161).

Most discourse analyses of classrooms take the view that the proceedings in a lesson are uniquely determined by the teacher, and that the learners as one single many-headed conglomerate are nothing but the passive recipients of this determination. For the learners the game is fixed and all they can do is sit there and wonder, trying to provide the appropriate noises as indicated by meagre clues the teacher throws their way. Indeed, at times this appears to be an accurate reflection of the state of affairs, as the excerpt from Adelman in Box 6.4, from a conversation between a researcher and some students, illustrates:

BOX 6.4

GIRL: You don't really know what you are meant to be
                doing.
INTERVIEWER: Yes
GIRL: . . . at the time.
INTERVIEWER: Sorry? Say that again?
GIRL: You don't know what you're meant to be doing at the
                time, if you're meant to be talking about the pool . . .
GIRL 2:   . . . pond or the village life or what.
INTERVIEWER: Oh, you don't quite know how to respond sometimes
                to his questions. Did you feel that that time then?
GIRL: Oh yes.
GIRL 2:   Yes.

                                        (Adelman 1981, pp. 92–3)

If this state of affairs occurs with some regularity in native-language classrooms, it is possible that it occurs even more frequently in second-language lessons.

However, it does not occur all the time, and an analysis of classroom patterns must show what factors influence its occurrence. In terms of our analysis so far it can be hypothesized that such confusion can arise when some activity is prespecified, i.e. is nonlocal in that it has been planned beforehand by the teacher, when some content matter must be transmitted (topic orientation) in a certain way, i.e. through a series of questions and answers (activity orientation), and when the learners' participation is not determined by the rules and constraints of ordinary conversation. This is typically the case in an interaction type 3.

We can summarize the various elements that play a part in the construction of classroom activities in the form of a table, as below. In this table I add, as a final column, the notion of participation structure that I propose for the L2 classroom, and a more detailed description of these structures will be given subsequently. The table will become clear by consulting it while reading through the description of ITs and PSs following it. It is especially important to focus on how interaction types and participation structures are systematically related in this description.

TABLE 6.1	Prespecification		Academic		Social	Participation structure
Interaction Type	predominantly local	non-local	orientation topic	activity	rules and constraints	primary – secondary speaker
IT 1	+	−	−	−	+	PS 1: T/L–L/T
IT 2	−	+	+	−	−/+	PS 2: T–(L)
IT 3	−	+	+	+	−	PS 3: T–LL/L
						PS 4: T–L
IT 4a	−	+	−	+	−	PS 4: T–L
IT 4b	−/+	−/+	−/+	+	−/+	PS 5: L–L/(T)

I will now provide a more detailed description of the interaction types which takes into account their identification in the previous section as well as the information we have been able to add in this section. This description performs a crucial task which is to link systematically participation structures to interaction types. This link is essential if the model is to be directly useful for L2 classroom research.

IT 1 (conversation)

Prespecification: The construction of conversation is predominantly local, since the participants' contributions cannot be predicted. This is so even if the teacher has planned the conversation, in the sense of having decided to get the learners to talk about, say, last night's party. If during the conversation other topics come up the teacher will go along with them, since the aim is to establish 'informal talk', not getting information about a specific topic. Indeed, if a specific topic is enforced by the teacher, the activity will change into an IT 2 or IT 3.

Academic orientation: The focus is neither on a specific topic or instructional content nor on specific activity rules. Anyone can contribute when the floor is available.

Social rules and constraints: The usual rules for conversation are in operation regarding self-selection, topical coherence, non-interruption, politeness, etc.

Participation structure: Both teacher and learner can be primary speakers (i.e. have rights to select, address, change topic, etc.). The teacher must show restraint and not want to control too much, since this would change the activity into an IT 2.

IT 2 (telling)

Prespecification: Predominantly non-local, since the teacher has decided that some information has to be imparted to the learners. It can be local at times when some prior talk makes the giving of information (e.g. about some grammatical point) relevant.

Academic orientation: The focus is on topic, since the main objective is to provide some information.

Social rules and constraints: The rules and constraints may not be relevant if the teacher says, for example, that students should keep their questions till the end, or just be quiet and pay attention. However, more usually social rules and constraints apply in terms of giving appropriate listening responses, and asking for clarification, confirmation, adding information, etc. Learners self-select to participate overtly. However, usually only a limited kind of participation is possible.

Participation structure: The teacher is primary speaker, learners optionally self-select to provide listening responses, initiate repair, add information, etc. No topic-change or allocation of speaker other than teacher is open to learners.

IT 3 (elicitation)

Prespecification: Predominantly non-local, since some content matter has been analysed and sequenced and it has been decided that it must be systematized in some way by a process of asking and answering questions.

Academic: The focus is both on topic and on activity, since some information must be collected and presented, and this must be done in a recitation format. The only variation is that learners may volunteer to answer (undirected questions) or be specifically allocated turns (hence the two participation structures available for this

IT – see below).

Social rules and constraints: Do not apply, since the teacher controls participation. Learners may request clarification, etc., but only at appropriate times, e.g. during a switch between dyads. At times teacher or learners insert sequences of IT 1 or IT 2 to temporarily break out of the lockstep.

Participation structure: Two PSs are possible, depending on whether the teacher asks undirected questions (followed by self-selection or bidding) or specifically allocated ones.

IT 4a (ritual)

Prespecification: Predominantly non-local, since we are here in the realm of repetition, minimal pair practice, substitution drills, and the like.

Academic orientation: The focus is on activity, on doing the right thing at the right moment, as indicated by the rules.

Social rules and constraints: Do not operate, since they have been superseded by ritual rules and constraints ('if I say A, you say B, okay?').

Participation structure: Identical to that in the specific allocation option in IT 3, with the proviso that chorus responses are also possible.

IT 4b (group work)

This interaction type can turn into any of the previous ones, depending on the type of task that is set, and the way it is conducted. In terms of sequential placement and cyclical lesson rhythm it occupies the same slot as IT 4a, and this is the main reason for calling it IT 4b rather than IT 5 or some other name. In terms of interaction potential it can be anything it is allowed to be; its major defining characteristic in terms of participation structure is that the learner is primary speaker. A lot depends on how closely monitored the group is by the teacher: if the teacher visits the group and becomes primary speaker, the participation structure ceases to be PS 5, but rather turns into one of the other structures. This accounts for the frequent observation that when a teacher visits a group a sudden change in interaction takes place.

The above relates interaction types (IT) to participation structures (PS). It appears that the varying configurations of speaking rights and duties of the learners can be consistently related to the type of interaction that is taking place. This in turn means that when a certain orientation is manifested, a specific set of rules and constraints tends to operate which may either encourage or discourage participation on the part of the learner. What is said, when it is said, and how it is said, by whom, can therefore be more or less predictable, depending on what kind of activity is in progress. We are not yet saying that one way of participating is better – in terms of learning – than another, but we are able to identify the ways of participating and link them to different purpose-oriented procedural sequences.

It now remains to describe the participation structures in more detail. I will use the letters L and T to refer to different roles and possibilities for learners and teachers, the horizontal dash to separate primary speaker and discourse controller from the secondary speakers and attenders, the oblique slash to indicate the possibility of shared roles, and brackets to indicate optionality of active involvement. This notational shorthand is intended to indicate the unmarked division of labour in the different structures, though of course departures from this are always possible and perhaps not uncommon. Further detailed analysis will no doubt show that at times a differentiation between addressee, audience and respondent is relevant, and also a distinction between primary speaker and controller of discourse, but these distinctions are incidental to the present exercise.

The participation structures in the L2 classroom can be described as follows:

PS 1: T/L – L/T: A conversation in which either teacher or learner can introduce topics, self-select, allocate next speaker, etc.

PS 2: T – (L): The teacher has some information to impart, and the learners' task is to assimilate this information. The teacher wishes to impart the information as efficiently as possible, the learners must indicate that they are attending and that they understand (listening responses), request clarification, and bring up relevant additional points as appropriate. Learners self-select.

PS 3: T – LL/L: The teacher elicits information by asking un-directed questions to the whole class. Learners volunteer answers by selecting to speak (sometimes resulting in chorus responses or overlapping answers), or by bidding for turns, e.g. by raising their hand. This is a vulnerable configuration since, if intelligibility falls below a certain level, it will be converted into PS 4 or PS 2.

PS 4: T – L: The teacher allocates specific learners, either to respond to an informational question (IT 3) or to perform some (linguistic) action (IT 4a).

PS 5: L – L/(T): The learners work in groups on a task that has been prespecified to a greater or lesser extent. The teacher may wander in and out of groups, taking part in a non-primary sense. When the teacher takes part in a primary sense (e.g. by becoming controller of turns) the structure ceases to be PS 5 for that portion of time.

Discourse boundaries

Using the information from interaction types and participation structures it will be possible in most cases to divide the lesson into its constituent sequences or episodes. This means that the identification of such episodes is not uniquely dependent on the location of boundaries and frames, as it is in e.g. Sinclair and Coulthard 1975. However, as I have indicated earlier, it is of interest to study the ends and beginnings of episodes since they often provide important information about the management of classroom affairs. In general, the first thing we want to do with a transcribed lesson is to look for natural breaks in the stream of interaction and thus divide it into smaller sections. Also, a teacher examining a recorded lesson may wish to focus on a certain activity and look for the most efficient ways to find the beginning and end. On the surface, boundary markers appear to be unambiguous markers of change, and indeed they often are. However, it is important to note that the items which commonly mark boundaries can also fulfil other functions. Therefore, they are not foolproof indicators of 'new business'. Further evidence of change must always be obtained.

It might be expected that, in general, a boundary between two episodes would consist of two parts: closure of one episode followed by opening of the next episode, and that both would be overtly manifested in the discourse. This appears not to be the case: a common method of closing an episode is by opening the next one. At times there may be indications that an episode is ready to be closed, e.g. through such utterances as: 'Any more questions?', 'Anything else?', but such utterances are more appropriately termed pre-closings than closings (see Schegloff and Sacks 1974, p. 246). Such pre-closings strictly speaking give learners the opportunity to ask for a continuation of the episode the closing of which is proposed, but in most cases the 'All right?', etc. is followed immediately by introductory statements concerning the next episode.

In many cases it turns out that there appear to be no surface indications of closure or imminent closure, but rather the opening of the next episode simultaneously does the work of closing. The reason for this is not hard to find: closings in lessons are often not negotiated matters to be decided between the participants, but are simply executed by the teacher through the starting of the next episode. The teacher does not have to propose closure to the learners, but rather just closes – such is the power of authority. For instance, here is a boundary between an IT 2 and an IT 4:

EXTRACT 6.11

```
1 T  so you can make it longer and longer      allright?
2 L                                       ⌜yeah yeah⌝
3 T  okay let's just go through these if I say
     ((see Extract 6.2 for a continuation))
```

Sometimes boundaries can constitute topic-oriented (if we regard 'procedural information' as a topic) episodes in their own right. Thus the boundary between an IT 4a and an IT 4b (group work) was executed in the following way:

EXTRACT 6.12

```
1 L8  excuse me, can you help me, how- do- I- get- to the theatre?
2 T   good. all right. now I want (you) to just break up in threes and
      I just want you to practise . .
      (line omitted)
         .
         .  ((12 lines omitted))
         .
      or one person can say London, and the other people can ask the
      questions . . all right?      (it's) just a=
3 L                            ⌜(right)
  T   =very short practice, you three- you three- you three- and you
      three
4 LL  ((noises, chairs, movement))
```

The next extract illustrates a boundary between an IT 3a and an IT 4a, or a change from eliciting ways of giving directions by means of undirected questions to practice in giving directions by means of specific allocation. This boundary is executed as follows:

EXTRACT 6.13

```
    1    LL  it's on your left
    2    T              ⌜and it's on your left . . . . . . ((drawing on
                        board)) . . .
→   3    T   there we are    all right?    so. could you tell me=
    4–5  L             ⌜yes         ⌜yes
         T   =the way to the bus station please Jaap?
    6    L9  e:r . .
    7    LL  ((laughter))
```

A plausible explanation for the laughter in 7LL, and for L9's hesitation in 6L9 is that the sudden switch in activity has taken L9 and the rest of the class by surprise. In any case, the change from elicitation of information to teacher-guided practice is only minimally marked by 'so'.

Other boundaries tend to follow similar patterns, being more or less prolonged or marked, depending on the procedural information or prefacing that is deemed necessary by the teacher. In most cases there are some of a limited set of boundary markers or *frames* (cf. Sinclair and Coulthard 1975) which accompany such boundaries, but it would be wrong to assign episodes purely on the basis of such markers: as suggested before, they may be absent in the case of some episode boundaries, and they may be present in cases of quite minor shifts, such as dyad-change and minor topical shifts. Rather than calling them frames, these items are more properly termed *decision markers*: they indicate a decision point reached or manifest a decision just made by the speaker. At times this decision may relate to an activity or topic switch, at other times it may merely mark a cognitive or strategic decision with minor consequences in interactional terms. The following extract is an example of the latter:

EXTRACT 6.14

   1 T   can you say it again? . . excuse me . . . and again, Jaap?
   2 L9 excuse me, can you tell me the way to the cinema
→ 3 T   okay. now, ex- it's excuse me, can you tell me the way to the cinema? all right? can you tell me the way to the cinema? just drops a little at the end, can you say it again?

Decision markers are a small set of items, all uttered with a falling intonation, and followed by a brief pause. Typical items are: 'okay.' 'now.' 'all right.' 'so.' 'well.' and combinations of these.

I have mentioned that not all major boundaries are overtly marked by such items, and this may seem surprising since the change from one interaction type to another must constitute a major decision point in a lesson. In one lesson, the one from which most examples in this section are drawn, I identified three (out of sixteen) episode changes that were not overtly signalled by decision markers. Upon inspection it appeared that in all three cases the preceding episode was an IT 2 (dealing with procedural information) and the following episode was an IT 4b (group or pair work). This suggests that these preceding procedural episodes are subsidiary to the following task, and may be considered as boundary *episodes*. They in themselves indicate, in their occurrence, that a major new stage in the lesson is reached, and as such explicit decision markers may not be relevant.

In summary, we can not rely on decision markers for evidence of episodic boundaries, since at times their function is carried out by entire subsidiary episodes, while at other times they do not mark episodic changes at all. Unless there is evidence from discourse orientation and participation patterns, no switch or change can be assumed. The analysis in the previous sections allows us to rely on *structural* evidence *within* the unitary sequences to identify those sequences, and call them *episodes* with characteristic properties in terms of both purposeful orientation and participation structure.

Conclusion

In this chapter I have analysed the second-language lesson in terms of its overall organization. Whereas Chapter 5 studied the issue of participation from the bottom up, as it were, I have turned here to a different angle of vision, from the top down. I believe that the two ways of viewing produce consistent and converging evidence, which I would like to summarize in a few major points. I will come back to some of the suggestions made here in Chapter 8.

1. It is true that at times the learners' participation is entirely predetermined, and that they are told what to say and when, and always to the teacher. However, this is not always the case, and I have shown what the circumstances are that specify predetermination and restriction, as well as those that encourage creative contributions.

2. The teacher controls classroom interaction, undoubtedly, almost all the time. This is not necessarily a negative comment, since without this control there might be no lesson or, to come back to Stevick's terms, without control there might be no initiative. By looking at the places in a lesson where control can be usefully relaxed to allow more initiative, the teacher can work towards achieving a balance between these two forces, and steer a course between ritual and free-for-all.

3. There are sound reasons for everything that occurs in standard L2 lessons, even for those things methodological fashion may discard as wasteful. We are just at the beginning of classroom research where we can describe what actually goes on, but not yet whether that is 'good' or 'bad'. At times teachers are told that it is easier to learn a language outside the classroom than inside it, but we should be careful not to reject many years of grassroots

experience and accumulated practice out of hand. The only justification for taking classroom lessons is that they are a shortcut to language learning, and to be this they must be different from what goes on outside. In some way they must economize, concentrate and cut corners. Therefore the classroom can never just be a replica of the outside world.

4. The classroom is not a world unto itself. The participants (teacher *and* learners) arrive at the event with certain ideas as to what is a 'proper' lesson, and in their actions and interaction they will strive to implement those ideas. In addition the society at large and the institution the classroom is part of have certain expectations and demands which exert influence on the way the classroom turns out. It is in this sense that a lesson is organized according to nonlocal forces.

5. The classroom is also a social group (Breen 1985b) which establishes its own rules and constraints, to some extent different in each and every different classroom, but conforming to certain basic rules and norms of human conduct, partly of a very general nature, partly specific to a setting in which pedagogical purpose predominates. In this sense the classroom is locally organized. This interplay between local and nonlocal ingredients allows for a significant degree of improvisation and variation.

Notes:

1. See Hurtig's axiom: 'Discourse boundaries in and of themselves cannot constitute an adequate discourse theory.' (1977, p. 95)

7 The organization of repair in second-language classrooms

Introduction

In this chapter I want to take a detailed look at an area of classroom work which, perhaps more than any other in the eyes of most people inside and outside the profession, is characteristic of the language classroom: dealing with problems of language use. An ethnographic approach to the issue shows that this is not simply a matter of learners committing errors and teachers correcting them in various ways. It is rather, as Extract 7.1 illustrates, a matter of continuous adjustment between speakers and hearers obliged to operate in a code which gives them problems. This adjustment-in-interaction may be crucial to language development, for it leads to noticing discrepancies between what is said and what is heard, and to a resolution of these discrepancies. In order to investigate what happens when people repair their own and each other's language, we will have to go beyond a mere focus on identifiable linguistic errors, although in a second-language classroom such errors will naturally be frequent, and hence merit attention.

Although ethnographic study describes what occurs rather than what 'ought to' occur, certain questions about frequent patterns of repairing and correcting in classrooms will be raised regularly in this chapter, and it will be useful to keep these questions in mind, even if no clearcut answers can be provided at this point. Some of these questions are:

1. Should repairing aim to provide correct linguistic models, or just focus on meaning and understanding?
2. Should teachers withhold repair to give learners an opportunity to monitor their own performance and to do their own repairing?
3. What kinds of repair are 'legitimate' in a classroom, over and above the repairs common in non-pedagogic discourse?
4. In what ways does repairing by the teacher and by other learners assist the learner's language development, and in what ways may it hinder this development?

EXTRACT 7.1

```
 1  T   what do you do
 2  L5  I am an architect
 3  T   uhuh I am an architect
 4  L   (are you) building?
 5  LL  ((unint  – – –))
 6  T   exactly
 7  L6  ya!
 8  LL  building/building
 9  L2  are you building – no!
10  LL  no ((laughter))
11  L2  she's a woman
12  LL  ((laughter))
13  L2  yes! are you building?
14  L9  no
15  L5  building?
16  L3  it's builder
17  L   it's wrong
18  T   a builder?
19  LL  ///builder///
20  L   design
21  T   designer
22  LL  ///designer///
```

An overview of repair in classrooms

The errors made by language learners have always been a central point of interest for teachers and researchers. In the grammar-translation days, errors generally indicated rules insufficiently learnt or knowledge imperfectly assimilated. In the audiolingual days errors were regarded as cracks in the foolproof stimulus-response-reinforcement sequence, to be avoided as much as possible. Later on, in· the late sixties and early seventies, a number of teachers began to realize that errors were perhaps not just aberrations, admissions of guilt or inadequacies, or failures in the pedagogic system, but might be evidence of the learners' creative efforts to build a new linguistic structure, in similar ways to children learning their first language. The collection *Error analysis*, edited by Jack Richards (1974), still stands as a landmark to signal this new awareness. Following it attempts were made to determine which types of learner errors were most or least indicative of learning (or 'progress'), and the ways in which errors are or should be selectively treated by the teacher were examined. Subsequently, after a period of widespread dissatisfaction with error analysis research, the field of error correction as an inter-active process between non-native and native speakers has in recent years been receiving increasing attention from L2 researchers.

Conversational analysis (see Schegloff, Jefferson and Sacks 1977; McHoul forthcoming) shows that trouble in talk also occurs in natural conversation, and that speakers and hearers have specific ways of dealing with it. Furthermore, caretakers and the small children in their charge also spend much time in sorting out communication trouble between them. The ways in which this is done may be similar or very different from the ways in which it is done in L2 classrooms, or perhaps they are similar sometimes and different at other times. There is no doubt that it is important to find out how trouble is repaired in L2 classrooms, as a precursor to finding out how repairing may assist in L2 development. To do this, a simple tabulation of types of error and types of treatment is not helpful. Rather, we must focus on the processes of adjustment between speakers and hearers, and this requires a micro-ethnographic approach to the issue.

This is the approach I will use in this chapter to demonstrate that repair makes L2 use in the classroom significantly different from ordinary L1 discourse, informal L1 or L2 (or mixed L1-L2) discourse, and also from L1 use in L1 classrooms. To do this I shall use a number of extracts from transcribed L2 classroom talk which are placed at the most appropriate points in the discussion. However, the many different aspects of repair will make it necessary to refer to many extracts several times in different places, and cross-referencing is therefore frequent. Unfortunately, this will mean some jumping back and forth, and I ask the reader's forbearance. I have tried to reduce it to the minimum, but short of repeating extracts several times there is no alternative.

In the language classroom learners may show in their use of the target language how they are creatively constructing a new language system. Repairing, as one of the mechanisms of feedback on interactive applications of this interim system, is likely to be an important variable in language learning. Although it is not a sufficient condition, we may safely assume that it is a necessary condition. If, as Lyons (1968, p. 90) suggests, language in communication can be regarded as a homeostatic (self-regulating) system, then the regulating is done by constant feedback and monitoring by all participants. Some of the monitoring is done by the speaker and hearer internally, using internal (stored) and external (contextual) resources, some of it is done interactionally, in a cooperative effort between speaker, hearer and audience (if there is one). Both kinds of monitoring are essential ingredients in learning, but direct empirical evidence is by and large only available for the second interactional kind, since it is overt (although surface signals such as hesitations and word replacement often indicate the occurrence of internal monitoring).

What is repair?

The first task that a study of repair in L2 classrooms must face is a clear delimitation of the domain that is to be covered by the term. Repair can potentially cover a wide range of actions, including statements of procedural rules, sanctions of violations of such rules, problems of hearing and understanding the talk, second starts, prompting, cluing and helping, explaining, and correction of errors. A full and exhaustive discussion will not be attempted in this chapter (see Chaudron 1977 for a comprehensive treatment of corrective actions), but an important relation that must be clarified is that between *repair* and *correction*. In Schegloff, Jefferson and Sacks 1977 (hereafter Schegloff *et al.*) this relation is expressed as follows:

> We will refer to 'repair' rather than 'correction' in order to capture the more general domain of occurrences. Self- and other-CORRECTION, then, are particular types in a domain more generally formulated by a distinction between self- and other-REPAIR.
>
> (Schegloff *et al.* 1977, p. 363)

This means that repair is the generic term and that correction is one type of repair, namely the replacement of an *error* (whatever that is) made by the speaker, i.e. *error-replacement* (Extract 7.26:9T). Another major type deals with problems of speaking, hearing and understanding the talk (the main focus of Schegloff *et al.*).

The issue of repair is thus much broader than the mere correction of errors. Particularly since it may not be at all easy to define the term *error* clearly (as Day *et al.* point out, 'error tends to be a subjective judgment' – 1984, p. 20), repair will be taken in this paper in its generic sense, including the correction of errors, but also other phenomena. In this general sense repair can be defined as the treatment of trouble occurring in interactive language use.

In the L2 classroom the focus has generally been on errors committed by the learners and on the correction of these errors, since these phenomena occur frequently.[1] This is quite different from general conversation where overt correction of errors is rare. Error, whether of *fact* (e.g. stating that which is not the case), *reasoning* (defects of logic, argumentation, appraisals of cause-effect) or *language* (syntactic, phonological, stylistic, discoursal) indicates lack of competence in some respect, and the commission as well as the imputation of error is potentially face-threatening. Now, in ordinary L1 conversation, many people 'commit' errors of all three types mentioned regularly, but the mechanism of repair is organized in such a way as to avoid the face threats and loss of face that might result from overt correction. Generally, hearers, upon hearing an error, leave it up to the speaker to do something about it, in other words, they expect speakers to do their own repairing (or correcting). The time allotted for this self-repair is limited: Schegloff *et al.* estimate it to last up to and slightly beyond the end of the speaker's current turn. If no self-repair occurs within the allotted time the hearer may (if it is considered appropriate) do something about the problem since, apparently, the speaker cannot or will not do it. What follows may be the initiation of a correction, or a straightforward correction, but more likely the hearer will treat the problem as if it were a problem of hearing or understanding the talk. The hearer in effect ostensibly takes the 'blame', thus minimizing face threat.

In the L2 classroom the situation is different. In the first place, more problems needing repair occur, since the participants are not yet fully competent users of the target language. Secondly, the pedagogical orientation of talk in the L2 classroom justifies the overt correction of language use that does not conform to the learning aims. Thirdly, the learners are not ordinary people communicating while they go about their daily activities, but are members of the classroom community, which has its own rules as to what is appropriate and what constitutes face threat. It would, therefore, be unrealistic to expect in the classroom the same rules and procedures that apply outside it. This is probably unproblematic in most kinds of classrooms, but in the L2 classroom it creates a paradox. This paradox is that, in order to become a competent member of a speech community, one must participate in the affairs of that community. Also, in order to develop communicative competence one must learn to use the language code the way it is supposed to be used. I assume that it is supposed to be used in the way that people making everyday conversation use it. This crucially involves letting speakers do their own monitoring and repairing, rather than doing it for them. How this self-monitoring and self-repair is developed is a major issue for investigation, requiring evidence not only from ordinary conversation between competent speakers, but also from parent-child and native-non-native interactions in natural settings. Wells, for example, notes that parents often show explicit didactic concerns when interacting with their children (1985).

Before going on to look at the issue of repair from different angles, it will be necessary to examine the role of repair in classroom and non-classroom interaction in some more detail.

The place of repair in interaction

If we regard talk as an interactive process maintained by two or more people, it is reasonable to suggest that its forward motion is propelled by the sequential or cyclical operation of at least four systems: planning, execution, interpretation and adjustment.

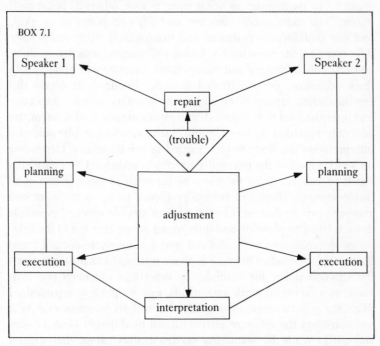

BOX 7.1

The system of adjustment, which can also be referred to as monitoring or matching, has as a subsystem the process of repairing, which occurs subsequent to the occurrence of a trouble spot or source. Repair is thus retrospective and, when done interactively, largely public and overt. It is done selectively, i.e. not everything that could be repaired is in fact repaired, and it can be done by the originator of the trouble spot, by another participant, or by both parties cooperatively. There is thus variation in repair activity, yet it is assumed that this variation is systematic. Schegloff *et al.* note a strong preference for self-repair in conversation, while Day *et al.* (1984) note the occurrence of off-record and on-record repair, defined in terms of ambiguity and considerations of face, notions familiar from the work of Brown and Levinson (1978), among others. In classrooms, as McHoul (forthcoming) suggests, roles are clearly defined, and it is the learner who has the trouble, and the teacher who resolves it.

Before going on to describe the phenomenon of repair in L2 classrooms in detail, I will, in line with suggestions made in the first part of the book, surround the notion with some intuitive observations. Our status as experienced conversationists, for example, leads us to suggest that, in L1 discourse, certain aspects of interactive talk are regarded by participants as being more private, others as being more public. The more public ones are anybody's property, so to speak, and can therefore be evaluated and manipulated freely and openly. The more private ones have a 'hands-off' warning attached to them, and can only be judged and manipulated – privately or publicly – by their originator, or else treated covertly. Intuitively it seems that certain surface aspects of execution, the interface between execution and interpretation (e.g. channel), and most interactive adjustment, are generally regarded as being public matters, whereas planning and interpretation are likely to be regarded as private affairs. Depending on which aspect of the interactive process is addressed by a particular repair procedure, it can therefore be regarded as more or less of an (inappropriate?) display of private problems, or as an intrusion into another's private domain. Certain types of trouble sources, especially those relating to planning and interpretation, are best left to the originator to repair, or else modulated into a non-private domain (most commonly, channel). Others, e.g. those relating to channel problems (background noise, for example) or superficial execution problems (such as a failure to mark agreement), may be publicly repairable. I think the general sense of this intuitive analysis becomes evident if one considers the different effects caused by different kinds of slips and gaffes made by politicians or newscasters: those that suggest incompetence or worse can cause considerable embarrassment (see Goffman's insightful description of *radio talk*, 1981). These and possibly other considerations point to the existence of an intricate system of repair in conversation, and since trouble in talk is so common, it is an essential and integral part of interaction.

The role of repair in language learning is hardly more straightforward. Given that adjustment in general is essential for communication to occur (it can be regarded as the nerve system of talk), repair is in a sense a mechanism to correct for imperfect adjustment. In other words, the better we are at adjusting, the less we are likely to have to rely on repair. In this sense, repair, in the context of not-yet-competent interactants, is a stop-gap procedure to compensate for lack of ability to adjust appropriately. Adjustment itself is especially crucial in non-native interaction, since there are likely to be problems of planning, execution and interpretation. If this is so, we may ask ourselves if repair, apart from being necessary for communication to take place, may have specific learning value, i.e. is useful *input*. If we assume that it is useful input, we may next examine if the types of repair common in competent native-speaker conversation (e.g. the preference for self-repair) are most conducive to the development of adequate adjusting ability, or if some L2 classroom-specific type of repair (e.g. routine correction of linguistic problems) might be more beneficial. In order to address these questions, we need much descriptive and analytical information about repairing in ordinary native-speaker interaction, about native-language child-adult inter-action, and about actual repair work as carried out in second-language classrooms.

A framework for the study of repair

As mentioned earlier, repair in L2 classrooms includes a wide range of phenomena, reflecting all the different kinds of things that teachers and learners do in the classroom. We cannot exclude from consider-ation the things that native speakers do in conversation, since they too may occur in the L2 classroom.

For convenience, the variety of repair activities in the L2 classroom may be grouped into three broad macro-categories of language func-tions which reflect the range of purposes of the participants. In earlier work (van Lier 1984) I referred to these functions of language as *goal*, *mediator* and *regulator*, but following Ellis 1984a, and to avoid the proliferation of terminology, I shall use the terms *medium-oriented*, *message-oriented* and *activity-oriented* goals, though my conception of the functions indicated is slightly broader than Ellis's:

Medium-oriented: a focus on the forms and/or functions of the target language (see also Extracts 7.5, 7.10).

EXTRACT 7.2

1	L2	I was listening		listening	
2–3	L1		⌐in the ra-⌐	⌐to the radio in (bed)	
4	L2	oh ja			
5	L1	while you having a bath			
6	L2	and you and you was having			a bath
7	L1			⌐you were-were *ha*ving⌐	

Message-oriented: a focus on the transmission of thoughts, information, feelings, etc. (see also Extracts 7.11, 7.28).

EXTRACT 7.3

```
1 E   what do you think is the main problem in the future.
2 F   in the future ..
3 E   m:
4 F   listening to the class an:    technical words
5 E                                ᶜm:?
6 F   como? ((tr: what?))
7 F   technical words
8 E   technical words
```

Acitivity-oriented: a focus on the organization and structure of the classroom environment, rules for the conduct of activities, etc. (see also Extracts 7.18, 7.21).

EXTRACT 7.4

```
1 T    o::h okay. Ruben how about number five ...
2 L7   five oh
3 T         ᶜnumber ...        I'm sorry .. four okay yeah
4 LL              ᶜ/four/four/ᴣ
```

Over and above these three macro-categories which at any particular time can be seen to operate in the classroom (at least whenever inter-action is pedagogically oriented), it must be borne in mind that the ostensible purpose of the gathering of the participants is the learning of language so that, even when language is used in its message-oriented or activity-oriented sense, participants may be aware that the ultimate aim is to use the language profitably as input.[2] This means that medium-orientation may be inserted at intervals, or may be noticeable, in activities that are message- or activity-oriented (see e.g. Extract 7.27, where a medium-oriented repair (5T) occurs in a message-oriented sequence).

The purpose-orientedness of the L2 classroom setting is likely to influence the kinds of repair work that are undertaken, both in terms of the kinds of trouble that are considered suitable candidates for repair, and the ways in which the repair can be done. There are thus likely to be kinds of repair work in the L2 classroom that are specifi-cally pedagogic in nature, and we may term these kinds of repair *didactic repair*. In addition to didactic repair we are likely to find instances of repair that is common to all face-to-face interaction and that addresses problems of *the talk*. We may call this kind of repair *conversational repair*, and for its description we may use studies such

as Schegloff *et al.* as a starting point. If this distinction is a valid one
we should be able, in an analysis of L2 classroom talk, to find these
two orientations operating at different times and relatively independently of each other. We might expect that, when type of interaction
approaches ordinary L1 discourse, conversational repair is more
salient than didactic repair, and that when an activity type is classroom specific, didactic repair is more prominent. A first step, given
the framework so far, might be to see if the three macro-functions
are likely to lead to either didactic or conversational repair, e.g. if
medium-oriented repair is predominantly didactic, and message-
oriented repair largely conversational. However, we would then be
in danger of linking type of repair to type of trouble source, and this
would lead us back to all the perennial problems faced by traditional
error analysis. It is clear that medium-, message-, and activity-oriented
troubles can all be treated and resolved in either conversational or
didactic ways, and a valid description will show what is different
about these ways and how to identify them in interaction. In order
to move ahead in the search for a framework, it is crucial to realize
that the didactic-ness or conversation-ness of a repair procedure lies
not in the type of trouble that is addressed, but in the way it is
addressed, i.e. whether a word is offered when a speaker hesitates,
a proposition denied, a request for clarification or repetition made,
a clue given, etc. It is only in this way that the didactic nature of
repairs illustrated in, e.g. Extracts 7.5, 7.9, 7.10, 7.15, and the
conversational nature of repairs in, e.g. Extracts 7.11, 7.12, 7.23,
7.25, can be described.

A preliminary analysis of the L2 classroom data quoted in this
chapter, plus intuitive reflection on general conversation, suggests
that the single axis didactic-conversational is not sufficient to build
a conceptual framework that can be of use later on. We can note,
for example, that hearers sometimes do repair to help speakers
produce utterances they have problems with, or to make sure that
speaker and hearer are on the same 'wavelength', and that at other
times hearers do repair to tell speakers they are wrong, made a
mistake, etc. This leads me to the proposal of a second axis, intersecting with the first, which distinguishes repair which is designed
to help, enable, support, and repair which is designed to evaluate,
challenge, contest. This distinction must not be seen as one which
separates the 'nice' from the 'nasty', the supportive from the critical,
or the constructive from the destructive (although such notions at
times may enter), but rather in terms of the sequential implications
a repair initiative may have for the interaction (that is, at what point

the repair will be initiated, and what further work the initiation requires), as the discussion in the next section will show. I will therefore use relatively neutral terms to refer to this axis: *conjunctive* versus *disjunctive* repair. Clear examples of conjunctive repair can be seen in Extracts 7.2, 7.4, 7.16, 7.25; of disjunctive repair in Extracts 7.18, 7.26, 7.27. My claim here is that the framework created by the intersection of the two axes is valid for all repair in interaction, but that it is particularly relevant to the description of L2 classroom repair. It can be shown visually as follows:

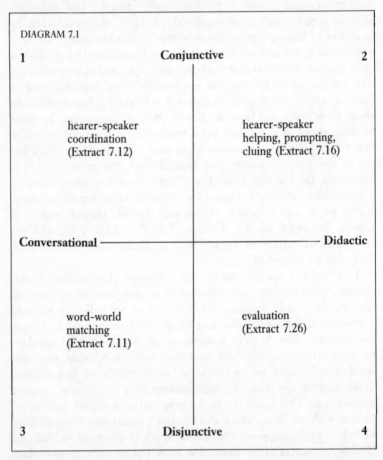

DIAGRAM 7.1

1   **Conjunctive**   2

hearer-speaker
coordination
(Extract 7.12)

hearer-speaker
helping, prompting,
cluing (Extract 7.16)

Conversational ———————————— **Didactic**

word-world
matching
(Extract 7.11)

evaluation
(Extract 7.26)

3   **Disjunctive**   4

The framework suggested distinguishes between four types of repair, and a movement from 1 to 4 implies two things: firstly, increasing status- or role-marking or inequality, and secondly, increasing likelihood of threat to face. Both in the classroom and in non-pedagogical settings all four types of repair are likely to occur. However, in accordance with contextual appropriacy, a type of repair may be modulated *downwards* (in terms of face-threat) to the next type below or another type further down. So that, if we want to tell a speaker a mistake was made (type 4), we may suggest factual or other counterevidence (type 3). We may also put in a word here or there gently suggesting that we may be able to expand or help out or, conversely, withhold the proper listening responses in the proper places (type 2). Finally, we may pretend that we did not hear or understand properly, and request a re-run or paraphrase (type 1). Meanwhile, the speaker will often be aware that a lower-type repair *may* really mean that a higher-type repair is being done. The indirectness of downward modulations allows for avoidance of interactional conflict. This framework begins to show the dynamics of repairing in interaction and, furthermore, avoids the assumption that repair is necessarily disruptive, a side sequence inserted in the stream of discourse (or a 'pushdown routine' – see Varonis and Gass 1985).[3]

The framework addresses interactive, or other-repair, which is done in combination with or instead of self-repair.[4] Self-repair is preferred in conversation, i.e. speakers are generally given the chance to repair their own troubles before other-repair is initiated. In L2 classrooms self-repair also occurs (e.g. Extracts 7.6, 7.8, 7.14:3L2) but, as a cursory examination of the data shows, other-repair is particularly frequent. The question arises if, in the L2 classroom, other-repair *replaces* or *interferes with* self-repair to some significant extent, and if this is detrimental to the learners' interlanguage development. In general, the framework outlined above raises a number of questions which descriptive L2 classroom research can address, and a few of the more salient ones are summarized below.

1. Is conversational repair in the L2 classroom identical to that in L1 discourse, both in terms of the kinds of trouble source it addresses and in terms of the ways in which it deals with those trouble sources?
2. Alternatively, does the L2 classroom environment transform conversational repair in classroom-specific ways, e.g. by ignoring the preference for self-repair?
3. Can we find empirical evidence for a basic difference between didactic repair and conversational repair in the L2 classroom, in the kinds of trouble source addressed and in the ways of dealing with them?
4. Can we find systematic differences or similarities between repair in the L2 classroom and repair in the L1 classroom, i.e. is there

a type of repair that is classroom-specific while not being *L2 class-room*-specific?

5. Can we, at least intuitively, identify kinds of repair, or ways of repairing that are more conducive to language learning than others?

6. How can we empirically investigate the learning value of different ways of repairing or aspects of repair?

7. Are valuable repairs exactly those that we have called conversational repair, or do they include repair work that also occurs in the L1 classroom, i.e. didactic repair that is common to all educational settings, or do they include also repair work that is L2 classroom-specific?

8. Do different participation patterns (e.g. group work) lead to different ways of repairing?

Sequential aspects of repair in second-language classrooms

So far I have essentially explored the concept of repair in L2 classrooms in a top-down manner, and this has resulted in a conceptual framework and a series of questions. It would now be possible to construct a classification or coding model, and apply this to different data to test its sorting capacity. However, I feel that this would be seriously premature, since the data could no doubt be made to fit into the particular pigeonholes created, if necessary in Procrustean fashion, without in any way providing more information about what is actually done when repairing is being done in the classroom. It is advisable now to turn to a different mode of viewing, from the bottom up, to see how participants deal with their own and each other's troubles in the L2 classroom. To this end, a sequential analysis of L2 classroom repair will now be illustrated.

As we have seen, repair work can be done by self, by other, or by both in cooperation (leaving aside for the moment the potential involvement of third parties, which is by no means uncommon). Schegloff *et al.* suggest four trajectories for repair procedures, based on the sequential positions in which self- and other-initiation and self- and other-repair occur:

a) same turn (ST)
b) same-turn transition space (TS)
c) next turn (NT)
d) third turn (TT)

One single repair procedure takes place within a sequence of minimally one turn, and maximally three turns. It is, of course, possible that repair is done on trouble that occurred several or many turns before, but this happens rarely (though see Extract 7.30), and need in any case not be accounted for in a sequential description. The full repair format can be expressed schematically as follows (I disregard, for the sake of convenience, the position of same-turn transition space; as I shall show, this position may not be identifiable in L2 classroom discourse):

Turn 1: trouble source —— (initiation) —— (repair)   SELF
Turn 2: (initiation) —— (repair)   OTHER
Turn 3: (initiation) —— (repair)   SELF

Everything is optional in this format except for the trouble source itself. Constraints are that at least one of the optional elements does in fact occur, and only one instance each of initiation and repair can occur. Repair can and frequently does occur without any separately identifiable initiation, but if initiation occurs without a repair following it, the repair remains unfinished, i.e. there is no satisfactory repair outcome. An example of unsatisfactory repair occurs in Extract 7.29. The format is recursive in that a repair may be unsuccessful, and re-initiations and re-repairs can be made, similar to the bound exchanges in Sinclair and Coulthard (1975) and Mehan (1979).

Table 7.1 (p. 194) lists all the sequential possibilities for repair work, yielding six trajectories (or repair routes) within the three-turn format.

Note that I use the term *initiation* only in those trajectories where initiation and repair are conducted by different participants. The reason for this is that in most cases it is impossible to distinguish two separate repairing actions when one person carries out the repair. I thus define initiation as a request to the interlocutor to do repair, i.e. as *an interactive action*, rather than merely as 'the beginning of a repair'. This is necessary if we want to avoid calling pauses, pause fillers, turn-holding devices, etc. initiations. Although these items frequently occur at the beginning of repairs (as 'editing terms', see Levelt 1983), their function is not necessarily to initiate repair, but often also to regulate turn taking.[5]

I shall now discuss each of these trajectories in turn, using examples of transcribed L2 classroom data as evidence.

TABLE 7.1 Repair trajectories

Trouble source	Initiation self	other	Repair self	other	Trajectory
1			1		T.1: same-turn self-repair
1			TS		T.2: transition-space self-repair
1			3		T.3: third-turn self-repair
1		a) 1 b) 2	1 3		T.4: other-initiation/self-repair
1				a) 1 b) 2	T.5: other-repair
1	1			2	T.6: self-initiation/other-repair

Note: Numbers and letters (TS = transition space) in the columns refer to the turn in which the repair part occurs. Thus trouble source always occurs in turn 1 of a repair sequence.

1. Same-turn self-repair

This trajectory occurs frequently in the classroom data, both for teachers and for learners. As regards the latter, it may be expected that L2 learners have relatively more speech-production (including word-search) problems than native speakers, so that self-repair is likely to be more frequent in this group of speakers than in native speakers. We thus note many instances of hesitations, filled or unfilled pauses (e.g. Extract 7.5: 1L12), word replacements (Extract 7.6), rephrasing (Extract 7.8), try-marking (Extract 7.21: 1L10) and so on.

EXTRACT 7.5

→ 1 L12 excuse me e:r which way: e:r . . . is the way to=
   2 T   ᶜuhuh
    L12 = the bus station

EXTRACT 7.6

L5 excuse me, can you help me, ca– er could you tell me where's the theatre please

EXTRACT 7.7

T okay. now I'm going to give you *one more* way of asking directions which– or *two* more ways in fact– excuse me, can you help me ((cont))

EXTRACT 7.8

L1 excuse me, I'm looking e:::r– I'm sorry– excuse me can you help me the way e:::r

However, it can be noted that the frequency of self-repair varies considerably with the type of activity that is being conducted: at certain times during a lesson it may be frequent, at other times it is virtually absent. In general, where learners self-select e.g. in order to offer candidate responses to undirected (i.e. not directed at one specific learner) teacher elicitations, learners tend to produce verbally minimal contributions (see Extract 7.29; this also occurs in similar activities in native-language classrooms, see, e.g. Sinclair and Coulthard 1975; Sinclair and Brazil 1982). Where learners are required to produce longer utterances in a slot-and-filler, teacher-to-learner format (see Extracts 7.5, 7.26), trouble sources frequently occur, but in these cases the teacher tends to provide repair, repair-initiations or prompts before the learner gets a chance to initiate self-repair. By far the greatest incidence of self-repair in the data I have examined occurs in group and pair work, where it occurs perhaps more frequently than it would in general conversations in the target language, since in these situations the learners are often required to produce utterances and sequences of utterances of a complexity they would not generally attempt outside the classroom. Moreover, when the task is medium-oriented, specific form-related trouble is routinely repaired regardless of whether or not it affects intelligibility (see Extracts 7.2, 7.10, 7.14).

2. Transition-space self-repair

The term transition space refers to the moment when a turn 'looks like' it may be completed (see Sacks *et al.* 1974). It is the slight gap or split-second moment when either another participant becomes speaker, or present speaker continues.

Schegloff *et al.* argue that there is a massive preference for self-repair in conversation, so that 'others "withhold" repair initiation from placement while trouble-source turn is in progress' (p. 373). They continue:

> Indeed, other-initiations regularly are withheld a bit PAST the possible completion of the trouble-source turn; not only does a withhold get them specifically positioned in next turn, but it can get 'next turn' itself delayed a bit. In such cases, other-initiations occur after a slight gap, the gap evidencing a withhold beyond the completion of trouble-source – providing an 'extra' opportunity, in an expanded transition space, for speaker of trouble source to self-initiate repair.
>
> (Schegloff *et al.* 1977, p. 374)

In the present data this trajectory does not occur. Though more data would be needed before a claim could be made that it does not occur in L2 classrooms *per se*, I think several reasons can be advanced for its absence in general. In the first place, the way to tell when a turn has come to an end in the L2 classroom is not normally by means of the usual turn signals, or even message or syntactic completion, but rather by means of the teacher's orchestrations, the rules of the activity, and the demands of the task. Hence transition is in classrooms often a much less negotiable and more clearcut issue than in general conversation with the result, for example, that intra-turn pauses do not generally pose a floor-threat in the classroom in the same way that they do in general conversation. They do lead to frequent helping, prompting and correcting, but this does not usually involve loss of turn or floor. In turn-taking terms, the transition-relevance place (Sacks *et al.* 1974) is suspended.

Secondly, withhold of other-initiation, by teacher and learners alike, is not in evidence to any significant extent. Indeed, as we shall see, other-initiations routinely occur *while* trouble-source turn is in progress, i.e. as *intra-turn repair*. This particular repair procedure is made possible by the fact that face risk due to other-repair can be regarded, in the interests of language learning, as being officially suspended in the classroom.

3. Third-turn self-repair

For essentially similar reasons to those proposed for the absence of trajectory 2, no instances of this trajectory occur in the data examined (see also McHoul forthcoming, where similar comments are made about native-language secondary school data).

4. Other-initiation/self-repair

This trajectory occurs in two sequential environments:

a) same-turn initiation/same-turn repair;

b) next-turn initiation/third-turn repair.

Together with the next, this is a particularly frequently occurring repair trajectory in the data. It occurs when problems of hearing or understanding the talk are in evidence (see, e.g. Extracts 7.3, 7.23, 7.27) and for procedural problems. In this sense it is arguably the most common trajectory of interactive (i.e. actively involving hearer) repair in conversation where, given some trouble, the hearer initiates repair, but leaves it up to the speaker to carry out the repair. It also occurs frequently when linguistic and/or subject-matter problems need repairing and, rather than just doing the repair, an initiation is done in the form of prompting, cluing or helping (see Extracts 7.9, 7.10 below).

EXTRACT 7.9

```
       1 T    dark hair and something else though
       2 LL   /((unint))/(rich)/dark hair/((unint))
  →    3 T    nearly there
       4 L9   uh ... fairly dark .. (fairly) ((unint))
  →    5 T    no ... what kind of hair does Elly have
       6 LL   fair
  →    7 T    fair hair and? ...
```

EXTRACT 7.10

```
       1 L1       they are watch televi- television
       2 T        okay now. yesterday at eight o'clock .. they ..
       3 L1       they are     they watches     watched     they were=
  →  4-5-6 T       ʳthey-        ʳthey:::-        ʳthey ((unint))
       L1       = ... watching
```

It will be of interest to compare this trajectory with the next: other-repair, since considerable pedagogical differences are likely between doing repair for the speaker, and getting the speaker to do repair. In general, it appears that trajectory 4 occurs most frequently when the trouble source is related to the orientation (message or medium) of the task, whereas trajectory 5, particularly 5a, is used to resolve trouble which is not directly related to the aim of the activity. In a message-oriented activity, medium-related trouble is often resolved through trajectory 5a, and I would expect the reverse to hold true as well. This makes sense since a trajectory 4 takes more time and effort than a trajectory 5, and most time and effort will be spent on those troubles which directly relate to what the activity is about. All other kinds of trouble will be dealt with swiftly so as not to lose sight of the aim.

Other-initiations can be done by means of questioning repeats of the trouble-source item (Extracts 7.27, 7.30:10L1), devices such as 'Huh?', 'What?' (Extracts 7.3, 7.23:5T), or more explicit requests for reruns or clarification (Extract 7.14). The line between this and the classroom-specific phenomenon of prompting or cluing is thinly drawn, if at all. In the latter case, the initiation itself offers some information as regards the desired outcome, as in Extract 7.9:5T. However, as in Extract 7.10, it is not always clear whether the teacher's repair initiations constitute prompting or not. In favour of regarding them as such is the argument that they do point the learner to the specific word that is in need of repair. For some further examples of trajectory 4 see Extracts 7.11, 7.12, 7.13 and 7.14. It may be of interest to note that Extract 7.13 is an example of procedural repair: L1's contribution, though informationally correct (as it turns out), is offered partly in Dutch, and the teacher cannot or will not accept it in this form. Finally, Extract 7.15 shows three other-initiations (4T, 6T and 8T) and withholding of other-repair, thus eliciting the desired item in 9L (provided that this does in fact contain the right response).

EXTRACT 7.11

   1 T   *thin* face
→ 2 L   ((softly)) what is thin uhm: what is thin
   3 T   ((gestures)) fat . . . thin=
   4 L   ᶜa:h
   5 LL =//thin//((laughter))//

EXTRACT 7.12

   1 L1 e::::r . . . can you tell me the way . . to the
           (market) square?
→ 2 L2 to the?
   3 L1 (mare)? market square?
   4 L2 market square?
   5 L1 yes

EXTRACT 7.13

   1 L1 oh een beweeglijke mond . . een mouth . een mond
→ 2 T   yes okay can you say it in English

EXTRACT 7.14

<pre>
     1 L2   what were you doing- what were *you* doing while
             I: . . . while I was having a bath
→ 2 L1   can you say again?
     3 L2   yes, what was you doing . . . what- what were you doing . .
             when I was having a bath
</pre>

EXTRACT 7.15

<pre>
     1 T   uhuh so how does he do his job?
     2 L   he's good=
     3 L   =he's good
→ 4 T   yes he does his job . . .
     5 L3   very good I=
→ 6 T   =he does his job-
     7 L   ((unint))
→ 8 T   he does his job . . .
     9 L   ((unint))
    10 T   yes he does his job *well*
</pre>

5. Other-repair

Other-repair can be done *while* trouble-source turn is in progress or in next-turn position. Similar to trajectory 4, this trajectory can thus be divided into two sub-types:
a) same-turn other-repair;
b) next-turn other-repair.
The former, according to Schegloff *et al.*, does not occur in conversation, and if this is the case, it must be regarded as didactic, or classroom-specific. Interestingly, McHoul (forthcoming) reports its absence also in L1 classrooms so that, on the basis of this evidence, it may be an L2 classroom-specific way of repairing. It occurs frequently in the data, and may often informally be called *helping*. Helping can be distinguished from prompting or cluing by regarding as instances of the former only those cases where a candidate replacement or candidate item for the trouble-source item is offered. Both learners and teachers frequently do helping, particularly when the focus is on the production of complex linguistic strings. It may be done in the interest of the smooth production of the response, is thus often done instantaneously, and focuses on minor items in a longer, compléx utterance. There is in these cases no evidence of a desire to take the floor on the part of the repairer, and the original speaker continues the turn, or promptly starts a new turn. Whether or not a sense of interruption is felt cannot usually be determined by inspection of the data. Ostensibly, this trajectory can be regarded as a way

of facilitating the ongoing execution of some complex task. Examples can be found in Extracts 7.16, 7.17 and 7.18. Extract 7.18 illustrates not a linguistic trouble source but a procedural one. The teacher's intended activity is 'repeat after me', whereas L9's interpreted activity is 'produce the appropriate response'. This extract shows how such activity confusion can occasion considerable repair work in L2 classrooms (see Chapter 6). It may not be easy at all times to switch from one activity frame to another, hence the considerable procedural explicitness that accompanies most activity switches.

EXTRACT 7.16

```
    1 T    good. okay. can you help me, can you tell me the way to the
           theatre please?
    2 L12  can you help me, can- you:- . .=
→   3 L                               ᶜtell ((whispered))
→   4 L                               ᶜtell me the way
      L12  =tell me the way to the theatre please?
```

EXTRACT 7.17

```
    1 T    Gerda. can you tell me the way to the bank please?
    2 L1   yes straight . along the street
→   3 T    straight along this road
    4 L1   this road
    5 T    uhuh
    6 L1   e:n:: den to: the: traffic lights
    7 T    okay
    8 L1   and then . . . (str-)=
→   9 T    =straight along this road- *till* the traffic lights
```

EXTRACT 7.18

```
    1 T    I'm fine thanks and you? can you say that? I'm fine thanks and
           you?
    2 L9   e:r I'm fine too
→   3 T    okay can you just repeat that sentence, I'm fine thanks and
           you?
    4 L9   . . . e:rm ((unint))=
→   5 T    =((unint)) just repeat that sentence, I'm fine thanks and you?
    6 L9   I'm fine thanks and you?
```

When other-repair occurs in next-turn position, i.e. in the turn *after* the occurrence of the trouble, it is often of course *third turn* in an exchange, i.e. the feedback or evaluation slot. Repairing is thus woven into the texture of exchange structuring, both as parts of moves, and as full moves.

6. Self-initiation/other-repair

This final trajectory is treated ambiguously in Schegloff *et al.*'s account. They do give one example:

> Other-repair can issue from self-initiation:
> B: He had dis uh Mistuh W- whatever k- I can't think of his first
> name, *Watts* on, the one thet wrote // that piece,
> A: Dan Watts.
>
> (Schegloff *et al.* 1977, p. 364)

Further on in their paper, however, Schegloff *et al.* assert that 'self-initiated repairs yield self-correction' (p. 377), and the issue of self-initiation/other-repair is not discussed further. McHoul (forthcoming), in a footnote, suggests that, although he has not seen any data confirming this, he has a suspicion that self-initiated other-correction does occur. It may be a special feature of L2 classrooms that this trajectory occurs there quite regularly, but I must admit to being surprised that it does not also occur with some regularity in general conversation or in other classroom data. That aside, it is reasonable to expect less competent L2 speakers to appeal to more competent co-interactants to provide linguistic support in the interests of the smooth running of the discourse. At times, as in Extract 7.19, such linguistic support is required in the face of a total linguistic or communication breakdown (although in this case the support, offered in 4L1, is not in fact used by L3); at other times it is overtly requested and readily obtained. In many cases it is the teacher to whom the request (or correction-invitation, in Schegloff *et al.*'s terms) is addressed, though in Extracts 7.20 and 7.21 it is addressed to a fellow learner.

EXTRACT 7.19

```
1    T    so. excuse me, how do I get to the railway station?
2    L3   oh        go-go (strong ma low)- no- go . . . =
3    LL      ⌜((laughter))⌝
     L3   =nou ik weet niet meer hoor ((tr: well, I don't
                              know it any more))
→ 4  L1   straight ahead
5    L3   go along      this street      (then your) one two three
6–7  T         ⌜uhuh          ⌜uhuh
```

EXTRACT 7.20

```
1  L1 (where is the way) is dat goed?* where is the way?
2  L  ja: where is the way to the cinema
                *((tr: is that correct?))
```

EXTRACT 7.21

```
1 L10 has (he) has (she) curly .. dark hair? . . . curly? is dat goed?*
2 L9  nou eh . . . . I can only say yes or no hehehehehe
                    *((tr: is that correct?))
```

In many cases the self-initiation of this trajectory is in the form of *try-marking*, i.e. the candidate item, or suspected trouble source, may be offered with tentative (rising) intonation (Extract 7.22), and may be preceded by hesitation markers and pauses, and followed by a brief pause. In other instances the speaker cannot produce the trouble-source item and invites (an)other participant(s) to supply it. This can be regarded as another form of helping: initiated or invited helping – see Extracts 7.23, 7.24 and 7.25.

EXTRACT 7.22

```
1 T can you tell me what are the three parts of the description she gives
     about this man=
2 L =his character?
3 T yes, character
```

EXTRACT 7.23

```
1 T  if you say .. eh let's take Saffron Walden as an
      example a:nd if you say        what amenities does=
2 L                              ᵗ((unint))ᴵ
  T  =Saffron Walden have . . . for tourists .. what amenities
3 LL =/oh/yeah/. .//((ehm))//((unint))//=
4 L5 =stores
5 T  hm?
6 L5 stores?=
7 L9 =voorzieningen ((tr: amenities))
8 T  shops?      shops? uhuh yes . . .
9 LL       ᵗ//yes//ᴵ
```

EXTRACT 7.24

```
1 T okay what's the next question
2 L6 uh:: who gave the staind (stained)? stained?
3 L                                      ᵗglass
4 T glass windows
5 L glass windows
6 L glass windows
```

EXTRACT 7.25

```
1 T Teresa how about number . . . five
2 L4                            ᵗfive
```

Repair and sequencing in discourse

Spoken interaction requires the integration of several cognitive and interactive processes or systems. During interaction, native speakers routinely monitor the integration of these processes and adjust simultaneously and instantaneously according to the demands of messages, settings and participants. This adjustment is essentially proactive, i.e. it is based upon predictions of what is appropriate and likely to occur, in other words, what is a fitting next contribution to the ongoing discourse. It is not likely that the integration of the different systems, and the continuous monitoring and adjustment, will be trouble-free, and the interactive system of repair deals with the inevitable remaining imperfections. Not-yet-competent speakers, such as L2 learners, are likely to have various problems with the different systems, their integration, and with the necessary adjustment. The system of repair is therefore likely to carry a heavier burden in non-native-speaker interaction than it does in native-speaker interaction. It is not certain that the existing system of native-speaker repair can cope with this heavier load without some modification. We might hypothesize that there is a basic rhythm to interaction that resists being slowed down or pulled out of joint by too much repair work (for the notion of rhythm in interaction, see e.g. Erickson 1981a; Gumperz 1981; Scollon 1981). Ordinary constraints such as the preference for self-repair and the concurrent withhold of other-repair may have to be relaxed in order to cope with increased trouble. If this is the case we should not expect or demand that the system for repair as outlined by Schegloff *et al.* remain inviolate in non-native-speaker interaction.

On the other hand, studies of informal non-native-speaker or non-native-speaker/native-speaker interaction indicate tentatively that, by and large, participants in such interaction observe the regularities suggested by Schegloff *et al.* (see e.g. Gaskill 1980; Schwartz 1980). Such studies do note the occurrence of other-repair (including error-replacement), but only as a last resort, after opportunities for self-repair have occurred.

To complicate matters, in conversations between native-speaker/non-native-speaker friends, Day *et al.* (1984) found that on-record correction was more common than off-record correction. Day *et al.* suggest that the closeness of the relationship made such on-record correction possible. Varonis and Gass (1985), furthermore, suggest that, especially in native-speaker/non-native-speaker conversations, at times lack of understanding may not be overtly expressed or even noticed.

By and large, it seems that in informal conversation there are constraints on massive repair, though intimacy may relax these constraints when non-native-speakers are involved. Summarizing, I suggest that factors influencing the occurrence of repair in informal settings fall into three basic types:

a) intelligibility and interpretability;
b) conversational rhythm and tempo;
c) face (distance, power and rank – see Brown and Levinson 1978).

In L2 classrooms, however, the case is different, since a fourth factor plays a role, namely, pedagogy. In view of the purpose of the pedagogical setting, it can be postulated that the decision: to repair or not to repair is based on criteria that differ from those operating in informal, non-pedagogic settings. Intuitively I propose to order these criteria, and the repair-decisions they lead to, in a hierarchical fashion, as suggested in Diagram 7.2.

A major question is, should repair in the L2 classroom follow the same rules and employ the same criteria as repair outside the classroom, or is it pedagogically justifiable for things to be significantly different there? In other words, taking the main differences to be in the *criteria* for repair and the *trajectories* for repair, leading to a prominence of didactic and evaluatory types of repair, are these types of repair beneficial for language learning, or should they be avoided? Are they perhaps beneficial and appropriate for certain types of activities rather than others?

These are complex issues, and conclusive answers are not available at this point. The next section will make some observations which will point to areas for further research.

Some pedagogical observations

1. Turns in L2 discourse, particularly learner turns during teacher-learner lockstep work, are not as uninterruptable by other-initiation and other-repair as turns in general conversation are (at least according to Schegloff *et al.*). They are generally allocated by the teacher, and this allocation remains in force until it is cancelled out, e.g. by another allocation. This means that interruptions for repair, error-replacement, helping, etc. do not constitute floor threats in the same way that such interruptions might in general conversation (the teacher is, after all, the official 'floor-keeper'). Moreover, the repair-related interruptions are generally designed to facilitate the ongoing construction of the turn, and in many cases they may be welcomed, if not actually invited, by the learner.

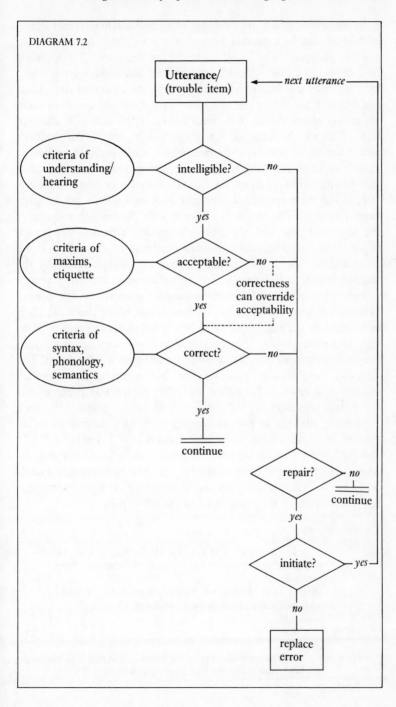

DIAGRAM 7.2

2. In sequences which are made up of several teacher-learner dyads, each dyad can be extended beyond the basic three-turn format by a series of repairs which can occur during the learner's responding turn or in third place (the evaluation slot). Since the learner's turn in these cases can be extended indefinitely, the notion of third-place evaluation is not always relevant, since evaluation can and does occur at various places during the construction of the learner's allocated turn. This can be seen in, e.g. Extract 7.26, where the teacher's repair initiations and error-replacements clearly fulfil an evaluatory as well as a (re-)initiating function. Repairing, correcting, evaluating and (re-)initiating overlap and are conflated (see also Chaudron 1977), and their sequential purposes and implications are in many cases identical. The teacher's concern with the smooth running of the sequence, and with the learner's smooth, effortless production of the target utterance, are evidenced overtly in Extract 7.26: 6T and also in 24T where the learner's pause occasions helping by the teacher, which in this case occurs simultaneously with the learner's restart. The teacher thus exerts sequential pressure on the learner to minimize intra-turn pauses and hesitations, since these are likely to be used by the teacher to produce intra-turn repairs and promptings of various kinds. Generally learners will want to avoid such frequent insertions, even though they do not pose a floor threat. The tolerance for intra-turn pauses varies, but in teacher-led recitation sequences it tends to be rather low. This means that opportunities for repair trajectory 1 (self-repair) tend to be reduced in such sequences, whereas in pair and group work they tend to be much greater. In extracts from group and pairwork, e.g. Extracts 7.12, 7.14 and 7.21, intra-turn pauses occur *both before and after* trouble sources, whereas in teacher-led sequences they tend to occur predominantly *before and not after* trouble sources. In the latter the learners are thus not given the time they may need to do self-repair.

EXTRACT 7.26

   1 T   okay so can we try and say now (Willy) can you say Brigitte
               was phoning her boyfriend ... while the children were
               watching TV
   2 L10 Brigitte *was*– Brigitte *was* phoning her– her boyfriend ...
               and- while the children were watching TV
   3 T   okay now.
   4 L9 ˈBrigitte–
   5 L   ((unint))
→ 6 T   ˈcan we make that a bit faster .. Brigitte was phoning
               her boyfriend while the children were watching TV

```
 7  L10   e:hh I can't say it so– so so quickly
 8  LL                              ⸢((laughter))
 9  T     Brigitte was phoning
10  L10   Brigitte was phoning
11  T     her boyfriend
12  L10   her boyfriend
13  T     okay stop. say: her boyfriend
14  L10   her boyfriend
15  T     phoning her boyfriend
16  L10   phoning her boyfriend
17  T     w'z phoning her boyfriend
18  L10   she was fa– phoning her boyfriend
19  T     okay. Brigitte was phoning her boyfriend
20  L10   Brigitte was phoning her boyfriend
21  T     good. while the children were watching TV
22  L     yes
23  L10   while the children were .. watching TV
→ 24  T                             ⸢watching TV
25  T     good. much better. ((to L8:)) Brigitte was phoning her
          boyfriend while the children were watching TV
```

3. Since anything can in principle be a repairable (or trouble source) it is impossible to predict if and when repair work will occur in a sequence of discourse. In principle repair can thus occur at any time during otherwise predictable and predicted sequences. By and large, people like some measure of predictability in their interaction, and classroom activities are no exception.

The predictive power of certain utterances across several subsequent turns (see Extract 7.5: 1T; see also Chapter 6) gives a sense of coherence and rhythm in sequences longer than two or three contiguous utterances. An activity is set up and turns are staked out, creating the expectation of a smoothly running sequence. At any point, however, such sequences can be extended or interrupted by repair sequences which can be regarded by the participants as annoying hiccups in the interaction. Perhaps in unconscious response to this certain repairs, particularly requests for clarification by learners, tend to be delayed to occur at the points where the teacher switches from one dyad to the next, in other words, at the end of a three-part exchange, or anywhere else where there appears to be a crack in the structure (and, one may ask, how many more potential repairs are never made?). This does not apply, it appears, to teacher-initiated repair, which routinely occurs in intra-turn position, nor does it apply to prompting or helping by learners, which again occurs routinely in intra-turn position.

It appears that certain types of repair need to be done in appropriate slots, in separate turns, while others are done within the turn in which the trouble occurs. The former generally deal with problems of hearing or understanding the talk, and with matters relating to content, whereas the latter deal with 'helping out' with speaking problems, and occur immediately after the trouble spot, without waiting for the turn to end. This is the same distinction, made earlier, between disjunctive and conjunctive repair, now presented in sequential terms. The upshot is that in eliciting or ritual sequences (IT 3 and 4a – see Chapter 6) there appears to be a constraint against exactly those types of repairs that are aimed at understanding what is going on, but not against those that keep the sequence going.

In repair work of the conjunctive (or 'enabling') type, repairable and repair are not related in the same way that two turns in discourse generally are. In particular, the repair does not address the content of the turn containing the repairable, but rather some superficial feature of that turn, usually of a linguistic or procedural nature. Humphrey, when discussing teachers' sanctions, calls this kind of connection *disaffiliation*: the repair utterance is responsive in some way to the trouble source, but 'generally oblivious' to the content of the trouble-source turn (1979, p. 129).

We might expect that, as learners become more fluent and capable of self-monitoring and adjustment, reliance upon this kind of repair would diminish. The danger is that this repair, perpetuated by the activities that promote it over disjunctive/conversational kinds of repair, may prevent the development of self-monitoring, and create a dependency in the learners upon immediate other-repair. The pedagogical question is thus if it would be beneficial to withhold such repair in order to promote the development of self-repair. The way to do so is not to advise teachers against doing intra-turn repair, or to prohibit cluing and helping by teachers and learners alike, but rather to examine activities carefully in terms of the kinds of repair they demand by virtue of their construction.

4. During L2 classroom work teachers frequently have occasion to routinely repair learners' utterances in L2 which are (perceived to be) in some way defective. Such routine repair, often in the form of a paraphrase of the defective utterance, is usually accepted without comment by the learners, and is evidence of the teacher's superior status as a competent or native speaker of the target language. A straightforward example of this occurs in Extract 7.27: 5T.

EXTRACT 7.27

```
1 T   ((to L8)) you're going to California?
2 L9  Californa?
3 T   California
4 L4  ((to L8)) how do you: going?
→ 5 T   how are you going?
```

At the same time such correcting-by-paraphrase may involve the teacher interpreting the learner's utterance in a certain way where, perhaps, several interpretations are possible. In Extract 7.28 the teacher repairs in this way an utterance that perhaps does not warrant repair (the person referred to *was* the organist), and the repair implies an interpretation which may be at variance with the learner's intended meaning.

EXTRACT 7.28

```
1 L6  and he was also or- or- organist
→ 2 T   yes the- he organized it . . . uhum
1
```

In Extract 7.29 the teacher's paraphrase in 11T involves a topic switch from the person's nose to his height, and this switch, assumed by the teacher to have occurred in 9L, is in fact not concurrently made by the learners, whose topic continues to be the nose. At the end of the extract the person's nasal characteristics remain unresolved. The confusion, while evident to the analyst, may be less clear to the participants. Although they may be aware of communication trouble, they may not know what causes it and consequently be unable to deal with it. It may be of interest to note that I have seen such communication problems occur with some regularity in teacher-learner sequences, but I have yet to see the first example from learner-learner group work.

EXTRACT 7.29

```
1 T   what kind of nose? does he have?
2 L   long .. long nose?
3 L1  long nose?
4 T   not a long nose
5 L9  big big nose?
6 L   thin?
7 T   no
8 LL  ((laughter))
9 L   very tall?
10 L  ((unint))
```

```
→  11  T    does she say he's tall? . . . . . . . . . medium
   12  LL                                          ⌈medium
   13  L    medium tall
   14  T    medium height . . .
   15  LL   ((unint))
→  16  L9   medium height nose
   17  T    medium height . . . .
   18  L    eh . . that was the nose
   19  T    yes what about his nose
   20  L    uhuh?
   21  T    what sort of *nose* does he have?
   22  LL   ((unint))
   23  T    did anybody get any other things down
```

5. Finally, a teacher may have problems in correctly assessing the force of a learner's repair-initiation. In Extract 7.30, 10L1 is treated by the teacher as a problem of hearing or an understanding check, whereas the later sequence shows that what was really at issue was a problem of understanding. Note that the learner does not interrupt the ongoing sequence (in the first part of the sequence) to initiate the appropriate repair: it is possible that such repair is felt to be sequentially inappropriate at this point in the sequence (see above). She remains in doubt about the problematic item until she can conveniently (i.e. without interrupting a sequence) ask the advice of her fellow learners.

EXTRACT 7.30

```
    1  T    Gerda. can you tell me the way to the bank please?
    2  L1   yes straight . . along the street
    3  T    straight along this road
    4  L1   this road
    5  T    uhuh
    6  L1   e:n:: den to: the: traffic lights
    7  T    okay
    8  L1   and then . . . (str-)=
    9  T    =straight along this road– *till* the traffic lights
→  10  L1   till?
   11  T1   yes
   12  L1   till the traffic light– and then
                .
                .
                .((two pages of transcript later))
→  13  L1   *till* wat is *till* eigenlijk ((tr: *till* what does *till* actually mean?))
   14  LL   /tot/tot/
   15  L1   oh
```

Conclusion

Problems occur in all kinds of talk, both in classrooms and outside them, but the ways in which they are dealt with vary according to the concerns of the participants and the nature of the problem. In this chapter I have tried to explore the process of repairing in L2 classrooms in two different ways, and to show how information thus obtained can lead to a framework for study. The description, partial though it is, shows that the issue is a complex one, and that much further analytical work is needed before classroom-based studies yielding easily quantifiable data can be undertaken. The model obtained through a top-down, conceptual study needs testing and refinement by way of micro-ethnographic study of more data, both in conversational and classroom settings. We need to look particularly closely at the relative benefits of self- versus other-repair in terms of language learning, and here psycholinguistic data, e.g. about learning styles and strategies, may be necessary.

The sequential study of the process of repairing shows that there is a heavy emphasis on other-repair in the classroom in contrast to non-classroom settings, where self-repair predominates. Where other-repair occurs in the turn following the problem turn, it can be regarded as either an evaluation in the traditional, exchange-structure sense, or as a kind of repair that is similar to conversational repair. When the other-repair occurs during the problem turn, it is generally aimed at helping in the production of that turn, but at the same time it may deny the speaker the opportunity to do self-repair, probably an important learning activity. I suggest that some delay of other-repair (both initiation and error-replacement) may be beneficial, since it would promote the development of self-monitoring and pragmatic adjustment which is essential to competence in the target language (and to socialization in general, as Schegloff *et al.* point out). The notion of *wait time*, proposed in Fanselow 1977b in terms of delayed evaluation, is of prime importance in the study of classroom repair. At the same time we must bear in mind that certain types of activity naturally lead to certain types of repair, and that therefore the issue of how to repair is closely related to the context of what is being done.

Research on learners' errors in terms of type and frequency, and on the errors that teachers correct and evaluate, is not sufficient if we want to find out which types of adjustment in interaction are beneficial to L2 development. It is of crucial importance to describe in detail *how* repairing in the L2 classroom is done by all participants, not just the teacher, and to understand why it is done in all the different ways that it is done. Ultimately our aim is to find the ingredients that make the classroom a cost-effective and hospitable place to learn language.

Notes

1. Erickson, talking about classrooms in general, says:
    ... lessons are speech events characterized by the presence of frequent cognitive and interactional troubles and repair work. (1982, p. 162)
2. See Willis 1981, in which activity-oriented language is systematically exploited as input.
3. See Schegloff 1979, where same-turn repair is treated as part of a 'syntax-for-conversation'. Schegloff primarily addresses self-repair, but I am here suggesting that, through repair, hearers can actively contribute to a speaker's construction of a turn.
4. Self-repair is by its very nature conjunctive.
5. Hesitation markers can often be regarded as turn-holding devices, see e.g. Duncan 1973.

8 Connections

Introduction

In this chapter I want to pull together some of the main strands of discussion that have arisen in earlier chapters. To begin with it may be useful to list some of the central points that have been touched upon in various places.

1. A basic assumption made throughout this book is that second-language development can and does occur in classrooms. I have also suggested that the classroom can be a particularly productive place for the investigation of the process of L2 development, since the participants are overtly concerned with that aim. It seems to me to make common sense that, when people are consciously trying to learn something, interesting data about that learning can be collected. At the very least we cannot summarily assume that *more* interesting information about learning can be obtained when they are *not* concerned with learning, but rather with doing something else. This does not of course mean that learners need to be concerned with language learning at all times in order to achieve progress. It does mean, however, that they are capable of special efforts which they believe will speed up their progress. These efforts, plus the efforts of teachers especially trained to promote them, are visible in the classroom, more so and in more concentrated form than in out-of-class interaction or simulated conversations.

In the L2 classroom, experimentation with the interlanguage and the trying out of insecure hypotheses is, officially at least, encouraged. This is not usually the case in out-of-class language use where, due to the pressure of getting things done, the learners may consciously avoid experimentation with language which is at the cutting edge of the developmental process. It follows of course that the L2 classroom, to do its job well, must promote such experimentation. If it does not, it loses one important advantage it has over out-of-class talk.

2. Second-language development, as all learning, does not consist of a succession of single learning events, but rather is a cumulative process. I have used Heath's view of learning as a sequence of acquisition → retention → extension (see p. 92). This process, or series of linked processes, relies on an interplay between cognitive and interactive work, that is, mental activities and social activities which fuel and inform each other. These activities can only occur in a context of meaningful (purposeful) participation in talk. Sometimes adherents of a communicative approach make the mistake of equating 'meaningfulness' with only those things that lend meaning to talk outside class, that is, the exchange of information, the obtaining of goods and services, and the performance of social tasks in life. Important though these are, we must not discard the meaning potential of specific classroom activities, including rituals, games and metalinguistic problem solving. Classroom authenticity may be as valid a criterion for language development as 'real-world' authenticity, so long as it allows for purposeful participation and involvement.

3. Some reports of classrooms and some models of classroom discourse give the impression that teachers and learners do the same things over and over again, warranting summary statements about 'typical' classrooms such as those quoted on p. 137. There may be many classrooms that are like this, though I have suggested that some models tend to make things look that way, forcing unruly bits of data into a rule-governed mould. L2 classrooms, at least all those that I have observed, luckily do not fit into such moulds. Many different kinds of talk go on at different times, leading to the different interaction types and participation structures described in Chapter 6. However, we may find that some of these may be richer – in terms of providing fuel for learning – than others, since they all lead almost inescapably to certain specific and different ways of dealing with phenomena, such as the initiative to speak and influence the discourse, topic change and management, monitoring and repairing, and so on. These phenomena do therefore not occur at random, dictated by the whimsy of teacher habits or talent, but rather as a result of the social context of the classroom and the sequences of activities that occur in it. Should we wish to recommend changes, we should therefore start with the basic patterns of interaction rather than with the superficial phenomena which become visible in their enactment.

Through CR, the stream of classroom discourse can be segmented, and different kinds of interaction isolated, which allow for distinct patterns of participation. By studying these different patterns in detail, their potential for providing learning opportunities can be assessed, and thus methodological recommendations for a cost-effective use of classroom time can be formulated.

4. It follows from point 3 that the teaching profession is ill-served by pedagogical recommendations which isolate specific observable phenomena, such as types of questions asked, time lapses between answer and evaluation, and so on, without showing how such phenomena flow naturally from the kinds of activities that are conducted. It makes no sense to recommend a change in those isolated aspects without addressing the underlying organizational character-istics of the activities themselves.

5. Classroom work is partly preplanned and partly locally constructed. I have pointed out that the preplanning is usually done by the teacher on behalf of all the learners, and that local assembly, or improvisation, occurs because plans are never watertight, as 'light relief', or because the learners do unexpected things (perhaps because they are insufficiently aware of what is 'supposed to be done'). It is predominently during unplanned sequences that we can see learners employ initiative and use language creatively, and for that reason it might be suggested that less or no prior planning should be done. There are indeed teachers who take a radical view, and who leave it up to the learners to decide what is to be done in a lesson. However, it might be too rash to assume that all provision of structure and sequence by the teacher is counter-productive (see the discussion about control and initiative in Chapter 3).

In the world outside classrooms we very often plan our encounters, and we feel that this helps us to control the outcome. This is obvi-ously true when we go for job interviews, loan applications at the bank, visits to parents-in-law, and so on. It is also often true in more casual encounters, for example when a colleague or friend comes our way, and we have about twenty paces to take before reaching greeting distance. Few encounters ever take place according to plan, but we do find the plans helpful nevertheless. The cognitive work we do to plan conversations and social transactions is complex and skilful. It utilizes fully whatever linguistic and pragmatic systems and mechan-isms we have mentally available. It is likely that this work can be extremely beneficial for language learners, and indeed may be a crucial vehicle for learning. It can be observed that children learning their first language often plan conversations and game-like interaction long before they are skilful users of complex syntax. Parents and caretakers help them in this planning by providing prototypical structures and gradually handing over slots and roles. I will return to this work, called *scaffolding* by Bruner (Ratner and Bruner 1978; Bruner 1983) later in this chapter.

This brings me to the observation that in classrooms learners are often merely asked either to react in accordance with imposed plans, or to produce language spontaneously, without the benefit of planning their interaction themselves. It seems reasonable to suggest that communicative activities should be designed so as to encourage active planning of both single utterances and sequences of utterances.

6. Classroom research ideally belongs to the teacher, and is the obvious meeting ground between theory and practice. The teacher can use classroom research for two immediately useful purposes: firstly, to improve the classroom lessons from one week to the next, and secondly, to make diagnostic assessments of the learners that enable individual courses of action far more productively than traditional tests are capable of. The two are, of course, related.

These points make a series of claims which the discussion in earlier chapters makes relevant, but which are of course not proven. As Mitchell (1985) points out in the conclusion to her state-of-the-art survey, classroom research so far is descriptive, and it is not known how much it may be able to contribute to our theoretical understanding of classroom learning issues (though the reader must note that the statement suggests a distinction between descriptive and explanatory research which I have questioned in earlier chapters).

In the remainder of this chapter I want to explore further the arguments advanced here by focusing on two basic concepts: *control* and *evaluation*. These concepts appear to be central, the first in that it determines type and amount of participation, the second since it addresses the immediate purpose of classroom research, so far as the teacher is concerned: feedback on the effectiveness of the programme, and information about performance and progress of learners.[1]

Control: teacher's gain, learner's loss?

On several occasions Widdowson (1981, 1983) has pointed out that the relationship between teaching and learning is not identical to that of complementary transactions such as giving and taking, buying and selling:

> To consider learning and teaching as converse activities of this kind is to suppose that the learner takes no more and no less than what the

teacher gives, that there is an equation between teaching action and learner reaction, and that knowledge is transferred intact and unchanged as if it were some kind of cash or some kind of commodity.

(Widdowson 1983, p. 7)

When someone does some buying this means that some selling also occurs. When learning occurs, teaching may or may not be in attendance. When teaching occurs, learning may or may not take place. The view that teaching is an action which results in learning has been described as a *deterministic* view in Chapter 4. Yet I would suggest that, ideally, teaching and learning in the classroom are aspects of one single process, which may be called language development. The central term in this process is learning rather than teaching, as reflected in common non-standard usage which uses 'learning' for both activities (and in other languages, e.g. Dutch, where *leren* can be used in both senses).

Most approaches to syllabus construction, and most lesson plans, sequence tasks and activities in terms of the amount of control that is exercised: tightly controlled activities specify contributions and limit participation by providing detailed instructions; less controlled activities allow for a variety of contributions and for varying amounts of initiative and choice. A concern for some degree of balance and sequence of control is evident even in some of the most progressive recommendations of the communicative approach: activities in a lesson move from controlled to free, from pre-communicative to communicative, so that the teacher starts out with complete control (over who says what, when, to whom) and gradually relinquishes that control to allow for true communication only during some final portion of the lesson (see Box 8.1).

Control and initiative

According to Stubbs (1983, p. 50) a major part of classroom teaching consists of monitoring the classroom talk:

> Teachers constantly check up to see if they are on the same wavelength as their pupils, if at least most of their pupils are following what they are saying, in addition to actively monitoring, editing and correcting the actual language which pupils use. Teachers therefore constantly exert different kinds of control over the on-going state of talk in the classroom.
>
> (Stubbs 1983, p. 50)

Stubbs calls the teacher's language of control *metacommunication*: communicating about communication, and lists eight kinds of meta-

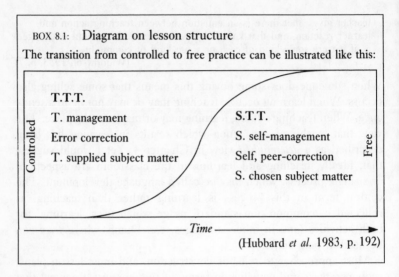

BOX 8.1:   Diagram on lesson structure

The transition from controlled to free practice can be illustrated like this:

T.T.T.

T. management

Error correction

T. supplied subject matter

S.T.T.

S. self-management

Self, peer-correction

S. chosen subject matter

Controlled — Free

Time

(Hubbard *et al.* 1983, p. 192)

communication which may be considered strategies of control (see Box 8.2).[2]

BOX 8.2   Metacommunication

Attracting or showing attention
Controlling the amount of speech
Checking or confirming understanding
Summarizing
Defining (including reformulating)
Editing (including evaluatory comments)
Correcting
Specifiying topic

(Stubbs 1983)

A number of studies have looked at the ways in which teachers in L2 classes structure their language, perhaps simplifying it in ways similar to those parents and care-givers employ with small children (Milk 1985; Chaudron 1983, forthcoming) to ensure comprehension. In Krashen's terminology (e.g. 1985) this leads to comprehensible input which is just one step ahead of the child or learner's current level of development $(i + 1)$. Such adjustment is largely intuitive and unpremeditated, and indeed there seems to be no way of scientifically specifying at any given moment what the right level might be. Stubbs's discussion of metacommunication adds to this automatic adjustment a range of conscious or routine-governed strategies to ensure that classroom interaction proceeds on task. These strategies may be as important as intuitive simplification in terms of providing comprehensible input. Gaies (1980, p. 90) calls the complex of a teacher's linguistic actions *input controls*, 'whose purposes are to facilitate communication and to maximize pedagogical effectiveness'. It is clear that the teacher's linguistic output will contain elements both of intuitive adjustment in the form of 'teacherese' or 'foreigner talk' and of conscious (or once-conscious) didactic strategies as illustrated by Stubbs's metacommunicative acts. However, it is unlikely that learners are mere passive recipients of such adjustments and strategies, but rather have certain means at their disposal to influence them and to indicate to the teacher if they are on 'the same wavelength' (Stubbs 1983, p. 50). In the above-mentioned study Gaies investigates the learners' *intake controls*, i.e. 'the ways in which learners regulate the manner in which and the rate at which content is transmitted by a teacher' (1980, p. 90).

Although Gaies's data derive from dyads and triads, i.e. from a teacher working with just one or two learners at a time, and thus may show significantly more intake control than would occur in ordinary classrooms, learners, collectively and individually, have a range of ways at their disposal to indicate to the teacher what should be done next to ensure smooth interactive progress. Gaies's taxonomy of learner intake control is reproduced in Box 8.3.

The specific types of intake control described by Gaies are all subservient to a teacher-controlled activity, i.e. they are *reactive* rather than *proactive*. They give evidence of some negotiation, but only in terms of surface aspects of an ongoing activity. They do not aim to shape that activity, merely influencing the rate and specific way in which it is conducted. In previous chapters I have suggested that learners also manage at times to change, initiate, terminate and temporarily suspend particular activities, and it is of interest to investigate why and how it occurs, and what happens when it occurs.

In Chapter 3 I mentioned Stevick's (1980) suggestion that in a classroom there is a balance between *control* and *initiative*. I want to return briefly to the discussion of control, constraints and resources, since there is no doubt that this issue is of central importance to CR. Though I make no pretence to resolve it, I hope these discussions will contribute to further work on the part of other second-language researchers and teachers.

The teacher exercises control in two ways: the structuring of classroom activity (sequencing of activities, length of time spent on each activity, what is to be done in an activity), and knowledge of results

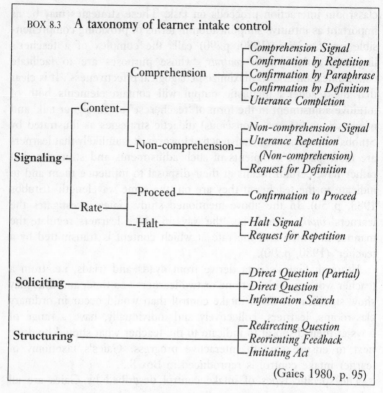

BOX 8.3   A taxonomy of learner intake control

Signaling — Content — Comprehension —
- Comprehension Signal
- Confirmation by Repetition
- Confirmation by Paraphrase
- Confirmation by Definition
- Utterance Completion

Non-comprehension —
- Non-comprehension Signal
- Utterance Repetition (Non-comprehension)
- Request for Definition

Rate — Proceed — Confirmation to Proceed

Halt —
- Halt Signal
- Request for Repetition

Soliciting —
- Direct Question (Partial)
- Direct Question
- Information Search

Structuring —
- Redirecting Question
- Reorienting Feedback
- Initiating Act

(Gaies 1980, p. 95)

or feedback (these are not Stevick's terms: he describes it as 'making it easy for the learner to know how what he has done or said compares with what a native speaker would have done or said' – 1980, p. 18). *Initiative* refers to 'decisions about who says what, to whom, and when' (*ibid*, p. 19). The relation between control and initiative is expressed by Stevick as follows:

> Seen in this way, 'initiative' and 'control' are not merely two directions along a single dimension. That is to say, 'control' on the part of the teacher does not interfere with 'initiative' on the part of the student: when the teacher tightens her 'control' of what is going on, she need not cut into the student's 'initiative'; often, in fact, she will actually increase it. Similarly, insufficient 'control' by the teacher may reduce or paralyze the 'initiative' of the student.

(Stevick 1980, p. 19)

We may relate this view of the interdependent nature of control and initiative to Giddens's view of rules as enabling and constraining resources simultaneously (see Chapter 3). However, Stevick's discussion suggests an unnnecessarily rigid division between control and initiative in terms of *roles*. In his description control is the teacher's domain, initiative the learner's prerogative. Later on in his book Stevick suggests that control, in both of the senses mentioned, can to a significant degree be delegated to the learners, but the dynamics of this delegation in terms of subsequent interaction remain unclear (see Allwright for further discussion on this issue, for example 1980, 1984). Of course, the connecting concept for both control and initiative is *responsibility*, and this gives an ideological rather than methodological flavour to the issue.

Of more directly pedagogical interest in the design and study of classroom work is Goffman's distinction of *system* and *ritual* constraints in interaction. It will be intrinsically simpler to focus in the classroom on the basic systematic requirements inherent in any communication, i.e. those things that are necessary for communication to be efficient. Such system constraints, in Goffman's description, include feedback capabilities, contact signals, turnover signals, repairs, formulations, conversational maxims, and so on, that is, those features of talk that are most usually addressed in conversational analysis. Goffman suggests that these constraints, though their realization may vary, are relatively culture-free.

In addition, however, social interaction requires another set of constraints (ritual constraints),

> namely, constraints regarding how each individual ought to handle himself with respect to each of the others, so that he not discredit his own tacit claim to good character or the tacit claim of the others that they are persons of social worth whose various forms of territoriality are to be respected.
>
> (Goffman 1981, p. 16)

The latter type of constraint is dependent on cultural definition, and may therefore cause considerable difficulty in cross-cultural communication. A problem with Goffman's distinction is of course that ritual considerations are commonly expressed through such systematic requirements as feedback signals, repair and so on (see the discussion of variable forms of repair in Chapter 7).

The above discussion of control and initiative, constraints and resources, makes it clear that social interaction is extremely complex and cannot be easily captured in terms of a simple model. This means that classroom activities cannot be compared in a straightforward manner with other social activities, but rather require in-depth study in their own right. In this respect CR is only at the very initial stages of development. Lest this sounds rather weak and unhelpful, it must be stressed that the charting of the problem is a crucial first step in research. If nothing else, it will prevent methodological approaches which are based on partial information and insufficiently analysed data.

Questions and control

A substantial proportion of classroom research has focused on the kinds of questions that teachers ask. There are many different ways of asking questions, and many different purposes for doing so. In the classroom certain specific types of questions are prominent, and although the same types also occur in non-instructional settings (for an in-depth study of types of questions see Goody 1978), they occur with different frequencies. A common distinction in classroom questions is between *display questions* (or known-information questions) and *referential questions* (or genuine information questions), where the asker does not already possess the information requested. In a study by Long and Sato (1983) it was found that L2 teachers ask many more display questions than referential questions, in contrast to out-of-class interaction between native and non-native speakers. This was so even though the lessons were purportedly communicative in orientation.[3] Why would teachers, even if they are convinced of the benefits of meaningful interaction, engage in so much questioning which is so obviously different from ordinary non-instructional discourse? Even an approach which calls itself 'the Natural Approach' (Krashen and Terrell 1983) recommends, in this instance for the purposes of lowering the 'affective filter', a series of display questions such as the following:

> Lets count the number of students with blue eyes. One, two, three, four ... Are there any others? (Jim). Oh, of course, we can't forget Jim. Yes, he has blue eyes. Now, who has brown eyes? Does Martha have brown eyes? (Yes). And what color is her hair? (Brown). Is it light brown or dark brown? (Light). Is she wearing a dress today? and so on ...
>
> (Krashen and Terrell 1983, p. 81)

Such questions have the professed aim of providing comprehensible input, and of encouraging 'early production'. I suggest that, by and large, what gives such question series their instructional, typically L2-classroom character is not so much that they are display rather than referential, but that they are made with the aim of eliciting language from the learners. Upon examination, it may well turn out that the teacher, and several of the students, did not know that Martha has brown eyes, and that this information was made available to all participants as a result of the question, which would make the question a referential one. Whether or not this is the case appears to be a perfectly trivial matter in interactional terms. In both cases the function of the question remains the same: to provide input, and to elicit verbal responses. What distinguishes instructional questions from conversational (non-instructional) ones is therefore not their referential or display nature, but rather their *eliciting function*. In interactional terms, the difference between the following (constructed) elicitations may be minimal:

a) *prompt or cue:*

    T   go to the theatre.
         yesterday. Martha.
    L   yesterday I went to the theatre.

b) *display question:*

    T   ((pointing to a picture)) Where did Martha go yesterday?
    L   She went to the theatre (yesterday)

c) *referential question:*

    T   Where did you go yesterday, Martha?
    L   (yesterday) I went to the theatre.

Although the linguistic form of the response may vary somewhat for different kinds of elicitations (we may add: 'Ask Martha what she did yesterday'; 'Did you stay at home yesterday, Martha?' etc.) the nature of the activity remains essentially the same: a verbal stimulus elicits a verbal response. To assume therefore that the display question is a major culprit of didactic (i.e. 'unnatural') discourse is simplistic. Instead, we must focus on the reasons why much of a teacher's discourse is aimed at eliciting certain kinds of contributions from the learners. Obviously, what is at stake here has much to do with the matter of control: control over the exact kind of language the learner is exposed to, and control over the contributions the learner can make in the classroom. That control can be as pervasive in referential questioning as it is, more blatantly perhaps, in display questioning or prompting and cuing. There may be good reasons for this control since we do not know yet if classroom-specific interaction is irrelevant to language development. It has a very long and venerable tradition, and before we reject it and replace it with alternative recommendations, we must make sure of its actual and presumed function.[4] The display-versus-referential distinction, seemingly so basic, may turn out to be irrelevant when more basic interactional issues are considered. It is for that reason that I have consistently warned against studies which isolate superficially identifiable features for quantitative treatment.

Many questions, even so-called 'pure' information questions, carry a control function. As Goody points out:

> Questions are speech acts which place two people in direct, immediate interaction. In doing so they carry messages about relationships – about relative status, assertions of status and challenges to status.
>
> (Goody 1978, p. 39)

Discourse studies, such as Goody's, of questioning strategies in practical everyday contexts, shed considerable light on the controlling power of questions. It is important to point this out here since the practice of questioning in L2 classrooms, pervasive though it is, has so far received only superficial treatment. If the power of questions is as strong as observations in other contexts suggest, it is a methodological tool that can be exploited in many different ways, including the promotion of language development. An analysis must go beyond simple distinctions such as display and referential questions, yes/no and open-ended questions, and so on, to investigate what different tasks questions set, and the different commitments they place on the answerer.

Such analysis is complex, since it may involve inferences about both the teacher's intentions and the learner's interpretations, and calls for a careful discoursal analysis of utterances. In terms of categorization, Bloom's taxonomy of educational objectives is still the most widely used resource for cognitive question types (Bloom 1956), though Mehan's classification of types of initiations is a practical alternative which is easier to handle, yet useful. Mehan distinguishes three types of initiations: elicitation, informative and directive. He further distinguishes four types of elicitation:

> *choice elicitation*: asks for agreement or disagreement (yes/no) or choice from a list provided by the teacher;
> *product elicitation*: requires a factual response such as a name, date, colour, place;
> *process elicitation*: asks for respondents' opinions or interpretations;
> *metaprocess elicitation*: asks students 'to be reflective about the process of making connections between elicitations and responses'.
>
> (Mehan 1979, pp. 45–46)

Another, even broader classification is provided by Redfield and Rousseau. In a meta-analysis of research on questions (1981) they divided question types into two groups: higher and lower cognitive questions. They concluded that higher cognitive questions produced better educational results. Of course, these results were not measured in interactional or language-learning terms, but no doubt similar studies in L2 classrooms would yield interesting information. The two types of questions were defined as follows:

> ... higher cognitive or divergent questions (are) those requiring that the student mentally manipulate bits of information previously learned to create or support an answer with logically reasoned evidence.
>
> Lower cognitive or convergent questions are defined as those calling for verbatim recall or recognition of factual information previously read or presented by a teacher.
>
> (Redfield and Rousseau 1981, p. 237)

Whichever classification is chosen, research into questioning in L2 classrooms must carefully examanine the purposes and the effects of questions, not only in terms of linguistic production, but also in terms of cognitive demands and interactive purpose (for further discussion, see Chaudron forthcoming).

Classroom rituals

Teacher-led classroom talk can be moved forward by a series of linked questions, much like a Socratic dialogue, by a series of instructions or directives for linguistic production, or by various kinds of talk that are closer to ordinary conversation or (narrative) exposition. As shown in Chapter 6, the parts learners can play in different forms of ritual vary according to interaction type. Basically, the teacher can either treat the whole class as a generic addressee, expecting answers in chorus or from individual volunteers, or select specific learners in a rotating-dyad format. There are of course variations on these themes, in the form of chain drills and other game-like activities with specific rules, but the basic characteristic is that participation is prespecified.

Boggs (1972) has shown that Hawaiian children contribute actively to chorus recitations but are reluctant to respond when they feel they are individually selected for special attention. Similar observations are made by Philips (1983), and my own observations in the Peruvian highlands also confirm a heavy reliance on spontaneous or orchestrated chorus, with only sporadic occurrences of specific allocation. The preference for collective interaction over individual teacher-learner dyads may be cultural, and needs to be taken into account when investigating multi-ethnic classrooms. In European/American style classrooms individual dyads (constructed through specific allocation, bidding or other forms of self-selection) are common, though chorus responding also occurs. The function of the latter in general subject classrooms may be to focus and coordinate attention, i.e. to prepare the class for a recitation activity. The following example from Sinclair and Coulthard illustrates such orchestrated attention-getting (though the responses are physical rather than verbal):

> Now. All eyes on me. Put your pencils down. Fold your arms. Hands on your heads. Hands on your shoulders. Fold your arms. Look at me.
>
> (Sinclair and Coulthard 1975, p. 90)

In the L2 classroom chorus responding fulfils a further function of preliminary production, a trial run – capitalizing on security provided by numbers – before further work, and perhaps as an aid to short-term memory.

For a chorus response to be successful the response must be entirely predictable so that all learners say the same thing. Imitation and repetition are thus common elements in chorus recitation, though also referential questions may elicit chorus responses, if the answer is sufficiently predictable due to prior discourse or a high degree of shared background knowledge.

Regardless of other possible developmental benefits, chorus sequences may create a sense of collaborative achievement which is important for creating social cohesion and a positive ambience. In the following extract a Peruvian teacher, in a Spanish-as-a-second-language lesson, skilfully creates a riproaring chorus which ends by children climbing on top of their tables and chanting at the tops of their voices. A parent or regional inspector passing within half a mile of the school house cannot fail to have been very impressed by the exemplary display of scholastic fervour broadcast across the otherwise silent pampa:

T	yo voy a ser Pepito, como me llamo?	I'm going to be Pepito, what's my name?
LL	Pepito	
T	como me llaman?	what do they (or you) call me?
LL	Pepito	
T	asi que todos saben, quien soy yo?	so that everyone knows it, who am I?
LL	Pepito!	
T	como me llamo?	what's my name?
LL	Pepito!!	
T	quien soy yo?	who am I?
LL	PEPITO!!	

A communicative purist may frown upon such chorus sequences as not being 'meaningful' or 'authentic' interaction, hence not conducive to language development. Yet I have frequently observed that learners enjoy chorus recitation (in moderation) and indeed, spontaneous choruses often develop in the classroom; in addition, 'private' imitation and repetition are common both in the classroom and in informal contexts. Learners repeat things in their heads constantly, and to be encouraged (allowed) to do so overtly is likely to stimulate auditory and motoric memory. Furthermore, I have observed that in teacher training, when exposed to unknown languages for the sake of experiment, trainees invariably indicate their preference for some chorus work. The consistent success of songs, rhymes and jazz chants further suggests that they may be a valuable aid in the development of the elusive yet central rhythm of language.

There may be several valid arguments for the maintenance of a ritual element in the language classroom, quite apart from any direct language-learning benefits. Classroom research is best served by being methodologically neutral, as recommended in the early chapters of this book. If we, on the basis of some theoretical model or pedagogical advice, recommend the abandonment of time-honoured practices, we may well be throwing out the baby with the bathwater. Throwing out chorus work, display questions, repetition, and so on, since they are not 'authentic' communication (that is, they do not occur in non-classroom settings; they may of course be authentic in the classroom context), may constitute premature surgery. If, as Breen (1985b) suggests, the classroom is a 'genuine culture', there is surely a place for ritual, routine and ludic elements, just as in any genuine culture and, crucially, as vehicles for socialization in any genuine culture. It must therefore be emphasized once again that classroom research must conform to the two central principles of ethnography: it must be *holistic* and *emic*.

A focus on tasks

An increasing emphasis on meaningful participation in interaction, coupled with the difficulties of establishing a valid syllabus based on linguistic (whether grammatical or functional) criteria for selection and grading, have led many teachers and researchers to propose a syllabus based on sequences of tasks. One of the earliest fully worked out projects is the multi-media course *Challenges* (Abbs *et al.* 1978 and 1982) which sequences tasks in such a way that the output (result, product) of one task becomes meaningful and necessary input to the next, thus creating chains of tasks which require a range of skills, and substantial cooperation between learners. Other more recent examples include the 'Bangalore project' directed by Prabhu

(1985) which, in Prabhu's words, employs

> problem-solving tasks ... without any language syllabus, pre-selection of
> language for particular activities or form-focused work ... with tentative
> results which indicate that unconscious grammar construction does take
> place from such teaching and that the resultant ability is more
> deployable than the result of more form-focused teaching.
>
> (Prabhu 1985, p. 171)

One of the potential shortcomings of the Bangalore project (though
much more information would be needed to confirm this) is that the
syllabus is based on specific content matter and the exchange of
information relating to this content matter. Therefore it addresses
some aspects of communication while possibly neglecting others. As
Brown and Yule point out (and as I have pointed out on several
occasions in earlier chapters), much of our day-to-day communication
is not aimed at transmitting information or discussing content-matter
problems, but rather at developing and maintaining social relationships and at self-expression (1983b). Brown and Yule thus
distinguish between *interactional* and *transactional* language use, and
argue that both require attention. In their proposals for a task-based
approach they argue therefore that both aspects of language use must
be taken into account in the design and sequencing of tasks. Of
specific interest are Brown and Yule's suggestions for the grading
and sequencing of tasks, since a syllabus must of course be more than
a random selection of tasks, however valuable and interesting they
may be. Brown and Yule's detailed discussion of criteria for the
design and selection of tasks is extremely valuable, especially if complemented with two further design features:

1. The use of chains of tasks, or tasks leading to other tasks, as
   implemented in *Challenges*; this can be a powerful motivating factor,
   as well as enabling a degree of work-sharing and individualization
   (for further discussion of this 'task-dependency principle' see
   Nunan 1985, p. 45).
2. The use of learner-produced and recorded interaction (discussions,
   role plays, etc.) as input, i.e. the recommendation made at various
   points in this book to build an element of ethnography into the
   syllabus (see further below).

If we regard task-based language teaching in this way, rather than
as mainly a problem of identifying suitable content matter, it may well
offer exciting new opportunities to exploit the full range of possibilities the classroom has to offer in terms of meaningful participation
in talk. It may well be that this is fully compatible with the role of
ritual outlined in the preceding section, especially if we resist the

temptation to equate task-authenticity (and hence relevance) with out-of-class authenticity.

Long (1985) makes some useful suggestions for a task-based approach, and warns against narrow definitions of tasks. However, his remark that he sees 'the primary function of the second-language classroom as being the provision of opportunities for natural second-language acquisition' (1985, p. 94), must be interpreted carefully. An analysis of tasks and 'naturalness' must address the following questions:

1. What is natural second-language acquisition?
2. What are appropriate opportunities?
3. Does the context have to be natural, the language, the purpose, or all of these?
4. If so, what aspects of the context, etc.?
5. Does the interaction have to be natural, the cognitive work, or both?

A task-based approach must avoid the temptation to attempt to force the 'outside world' into the classroom by hook or by crook, since this will not be possible. Worse, it is likely to be counterproductive in the long run. The validity of L2 classroom tasks is determined by the meaningful interaction they allow learners to engage in *in the classroom*, not by superficial linguistic or contextual similarities with target tasks.

Scaffolding

When children learn their first language they do not first learn sounds, then words, then sentences, and then finally apply this linguistic knowledge in their interaction with the social world around them. They begin by interacting with the meaningful people in their environment, and they converse, play games and engage in rituals long before they are able to utter their first recognizable words. Their caretakers typically spend enormous amounts of time in setting up and developing these interactions, and language develops along the way. This work is described by Bruner as follows (see also Ratner and Bruner 1978):

> One sets the game, provides a scaffold to assure that the child's ineptitudes can be rescued or rectified by appropriate intervention, and then removes the scaffold part by part as the reciprocal structure can stand on its own.
>
> (Bruner 1983, p. 60)

Scaffolding in this sense[5] is thus a process

> of 'setting up' the situation to make the child's entry easy and successful and then gradually pulling back and handing the role to the child as he becomes skillful enough to manage it.
>
> (*ibid*)

At the beginning of the conversation or game the parent typically takes both parts, but continually watches for signs that the child is able take a more active part. This 'handover principle', as Bruner calls it (q.v.), is crucial in the child's development of language and of social skills in general.

We may find this same process, perhaps in different guises, operating in L2 classrooms, though perhaps as teachers we can learn a few useful skills from studying the interaction between parents and children. This is not to say that we should imitate that interaction, but rather that there may be ways of structuring activities in such a way that a scaffold for the learners' participation is available, and a systematic way of disassembling that scaffold gradually. Typically, the models we use as presentation of new language or situations, often in the form of recorded dialogues, picture sequences, written texts or films, do not do this. Seeing or hearing others interact will not provide the crucial input that direct participation provides.

Language teaching methodology can benefit from a study of first-language scaffolding in two ways: a) A task-based approach can usefully experiment with ways to structure tasks with the principles of scaffolding and handover in mind, and b) CR can study in detail the ways in which classroom activities already tacitly employ such tactics, and build on them.

Evaluation, feedback and monitoring

In their discussion of a communicative curriculum Breen and Candlin regard *evaluation* as one of three essential elements of the curriculum process (see Box 8.4). The two kinds of evaluation mentioned are evaluation of learner and of *curriculum*.

I will first address the notion of evaluation of curriculum. It is crucial to Breen and Candlin's proposals that this evaluation be an integral part of classroom teaching and learning. How is such evaluation to be achieved, given that teachers have full schedules and time-consuming preparation and correction to do outside of class? I suggest that here CR will play a central role, and that it can be built into the cycle preparation → implementation → feedback. There may

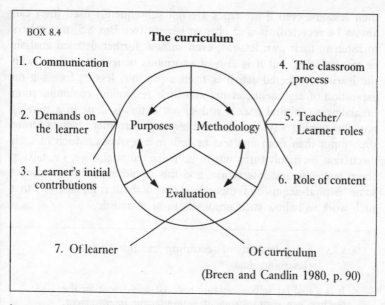

BOX 8.4

The curriculum

1. Communication

2. Demands on the learner

3. Learner's initial contributions

Purposes

Methodology

Evaluation

4. The classroom process

5. Teacher/Learner roles

6. Role of content

7. Of learner

Of curriculum

(Breen and Candlin 1980, p. 90)

be a number of different ways of building an element of classroom research into the curriculum process, and much inspiration can be derived from Hymes's recommendations on ethnographic monitoring (Hymes 1981), and particularly also from Stenhouse (1975, especially Chapter 10). Stenhouse mentions the tensions that can arise between the roles of teacher and researcher, but continues:

> I believe, however, that it is worth facing these tensions and attempting to resolve them. For in the end it is difficult to see how teaching can be improved or how curricular proposals can be evaluated without self-monitoring on the part of teachers. A research tradition which is accessible to teachers and which feeds teaching must be created if education is to be significantly improved.
>
> (Stenhouse 1975, p. 165)

There are now several examples of teacher-conducted CR in several different countries. Perhaps the most well-publicized project is the above-mentioned Bangalore project directed by Prabhu (1985), which is in effect a longitudinal monitoring of communicative principles applied in a number of classrooms through the use of content-based cognitively challenging activities.

An essential element in any classroom monitoring is the recording of interaction in that classroom, ideally on video, but usefully also on cassette tape if video is either unavailable or regarded as too intrusive. I consistently recommend to all trainee teachers that they record all their lessons, even if the tapes are not subsequently used (they can always be recycled). It is of obvious benefit (see Box 8.5) to teachers to listen to their own lessons, even without further detailed analysis or transcription, but it is also of enormous benefit to analyse, with the learners, selected activities from a previous lesson, focusing on exposition of arguments, errors and their resolution, communication breakdowns, cultural issues, and so on. If this is done in a suitably non-threatening way, learners and teachers reap more benefits from such input than from any text or task in a textbook. Much of such discussion inevitably turns out to be metacommunicative, i.e. talking about language and interaction, and this would appear to contradict some 'natural-acquisition' theoretical proposals. It is highly likely that such work will show such proposals to be simplistic.

BOX 8.5   Some benefits of recording and transcribing classroom data

1. It is a tool for self-monitoring and self-assessment for the teacher, hence an instrument in programme improvement.
2. It provides input for pedagogical and didactic discussion in L2 training courses.
3. It is a useful diagnostic aid for focusing on specific classroom problems.
4. It assists in the on-task and in-class evaluation of learner performance and progress.
5. It provides data for case study of specific learners or groups of learners who require special attention.
6. It can provide a cumulative data base for the study of interlanguage development and growth over a period of time.
7. It is a necessary tool for monitoring action research and classroom experiments, since it can focus on variables which other research does not or cannot control.
8. It provides input for learners to analyse interaction, and a means to monitor and discuss their own performance.

Evaluation of learners

The common way to evaluate learners' progress is through tests, quizzes and examinations. These are often institutionalized in the sense that schools and language institutes usually have their own sets of tests that are applied at specific intervals. In addition, many textbook series have their own batteries of progress or achievement tests and, of course, there are internationally recognized tests such as the

TOEFL, RSA, Cambridge, etc. There is no doubt that such tests fulfil important functions in providing feedback to the teacher, the institution, and the learner in terms of how individual learners or groups of learners are doing in relation to a larger population. However, they are by and large inadequate in terms of the learners' actual performance and progress, in interaction with peers and/or in target settings, so that they give only a very partial indication of communicative competence. Even those tests that include an element of speech production rely on responses to standard stimuli, which are recorded on tape and subsequently evaluated, so that true inter-actional ability and achievement in the target language is not, or only obliquely, addressed. Speaking into a tape recorder in reply to predetermined cues, or answering questions in an interview format, may introduce socio-psychological and cultural variables which interfere with performance, so that additional assessment is needed to compensate for testing bias. Such bias, which is inherent in any testing situation, however culturally sensitive it may be, is by now well-documented, for example in the work of Cummins (1984) and in numerous criticisms of Bernstein's work on restricted and elaborated codes (e.g. Stubbs 1976). An earlier penetrating analysis can be found in Cicourel *et al.* (1974):

> There tends to be a controversial discrepancy between what the teachers-as-indirect-researchers of their own settings tell us, and what we read about the child's performance on tests given under presumably controlled conditions.
>
> A central problem in education is the failure to compare information provided by the test with the information provided by the child's behavior in the classroom.
>
> (Cicourel *et al.* 1974, p. 300)

In a series of experiments with different tasks Brown *et al.* (1984) found that the quality of talk is much better when pupils talk to a friend from the same class than to an interviewer in an examination format (see also the notion of *communicative stress* discussed in Brown and Yule 1983b). It appears that formal tests do not adequately assess the ability to communicate, though there will be significant individual and cultural differences between different learners in the way they can handle oral test-taking and interviewing. Brown *et al.* also experimented with task formats where interlocutors were either present or absent. They note:

> We should also note that pupils perform better when they are talking directly to a friend than they do when they are asked to talk into a microphone so that the message could be played to a friend, who would then perform the task. We experimented with this mode of task

presentation because it is one which is apparently used quite a lot in some schools, particularly for assessment purposes. In general pupils produced less talk, and less adequate talk, when they spoke into the microphone.

(Brown *et al.* 1984, p. 37)

I should point out perhaps that Brown *et al.*'s pupils are teenagers in Scottish schools. They are therefore native speakers (though of a dialect that is significantly different from standard British English), but apparently their speaking skills are sufficient cause for concern for the Scottish Education Department to set up a study investigating issues of spoken English. The methods, techniques and task types, as well as the findings, of Brown *et al.*'s study are undoubtedly as relevant to second-language settings as they are to native-language ones.

Of special interest is Brown *et al.*'s detailed documentation of methods of scoring and assessment: various ways of unstructured and structured scoring are discussed, and they will be easily adaptable to L2 tasks conducted in the classroom. The reliability of assessment reported by Brown *et al.* is impressive, and since the scoring is criterion-referenced, such classroom task-based assessment would appear to possess a high degree of construct validity.

Conclusion

Control (and, as the other side of the coin, initiative) and assessment or evaluation are central to studies of second-language classrooms. The three aspects of interaction treated in detail in Chapters 5 to 7: active participation, participation structures and repair need to be systematically related to these two basic constructs in order to show how classroom interaction is organized and how this organization is a purposeful effort in which teachers and learners participate jointly. The following points summarize some of these relations:

1. Control can be shared by teacher and learners so that the discourse becomes less asymmetrical and more jointly planned. Planning then becomes a part of the interaction itself rather than being imposed from the outside, and learners are challenged to exercise their interactional competence. This would naturally result in a reduction in emphasis on elicitation and recitation, creating more space for other, more productive interaction types.

2. Certain activities with a ritual character may play an important role in classroom proceedings, primarily in terms of creation and main-

tenance of a socio-cultural context, but quite possibly also in terms of learning in more direct ways. Before rejecting such ritual work as chorus repetition, songs and chants in the interests of 'true' communication, classroom research must attempt to analyse the functions of classroom rituals in the social context of the class-room, and assess their potential benefits. An element of ritual in tasks and activities may also be specifically designed to take account of the ritual requirements of interaction described by Goffman (1981).

3. Questions are an important tool of power and control. The vast majority of questions are asked by the teacher, thus indicating the amount of asymmetry that exists in the average classroom. When control is delegated, particularly control over topic, the proportion of questions asked by learners can be expected to increase. Simultaneously, the floor will become a shared responsibility, and discourse will not only flow from and to teacher, but also between learner and learner.

4. In activities where the emphasis is on elicitation, a distinction between display and referential questions may be relatively trivial since the questioner's intention, and the learners' task, may be identical. Instead, questions may be classified in terms of their cognitive or interactional value. Most current classifications, including those based on Bloom's taxonomy, focus on the cognitive work that a question demands of its response. This is important, but a relevant classification for L2 classrooms will also emphasize the interactional work that a question requires. Many questions, both display and referential, are appropriately answered in ellipti-cal fashion, in one word or phrase. The shortness of a response bears no relation to the potential cognitive work required to produce it, but L2 questions may want to stimulate more elaborate linguistic production. Cognition and interaction, and systematic relationships between them, must therefore both be considered in an evaluation of question sequences. Elaborate production can of course always be enforced (e.g.: 'answer in a full sentence'), but such practices reduce initiative and transform elicitation into rote recitation.

5. Repair is also related to control. A teacher who rigidly maintains control over both topic and activity tends to use reactive repair strategies. As I have suggested, these strategies interrupt the flow of discourse, and most importantly, they stop the learners' inter-active work – and the cognitive work, if required – in its tracks. When control is shared, a type of repair is favoured which is

proactive, i.e. which aims to further the interaction *as it is developing*. The latter type of repair is similar to that found in natural conversation, and may thus be contrasted with specifically didactic forms of repairing. This distinction goes deeper than the one we usually make between form-oriented and content-oriented repair, though there will be strong correlates.

6. Classroom research is a natural vehicle for monitoring and feedback, and will almost inevitably lead to immediate adjustments. In its simplest form, the teacher records lessons and listens to (parts of) them in order to get a clearer picture of what happened and to assist in decisions on what should be done next. A second step would be to use classroom interaction as input to future activities, so that learners can systematically be trained to monitor their own interaction.

7. Classroom activities can be used to make criterion-referenced assessments of individual learners. A range of scoring techniques are available for this purpose. Brown *et al.* 1984 is a particularly useful guide to assessment on the basis of tasks, but many educational texts provide different kinds of scales, charts, questionnaires and other tools that can be used for a variety of purposes (an excellent practical guide is Cohen 1976). The point I wish to emphasize is that a learner's assessment should not be derived exclusively from standard tests, however useful and well-constructed they may be. Standard tests provide feedback to the world at large rather than to the learner. The classroom itself provides opportunities to let learners evaluate themselves and monitor their own progress. Self-evaluation is as yet a relatively unexplored (but see some of the contributions in Hyltenstam and Pienemann 1985), though promising pedagogical tool.

8. Through action research, i.e. studying activities through changing them and seeing the effects, the teacher can add an 'experimental' dimension to classroom research, rather than relying completely on *post hoc* inspection. Through the recycling process mentioned in point 6, the learners can be actively involved in such classroom experiments. Action research is of course nothing new, but it has not been in vogue in the social sciences for many years (for a survey, see Sanford 1981). The study by Brown *et al.* (1984) shows that it can be a powerful instrument in classroom research (see also Bialystok 1983a for an L2 based example of action research).

9. Finally, classroom research must not be swayed by particular pedagogical theories or models. While no researcher or teacher

can truthfully claim to be free of all bias and above subjective beliefs, an allegiance to the ethnographic ideals of *holistic* and *emic* enquiry will ensure that the whole context and the participants' perspective are kept central.

Unless this perspective is given prominence, educational research will remain particularly vulnerable to biases that derive from researchers' ideological beliefs and convictions. These biases are potentially as strong in quantitative as in qualitative research, and can only be avoided by a commitment to social context and to truthfulness to the data as they really are. Even though there may be no 'telling it as it is' (Stenhouse 1975), a principled approach to CR may come closer to 'seeing it as it is', and draw consequences that lead to 'doing it better'.

Notes

1. Much of what follows is directly relevant to syllabus design, but a full and coherent treatment of all the issues involved is not possible here. For an excellent discussion the teacher is referred to Nunan 1985.
2. Metacommunicative acts can be further subdivided, and analysed, as
   a) metalinguistic (correction of errors, linguistic explanation);
   b) metadiscoursal (confirming, requesting clarification, summarizing);
   c) metapragmatic (attracting attention, controlling speech).
3. Nunan (1987) also reports the persistence of traditional patterns of classroom interaction, despite an avowed commitment to the principles of communicative language teaching.
4. As Wells (1985) point out, parents also frequently ask display questions when interacting with their small children. They therefore play a role in first-language acquisition.
5. Note that this is a different interpretation of scaffolding from that which is suggested by Long and Sato (1984) and by Faerch (1985), where it refers in more general terms to collaborative features in native-speaker/non-native-speaker interaction and has no specific pedagogical purpose.

Appendix: transcription

A sensitive classroom ethnography cannot be conducted without recording and transcription of data. There are several reasons for this:

1. The observer needs an *estrangement device* which allows stepping out of the interaction and looking at it afresh from a detached viewpoint.
2. Analysis of interaction requires intensive immersion in the data; transcription, accompanied by multiple replays, provides such immersion.
3. Interesting phenomena often only come to light after detailed inspection of the data. That which appears at first sight incomprehensible or perfectly trivial can turn out to provide important clues to regular patterns.
4. Through recording and transcription the data become available to other researchers, who can therefore examine and criticize the analyst's interpretation.
5. Recorded and transcribed data allow for a comparison with other such data and can thus lead to cumulative research.
6. We observe selectively, and real-time coding merely enforces systematic preselection. Recorded and transcribed data, though also to some extent inevitably selective (see below), allow for an investigation of the entire interaction in its context.

Equipment and its operation

1. *Is audio recording sufficient? How important is video recording?*
The two most common ways of recording classroom interaction are *video* and *audio*. Video recording is preferable, since non-verbal behaviour is important for analysis. Of course, the purpose of the analysis will determine how important visual information is; at the very least it is extremely helpful, at times it may be indispensable. Availability and cost will often determine if videotaping is possible. Other considerations, such as difficulty of operation, or intrusiveness

of recording, can usually be overcome.

2. *What video equipment is best? How much moving around is necessary?*
When videotaping, a choice must be made between portable and stationary equipment. When recording classroom interaction, it is preferable to locate the camera in one fixed position in a corner in the back of the room, taking in the entire scene, especially if learners sit in a semi-circular arrangement. Sometimes the furniture can be rearranged somewhat to minimize the number of learners who can only be seen from behind. If learners sit in straight rows, it may be preferable to mount the camera in a corner in front of the room, but this usually means that the teacher will be out of the picture for part of the time. In practice the researcher must experiment with the best position of the camera, and compromises will have to be made. A wide-angle lens can increase the viewing area considerably, but the lighting will need to be checked. The camera should be mounted as high above the heads of the participants as possible, and since sophisticated tripods and extensions are usually not available, this may require some ingenuity, using curtain rails, portable projection screens, and so on. If at all possible, moving around with a handheld camera, focusing on different parts of the scene, zooming in and out, and so on, should be avoided since it is severely disruptive and imposes a haphazard kind of selectivity. Once the camera is located in one spot, focused and tested, it should stay there and not be touched for the entire period of recording. If possible, an extension microphone may be suspended above the heads of the participants, taped to the ceiling, since the internal microphone of the camera will be some distance removed from the scene of the action. So long as the equipment is positioned some distance above eye-level, it is not very intrusive, and the participants will rapidly come to ignore it.

3. *Can the class be moved to a room which is already set up for recording?*
Sometimes this is the only option available, but time must be taken to allow the teacher and learners to get used to the different environment. It may be necessary to schedule several sessions before usable recordings can be made. If at all possible, recording in the regular room is to be preferred.

4. *Should we audiotape as well as videotape?*
When videotaping, it is very useful to audiotape on a separate cassette recorder simultaneously. The reason is that some microphones of video cameras are not very sensitive, but more importantly, transcribing from audio is much easier than from video. Winding and

rewinding on a VCR is clumsy and time-consuming. In addition, most audio-cassette players have cue buttons that allow fast-review, some can be fitted with foot controls, and the better ones also have slow-down controls (important for timing overlaps, and useful for deciphering rapid speech). The videotape can then be used for global viewing and non-verbal information.

5. *What playback equipment is needed for transcription?*
Transcription involves frequent replaying of small segments, and good playback equipment is extremely valuable. A tape counter, pause and cue buttons are indispensable, and pitch control (a slowing-down mechanism) is very useful, as mentioned above. In the past I have found the Canon Repeatcorder very useful, since it has built-in repeat loops which, at the touch of a button, re-run one-, two-, or three-second segments of talk indefinitely. Sometimes it is necessary to hear an utterance many times before it becomes intelligible. If it remains unintelligible after many hearings it can be useful to call in someone else to listen to it, since a fresh ear may get it right the first time.

6. *What happens if videotaping is impossible or inconvenient?*
If it is not possible to videotape, any cassette recorder can be used to record from the middle of the room. Of course, the better the recorder, the better the quality of the recording. Stereo recorders (e.g. the so-called boom boxes) usually give better results in a classroom than mono recorders. In addition, two recorders can be used in one large class, so that one recording can be checked with another. Some recorders have sockets for extension microphones, and these can be helpful when recording group work. I often use small lavaliere microphones which can be clipped to a person's clothing or to the cover of a notepad in front of two or three learners.

The essential thing to remember is to choose the best equipment available, find the right place to put it, set the counter to zero, and then not tinker with it while the lesson is in progress. Most lessons are about 45 minutes in length, and for this reason it may be advisable to use C90 cassettes, so that the tape does not need to be turned over during the lesson. Although this tape is thinner than a C60, I have found that it is robust enough to be wound back and forth frequently on a reasonable cassette player. Even so, it is always prudent to make back-up copies.

7. *What can the observer do while recording?*
When audiotaping it is useful to use one's presence in the classroom

to note as much non-verbal information as possible, so that this can be added to the transcription later on. I usually prepare lined blank sheets with a minute-by-minute time count in the left margin (about five minutes per sheet is usually sufficient) and a vertical line in the middle of the sheet. On the left I record salient bits of talk (so as to provide a point of reference with the tape later on) and on the right I note all the non-verbal information I can, including what is written on the blackboard, pictures that are shown, and so on. These sheets are used when doing the transcription, and relevant information is transferred.

8. *How soon after the recording should the transcription be made?*
The transcription should be begun as soon as possible after the lesson, while the memory of the observation is still fresh. Minimally, the observation notes must be matched with the recording (remember to label and number both tape and notes immediately), and a skeleton transcription produced. Successive playbacks can then be used to flesh out the transcript.

9. *How serious is the 'observer effect'?*
Learners do not usually need much time to get used to observers and recording equipment, though a variable amount of time is needed for 'dummy recording', i.e. recordings which will only be used for testing and for allowing the learners to get used to being recorded. Teachers may take longer than learners to overcome their discomfort with being recorded, especially if there has been little liaison about the research between researcher and teacher. If teachers record their own lessons, with or without the presence of an outside observer, the problem will be minimized. Since ethnography relies on a relationship of trust between researcher and participants, this problem should be addressed before the research is begun.

Transcription

1. *How long does a transcription take?*
It is generally estimated that one lesson takes about 20 hours to transcribe, and in my experience this is about right. However, it must be noted that the product will be a rough working transcription, and that segments to be used for close analysis and presentation will still need polishing. A transcription is never finished. Labov and Fanshel found that, after years of working on one relatively short recording, they were still making non-trivial changes to the transcription (Labov and Fanshel 1977).

2. *Who should do the transcribing?*

Often assistants or secretaries are hired to do the transcribing, and the implication is that it is work which is preparatory to analysis, and thus can be delegated. However, the transcription process *is* analysis and interpretation and, as Ochs points out, it is 'a selective process reflecting theoretical goals and definitions' (1979, p. 44). Ideally it should be done by the researcher, but in any case in very close collaboration with assistants.

3. *How detailed should the transcription be?*

A transcript is by its very nature selective. It is possible to include all sorts of information and turn it into a complex notational system. However, for CR it is advisable to make the transcript *readable* and easy to follow. A working transcript should read like a script for a play and capture what was said and done during the interaction. Exact information (concerning, e.g. eye gaze, posture, intonation, and so on), can be added for specific purposes.

4. *How accurate should the transcription be?*

We should aim to include all that was said and by whom it was said. Many transcribers do not distinguish between different learners, just marking anything said by any learner by a generic 'P' for 'pupil'. This makes it impossible to differentiate between learners. Assignment of speaker can be problematic in the case of audio recording, when the transcriber is not familiar with the learners; in those cases the assistance of the teacher or learners in allocating utterances to individual learners should be obtained.

A transcription of a lesson can never be entirely accurate. The larger the class, the more difficult it will be to assign all utterances to their speakers, and to unravel simultaneous talk. A rule of thumb is never to guess, to mark all unintelligible talk as such, and to indicate when the speaker of an utterance cannot be identified.

Deviant pronunciation need only be recorded if it is an issue in the interaction, though at times phonetic transcription of some item can be useful.

If a word or segment cannot be deciphered with certainty this can be indicated by placing it between single brackets to show that this was what was probably said.

It is generally necessary to indicate pauses and overlaps fairly accurately. The most common way to do so is to use hooks to indicate onset and end of overlap, and periods to mark pauses. In my transcriptions I use one period for about one-third of a second, and three periods therefore indicate a pause of around one second.

5. *How much non-verbal information should be included?*

As mentioned before, the transcript must be readable and easy to follow. Therefore, only the most significant non-verbal information can be included, and this can be placed in double brackets showing that it is a comment on the verbal interaction. For example, if the teacher points to a particular learner: ((T points to L7)).

Transcription conventions

There is no uniform set of symbols used for transcription, since to some extent every transcriber uses a set that appears most convenient for the purpose of the research. Transcriptions of talk between parent and child often use a two-column format, one for the parent and one for the child, sometimes with a third column to note the non-verbal actions which in such interaction are of course vital (see Scollon 1976; Ochs 1979).

For the transcription of classroom talk it is generally most convenient to transcribe line-by-line, indicating speaker in the left margin, and numbering turns from beginning to end. Overlapping and concurrent turns can be indented to the exact point of onset relative to the line above. In the present book the conventions proposed by Jefferson (1978) are followed, with a few additions and simplifications that are convenient for classroom interaction.

The conventions are as follows:

T	:	teacher
L1, L2, etc,	:	identified learner
L	:	unidentified learner
L3?	:	probably learner 3 (L3)
LL	:	several or all learners simultaneously
/yes/yah//ok// ///huh?///oh///	:	overlapping or simultaneous listening responses, brief comments, etc., by two, three, or an unspecified number of learners
=	:	a) turn continues below, at the next identical symbol b) if inserted at the end of one speaker's turn and the beginning of the next speaker's adjacent turn, it indicates that there is no gap at all between the two turns
. , . . , . . . , etc.	:	pause; three periods approximate one second. These periods are separated from the preceding word by a space.

?	:	rising intonation, not necessarily a question
!	:	strong emphasis with falling intonation
OK. now. well., etc.	:	a period unseparated from the preceeding word indicates falling (final) intonation
so, the next thing	:	a comma indicates low-rising intonation, suggesting continuation
e:r, the:::, etc.	:	one or more colons indicate lengthening of the preceding sound
emphasis	:	italic type indicates marked prominence through pitch or amplitude
OK? so, next 'yes but-'	:	onset and end of overlap or insertion of concurrent turn; for convenience a space can be inserted in the turn above, but this does not indicate a pause unless marked by periods
. . . . .(radio)	:	single brackets indicate unclear or probable item
((unint)), ((coughs))	:	double brackets indicate (a stretch of) unintelligible (approximate length indicated), or comments about the transcript, including non-verbal actions
no-	:	a hyphen indicates an abrupt cut-off, with level pitch
yesterday Peter went	:	capitals are only used for proper names, not to indicate beginnings of sentences
[si:m]	:	square brackets indicate phonetic transcription

Bibliography

Abbs, B, Candlin, C N, Edelhoff, C, Moston, T and Sexton, M 1978 and 1982 *Challenges* Longman

Adelman, C 1981 On first hearing. In Adelman, C (ed.) *Uttering, muttering*: 78–97. Grant McIntyre, London

Alexander, L G 1968 *Look, listen and learn!* Teacher's Book 1. Longman

Allen, J P B, Fröhlich, M and Spada, N 1984 The communicative orientation of language teaching: an observation scheme. In Handscombe, J, Orem, R A and Taylor, B (eds.) *On TESOL '83: the question of control*: 231–2. TESOL, Washington D. C.

Allwright, R L 1975 Problems in the study of the teacher's treatment of learner error. In Burt, M K and Dulay, H C (eds.) *On TESOL '75: new directions in second language learning, teaching and bilingual education*: 96–109. TESOL, Washington D. C.

Allwright, R L 1980 Turns, topics and tasks: patterns of participation in language learning and teaching. In Larsen-Freeman, D (ed.) *Discourse analysis in second language research*: 165–87. Newbury House, Rowley, Massachusetts

Allwright, R L 1984 The importance of interaction in classroom language learning. *Applied Linguistics* 5: 156–71

Allwright, R L 1988 *Observation in the language classroom*. Longman

Allwright, R L and Bailey, K M forthcoming *Focus on the classroom*. Cambridge University Press

Andersen, R (ed.) 1983 *Pidginization and creolization as language acquisition*. Newbury House, Rowley, Massachusetts

Atkinson, J M and Heritage, J (eds.) 1984 *Structures of social action: studies in conversation analysis*. Cambridge University Press

Bailey, K M 1983 Competitiveness and anxiety in adult second language learning: looking at and through the diary studies. In Seliger, H W and Long, M H (eds.) *Classroom oriented research in second language acquisition*: 67–103. Newbury House, Rowley, Massachusetts

Bailey, K M 1985 Classroom-centered research on language teaching and learning. In Celce-Murcia, M (ed.) *Beyond basics: issues and research in TESOL*: 96–121. Newbury House, Rowley, Massachusetts

Bailey, K M and Ochsner, R 1983 A methodological review of the diary studies: windmill tilting or social science? In Bailey, K M, Long, M H and Peck, S (eds.) *Second language acquisition studies*: 188–98. Newbury House, Rowley, Massachusetts

Barnes, D 1975 *From communication to curriculum*. Penguin

Bateson, G 1958 *Naven*. Stanford University Press

Bateson, G 1979 *Mind and nature: a necessary unity*. Fontana, London

Beebe, L forthcoming *The social psychological basis of second language acquisition*. Longman

Bellack, A A, Kliebard, H M, Hyman, R T and Smith, F L 1966 *The language of the classroom*. Teachers College Press, New York

Beretta, A 1986 Toward a methodology of ESL program evaluation. *TESOL Quarterly* 20: 144–55

Bialystok, E 1978 A theoretical model of second language learning. *Language Learning* 28: 69–83

Bialystok, E 1983a Inferencing: testing the 'hypothesis-testing' hypothesis. In Seliger, H W and Long, M H (eds.) *Classroom oriented research in second language acquisition*: 104–24. Newbury House, Rowley, Massachusetts

Bialystok, E 1983b Some factors in the selection and implementation of communication strategies. In Faerch, C and Kasper, G (eds.) *Strategies in interlanguage communication*: 100–18. Longman

Bloom, B S *et al.* 1956 *Taxonomy of educational objectives. I: Cognitive domain*. Longman

Boggs, S T 1972 The meaning of questions and narratives to Hawaiian children. In Cazden, C B, John, V P and Hymes, D (eds.) *Functions of language in the classroom*: 299–327. Teachers College Press, New York

Bolster, A S 1983 Toward a more effective model of research on teaching. *Harvard Educational Review* 53: 294–308

Breen, M P 1985a Authenticity in the language classroom. *Applied Linguistics* 6: 60–70

Breen, M P 1985b The social context for language learning – a neglected situation? *Studies in Second Language Acquisition* 7: 135–58

Breen, M P and Candlin, C N 1980 The essentials of a communicative curriculum in language teaching. *Applied Linguistics* 1: 89–112

Brend, R M (ed.) 1974 *Advances in tagmemics*. North Holland, Amsterdam

Brewer, M B and Collins, B E (eds.) 1981 *Scientific inquiry and the social sciences: a volume in honor of Donald T Campbell*. Jossey-Bass Publishers, San Francisco

Brown, G, Anderson, A, Shillcock, R and Yule, G 1984 *Teaching talk: strategies for production and assessment*. Cambridge University Press

Brown, G and Yule, G 1983a *Discourse analysis*. Cambridge University Press

Brown, G and Yule, G 1983b *Teaching the spoken language*. Cambridge University Press

Brown, P and Levinson, S 1978 Universals in language usage: politeness phenomena. In Goody, E (ed.) *Questions and politeness: strategies in social interaction*: 56–289. Cambridge University Press

Bruner, J 1983 *Child's talk: learning to use language*. Norton, New York

Canale, M and Swain, M 1980 Theoretical bases of communicative approaches to second language teaching and testing *Applied Linguistics* 1: 1–47

Candlin, C N 1986 Explaining communicative competence: limits of testability? In Stansfield, C (ed.) *TOEFL Research Report 21: Toward communicative competence testing: proceedings of the 2nd TOEFL Invitational Conference*: 38–57. ESF, Princeton, New Jersey

Carrasco, R L 1981 Expanded awareness of student performance: a case study in applied ethnographic monitoring in a bilingual classroom. In Trueba *et al.* (eds.) *Culture and the bilingual classroom: studies in classroom ethnography*: 153–77. Newbury House, Rowley, Massachusetts

Carroll, J B 1981 Conscious and automatic processes in language learning. *Canadian Modern Language Review* 37: 462–74

Castro, O and Kimbrough, V 1980 *In touch* Teacher's manual 3. Longman, New York

Cathcart, R and Olsen, J W-B 1976 Teachers' and students' preferences for correction of classroom errors. In Fanselow, J and Crymes, R (eds.) *On TESOL '76*: 41–53. TESOL, Washington D. C.

Cavalcanti, M 1982 Using the unorthodox, unmeasurable verbal protocol technique: qualitative data in foreign language reading research. In Dingwall, S and Mann, S (eds.) *Methods and problems in doing applied linguistic research*: 72–85. University of Lancaster

Cazden, C B 1985 Classroom discourse. In Wittrock, M C (ed.) *Handbook of research on teaching*: 432–63. Macmillan, New York

Chafe, W L 1979 The flow of thought and the flow of language. In Givon, T (ed.) *Syntax and semantics 12: discourse and syntax*. Academic Press, New York

Chafe, W L (ed.) 1980 *The pear stories: cognitive, cultural and linguistic aspects of narrative production*. Ablex, Norwood, New Jersey

Chanan, G and Delamont, S (eds.) 1975 *Frontiers of classroom research*. NFER, Slough

Chaudron, C A 1977 A descriptive model of discourse in the corrective treatment of learners' errors. *Language Learning* 27: 29–46

Chaudron, C A 1983 Foreigner talk in the classroom – an aid to learning? In Seliger, H W and Long, M H *Classroom oriented research in second language acquisition*: 127–45. Newbury House, Rowley, Massachusetts

Chaudron, C forthcoming *Second language classrooms: research on teaching and learning*. Cambridge University Press

Cicourel, A V *et al.* 1974 *Language use and school performance*. Academic Press, New York

Clement, R 1980 Ethnicity, contact and communicative competence in a second language. In Giles, H, Robinson, W P and Smith, P M (eds.) *Language: social psychological perspectives*: 147–54. Pergamon, Oxford

Cohen, L 1976 *Educational research in classrooms and schools: a manual of materials and methods*. Harper and Row, London

Cohen, L and Manion, L 1985 *Research methods in education* (Second edition). Croom Helm, London

Corder, S Pit 1981 *Error analysis and interlanguage*. Oxford University Press

Corsaro, W A 1981 Communicative processes in studies of social organization. *Text* 1: 5–63

Coulthard, M and Brazil, D 1979 *Exchange structure*. Discourse analysis monograph 5, English Language Research, Birmingham

Coulthard, M and Brazil, D 1981 Exchange structure. In Coulthard, M and Montgomery, M (eds.) *Studies in discourse analysis*: 82–106. Routledge and Kegan Paul, London

Cronbach, L J 1982 *Designing evaluations of educational and social programs*. Jossey-Bass Publishers, San Francisco

Cummins, J 1984 *Bilingualism and special education: issues in assessment and pedagogy*. College-Hill Press, San Diego

Davies, A, Criper, C and Howatt, A P R (eds.) 1984 *Interlanguage*. Edinburgh University Press

Day, R R, Chenoweth, N A, Chun, A E and Luppescu, S 1984 Corrective feedback in non-native discourse. *Language Learning* **34**: 19–46

Denzin, N K (ed.) 1970 *Sociological methods: a source book*. Aldine, Chicago

Denzin, N K 1978 *The research act: a theoretical introduction to sociological methods*. McGraw-Hill

Dickerson, W B 1983 The role of formal rules in pronunciation instruction. In Handscombe, J, Orem, R A and Taylor, B P (eds.) *On TESOL '83: The question of control*: 135–48. TESOL, Washington D. C.

Dickson, W P 1982 Creating communication-rich classrooms: insights from the sociolinguistic and referential traditions. In Wilkinson, L C (ed.) *Communicating in the classroom*: 131–50. Academic Press, New York

Dulay, H and Burt, M 1975 Creative construction in second language learning. In Burt, M and Dulay, H (eds.) *New directions in second language learning, teaching and bilingual education*. TESOL, Washington D. C.

Duncan, S 1973 Toward a grammar for dyadic conversation. *Semiotica* **9**: 24–46

Dunkin, M J and Biddle, B J 1974 *The study of teaching*. Holt, Rinehart and Winston, New York

Dunn, R 1984 Learning style: state of the science. *Theory Into Practice* **XXIII**: 10–19

Edelsky, C 1981 Who's got the floor? *Language in Society* **10**: 383–421

Edmondson, W 1981 *Spoken discourse: a model for analysis*. Longman

Edwards, J R 1979 Judgments and confidence reactions to disadvantaged speech. In Giles, H and St Clair, R N (eds.) *Language and social psychology*: 22–44. Basil Blackwell, Oxford

Ellis, R 1984a *Classroom second language development*. Pergamon Press, Oxford

Ellis, R 1984b Sources of variability in interlanguage. Paper presented at the Interlanguage Seminar in Honour of Pit Corder, Edinburgh

Ellis, R 1985 *Understanding second language acquisition*. Oxford University Press

Ellis, R (ed.) 1987 *Second language acquisition in context*. Prentice-Hall, Englewood Cliffs. New Jersey

Erickson, F 1979 Talking down: some cultural sources of miscommunication in inter-racial interviews. In Wolfgang, A (ed.) *Research in non-verbal communication*. Academic Press, New York

Erickson, F 1981a Money tree, lasagna bush, salt and pepper: social construction of topic cohesion in a conversation among Italian-Americans. In Tannen D (ed.) *Analyzing discourse: text and talk*: 43–70. Georgetown University Press, Washington D. C.

Erickson, F 1981b Some approaches to inquiry in school-community ethnography. In Trueba, H T, Guthrie, G P and Au, H P (eds.) *Culture and the bilingual classroom: studies in classroom ethnography*: 17–35. Newbury House, Rowley, Massachusetts

Erickson, F 1982 Classroom discourse as improvisation: relationships between academic task structure and social participation structure in lessons. In Wilkinson, L C (ed.) *Communicating in the classroom*: 153–81. Academic Press, New York

Erickson, F 1985 Qualitative methods in research on teaching. In Wittrock, M C (ed.) *Handbook of research on teaching*: 119–61. Macmillan, New York

Erickson, F and Shultz, J 1981 When is a context? some issues and methods in the analysis of social competence. In Green, J and Wallat, C (eds.) *Ethnography and language in educational settings*: 147–60. Ablex, Norwood, New Jersey

Ervin-Tripp, S M 1972 An analysis of the interaction of language, topic and listener. In Fishman, J A (ed.) *Readings in the sociology of language*: 192–211. Mouton, The Hague

Faerch, C 1985 Meta-talk in FL classroom disourse. *Studies in Second Language Acquisition* 7: 184–99

Faerch, C and Kasper, G 1980 Processes in foreign language learning and communication. *Interlanguage Studies Bulletin* 5: 47–118, Utrecht

Faerch, C and Kasper, G 1983 Plans and strategies in foreign language communication. In Faerch, C and Kasper, G (eds.) *Strategies in interlanguage communication*: 20–60. Longman

Fairclough, N 1985 Notes on method in critical discourse analysis. *Lancaster Papers in Linguistics* 21

Fanselow, J F 1977a Beyond Rashomon: conceptualizing and describing the teaching act. *TESOL Quarterly* 11: 17–40

Fanselow, J F 1977b The treatment of error in oral work. *Foreign Language Annals* 10: 583–93

Felix, S 1981 The effect of formal instruction on second language acquisition. *Language Learning* 31: 87–112

Fishman, J A 1977 The social science perspective. In Troike, R C (ed.) *Bilingual education: current perspectives. Volume 1: Social science*: 1–49. Center for Applied Linguistics, Arlington, Virginia

Flanders, N 1970 *Analysing teaching behavior*. Addison-Wesley, Reading. Massachusetts

Gaies, S 1976 Gradation in formal second language instruction as a factor in the development of interlanguage. In St Clair, R and Hartford, B (eds.) *LEKTOS: Interdisciplinary Working Papers in Language Sciences*. Special issue: Error analysis and language testing. University of Louisville, Kentucky

Gaies, S 1977 The nature of linguistic input in formal second language learning: linguistic and communication strategies in ESL teachers' classroom language. In Brown, H D, Yorio, C A and Crymes, R H (eds.) *On TESOL '77: Teaching and learning English as a second language: trends in research and practice*: 204–12. TESOL, Washington D. C.

Gaies, S 1980 Learner feedback: a taxonomy of intake control. In Fisher, J C, Clarke, M A and Schachter, J (eds.) *On TESOL '80: Building bridges*: 88–100. TESOL, Washington D. C.

Gardner, R C 1985 *Social psychology and second language learning*. Edward Arnold, London

Gaskill, W H 1980 Correction in native speaker — non-native speaker conversation. In Larsen-Freeman, D (ed.) *Discourse analysis in second language research*: 125–37. Newbury House, Rowley, Massachusetts

Geertz, C T 1973 *The interpretation of cultures*. Basic, New York

Giddens, A 1976 *New rules of sociological method: a postitive critique of interpretive sociologies*. Hutchinson, London

Giles, H and Byrne, J 1982 An intergroup approach to second language acquisition. *Journal of Multilingual and Multicultural Development* 3: 17–40

Giles, H and St Clair, R (eds.) 1979 *Language and social psychology*. Basil Blackwell, Oxford

Givon, T (ed.) 1983 Topic continuity in discourse: a quantitative cross-language study. *Typological Studies in Language*, Vol. 3. John Benjamins, New York

Glaser, B and Strauss, A 1967 *The discovery of grounded theory: strategies for qualitative research*. Aldine, Chicago

Goffman, E 1974 *Frame analysis*. Harper and Row, New York

Goffman, E 1981 *Forms of talk*. Basil Blackwell, Oxford

Good, T L and Brophy, J E 1984 *Looking in classrooms* (Third edition). Harper and Row, New York

Goodenough, W 1981 *Culture, language and society* (Second edition). The Benjamin/Cummings Publishing Company, Menlo Park, California

Goodwin, C 1977 Some aspects of the interaction of speaker and hearer in the construction of the turn at talk in natural conversation. Ph D Dissertation, University of Pennsylvania

Goody, E N 1978 Towards a theory of questions. In Goody, E N (ed.) *Questions and politeness: strategies in social interaction*: 17–43. Cambridge University Press

Grice, H P 1975 Logic and conversation. In Cole, P and Morgan, J L (eds.) *Syntax and Semantics 3: speech acts*: 41–58. Academic Press, New York

Griffin, P and Humphrey, F 1978 Talk and task at lesson time. In Shuy, R and Griffin, P (eds.) *Children's functional language and education in the early years*. Final report to the Carnegie Corporation of New York, Center of Applied Linguistics, Arlington, Virginia

Gumperz, J 1981 The linguistic bases of communicative competence. In Tannen, D (ed.) *Analyzing discourse: text and talk*: 323–34. Georgetown University Press, Washington D. C.

Gumperz, J 1982 *Discourse strategies*. Cambridge University Press

Halliday, M A K 1970 Language structure and language function. In Lyons, J (ed.) *New horizons in linguistics*: 140–65. Penguin

Hammersley, M and Atkinson, P 1983 *Ethnography, principles in practice*. Tavistock Publications, London

Harris, Z 1951 *Structural linguistics*. Phoenix Books, Chicago

Hatch, E 1978 Discourse analysis and second language acquisition. In Hatch, E (ed.) *Second language acquisition*: 401–35. Newbury House, Rowley, Massachusetts

Haysom, J 1985 *Inquiring into the teaching process: towards self-evaluation and professional development*. OISE Press, Ontario

Heap, J L 1979 Classroom talk: a critique of McHoul. Unpublished paper, University of Toronto

Heath, S B 1982 Ethnography in education: defining the essentials. In Gilmore, P and Glatthorn, A A (eds.) *Children in and out of school*: 33–35. Center for Applied Linguistics, Washington D. C.

Heath, S B 1986 *Children at risk? Building investment in diversity*. Plenary Address, 20th TESOL Convention, Anaheim, California

Hockett, C 1968 *The state of the art*. Mouton, The Hague

Hubbard, P, Jones, H, Thornton, B and Wheeler, R 1983 *A training course for TEFL*. Oxford University Press

Huebner, T 1983 *A longitudinal analysis of the acquisition of English*. Karoma Publishers, Ann Arbor

Humphrey, F M 1979 'Shh!': a sociolinguistic study of teachers' turn-taking sanctions in primary school lessons. Ph D Dissertation, Georgetown University, Washington D. C.

Hurtig, R 1977 Toward a functional theory of discourse. In Freedle, R O (ed.) *Discourse production and comprehension*: 89–106. Ablex, Norwood, New Jersey

Hyltenstam, K and Pienemann, M (eds.) 1985 *Modelling and assessing second language acquisition*. College-Hill Press, San Diego

Hymes, D 1964 General introduction. In Hymes, D *Language in culture and society*: xxi–xxxii. Harper and Row, New York

Hymes, D 1969 Review of *Language in relation to a unified theory of the structure of human behavior* (Second edition) by K L Pike. *American Anthropologist* 71: 361–3

Hymes, D 1981 Ethnographic monitoring. In Trueba, H T, Guthrie, G P and Au, H P (eds.) *Culture and the bilingual classroom: studies in classroom ethnography*: 56–68. Newbury House, Rowley, Massachusetts

Hymes, D *et al*. 1981 *Ethnographic monitoring of children's acquisition of reading/language arts skills in and out of the classroom*. Vols I,II,III. Final Report to NIE, Washington D. C. (ED 208 096)

Jefferson, G 1978 Sequential aspects of storytelling in conversation. In Schenkein, J (ed.) *Studies in the organization of conversational interaction*: 219–48. Academic Press, New York

Keenan, E O and Schieffelin, B B 1975 Topic as a discourse notion: a study of topic in the conversations of children and adults. In Li, C N (ed.) *Subject and topic*: 335–84. Academic Press, New York

Kirshenblatt-Gimblett, B 1982 Contributions and caveats. In Gilmore, P and Glatthorn, A A (eds.) *Children in and out of school*: 254–6. Center for Applied Linguistics, Washington D. C.

Kohl, H 1965 *The age of complexity*. Mentor Books, New York

Krashen, S D 1979 The monitor model for second language acquisition. In Gingras, R (ed.) *Second language acquisition and foreign language teaching*: 1–26 Center for Applied Linguistics, Arlington, Virginia

Krashen, S D 1981 *Second language acquisition and second language learning*. Pergamon, Oxford

Krashen, S D 1982 *Principles and practice in second language acquisition*. Pergamon, Oxford

Krashen, S D 1985 *The input hypothesis*. Longman

Krashen, S D and Terrell, T 1983 *The natural approach: language acquisition in the classroom*. Pergamon, Oxford

Kuhn, T 1962 *The structure of scientific revolutions*. Princeton University Press, Princeton, New Jersey.

Labov, W 1966 *The social stratification of English in New York City*. Center for Applied Linguistics, Washington D. C.

Labov, W 1972 *Sociolinguistic patterns*. University of Pennsylvania Press, Philadelphia

Labov, W and Fanshel, D 1977 *Therapeutic discourse: psychotherapy as conversation*. Academic Press, New York

Lambert, W E 1963a Psychological approaches to the study of language. Part I: On learning, thinking and human abilities. *Modern Language Journal* **14**: 51–62

Lambert, W E 1963b Psychological approaches to the study of language. Part II: On second language learning and bilingualism. *Modern Language Journal* **14**: 114–21

Lambert, W E 1967 A social psychology of bilingualism. *Journal of Social Issues* **23**: 91–109

Lambert, W E 1974 Culture and language as factors in learning and education. In Aboud, F E and Meade, R D (eds.) *Cultural factors in learning and education*. Fifth Western Washington Symposium on Learning, Bellingham, Washington D. C.

Lambert, W E, Hodgson, R C, Gardner, R C and Fillenbaum, S 1960 Evaluational reactions to spoken language. *Journal of Abnormal and Social Psychology* **60**: 44–51

Lamendella, J 1979 The neurofunctional basis of pattern practice. *TESOL Quarterly* **13**: 5–19

Larsen-Freeman, D and Long, M H forthcoming *Introduction to second language acquisition research*. Longman

Leech, G N 1977 Language and tact. L.A.U.T. paper 46, Trier

Lett, J and Shaw, P 1986 Combining quantitative and qualitative program evaluation: a research report. Paper presented at 20th TESOL convention, Anaheim, California

Levelt, W J M 1983 Monitoring and self-repair in speech. *Cognition* **14**: 41–104

Levinson, S C 1979 Activity types and language. *Linguistics* **17**: 365–99

Levinson, S C 1983 *Pragmatics*. Cambridge University Press

Long, M H 1983a Inside the 'black box': methodological issues in classroom research on language learning. In Seliger, H W and Long, M H (eds.) *Classroom oriented research in second language acquisition*: 3–36. Newbury House, Rowley, Massachusetts

Long, M H 1983b Does second language instruction make a difference? A review of the research. *TESOL Quarterly* **17**: 359–82

Long, M H 1985 A role for instruction in second language acquisition: task-based language teaching. In Hyltenstam, K and Pienemann, M (eds.) *Modelling and assessing second language acquisition*: 77–99. College-Hill Press, San Diego

Long, M H, Adams, L, McLean, L and Castaños, F 1976 Doing things with words: verbal interaction in lockstep and small group classroom situations. In Fanselow, J and Crymes, R (eds.) *On TESOL '76*: 137–53. TESOL, Washington D. C.

Long, M H and Sato, C J 1983 Classroom foreigner talk discourse: forms and functions of teacher questions. In Seliger, H W and Long, M H (eds.) *Classroom oriented research in second language acquisition*: 268–85. Newbury House, Rowley, Massachusetts

Long, M H, Adams, L, McLean, L and Castaños, F 1976 Doing things with studies: an interactionist perspective. In Davies, A, Criper, C and Howatt, A P R (eds.) *Interlanguage*: 253–79. Edinburgh University Press

Lorenz, K 1971 A scientist's credo. In Lorenz, K *Studies in animal and human behaviour*, Vol. II: 1–13. Methuen, London

Lutz F W 1981 Ethnography – the holistic approach to understanding schooling. In Green, J L and Wallat, C (eds.) *Ethnography and language in educational settings*: 51–63. Ablex, Norwood, New Jersey

Lyons, J 1968 *Introduction to theoretical linguistics*. Cambridge University Press

Mackey, W F 1970 A typology of bilingual education. *Foreign Language Annals* 3: 596–608

Mann, S 1982 Verbal reports as data: a focus on retrospection. In Dingwall, S and Mann, S (eds.) *Methods and problems in doing applied linguistic research*: 72–85. University of Lancaster

McHoul, A W 1978 The organization of turns at formal talk in the classroom. *Language in Society* 7: 183–213

McHoul, A W forthcoming Notes on the organization of repair in classroom talk. In Schenkein, J (ed.) *Studies in the organization of conversational interaction*. Vol. 2. Academic Press, New York

McLaughlin, B 1985 Are immersion programs the answer for bilingual education in the United States? *Bilingual Review/Revista Bilingue* XI: 3–11

McLaughlin, M L 1984 *Conversation: how talk is organized*. Sage, Beverley Hills

Mehan, H 1979 *Learning lessons: social organization in the classroom*. Harvard University Press, Cambridge, Massachusetts

Milk, R D 1985 Can foreigners do 'foreigner-talk'? A study of the linguistic input provided by non-native teachers of EFL. Paper presented at the 19th Annual TESOL Convention, New York

Milroy, L 1980 *Language and social networks*. Blackwell, Oxford

Minsky, M 1975 A framework for representing knowledge. In Winston, P H (ed.) *The psychology of computer vision*: 211–77. McGraw-Hill, New York

Mitchell, R 1985 Process research in second-language classrooms. *Language Teaching* 18: 330–52

Moskowitz, G 1976 The classroom interaction of outstanding foreign language teachers. *Foreign Language Annals* 9: 135–43

Naiman, N, Fröhlich, M, Stern, H and Todesco, A 1978 The good language learner. *Research in Education* No. 7, OISE, Toronto

Nemser, W 1974 Approximative systems of foreign language learners. In Richards, J C (ed.) *Error analysis*: 55–63. Longman

Nunan, D 1985 *Language teaching course design: trends and issues*. National Curriculum Resource Centre, Adelaide

Nunan, D 1987 Communicative language teaching: making it work. *ELT Journal* 41(2): 136–45

Ochs, E 1979 Transcription as theory. In Ochs, E and Schieffelin, B B (eds.) *Developmental pragmatics*: 43–72. Academic Press, New York

Oosthoek, H and van den Eeden, P (eds.) 1984 *Education from the multi-level perspective: models, methodology and empirical findings*. Gordon and Breach Science Publishers, New York

Oreström, B 1983 *Turn-taking in English conversation*. C W K Gleerup, Lund

Peters, A M 1983 *The units of language acquisition*. Cambridge University Press

Philips, S U 1972 Participant structure and communicative competence: Warm Springs children in community and classroom. In Cazden, C B, John, V P and Hymes, D (eds.) *Functions of language in the classroom*: 370–94. Teachers College Press, New York

Philips, S U 1983 *The invisible culture: communication in the classroom and community on the Warm Springs Indian Reservation*. Longman Inc., New York

Pienemann, M and Johnston, M 1985 Towards an explanatory model of language acquisition. Paper presented at the Los Angeles Second Language Research Forum (Feb. 22–24), UCLA

Pike, K L 1982 *Linguistic concepts: an introduction to tagmemics*. University of Nebraska Press, Lincoln

Politzer, R L 1970 Some reflections on 'good' and 'bad' language teaching behaviors. *Language Learning* 20: 31–43

Prabhu, N S 1985 Coping with the unknown in language pedagogy. In Quirk, R and Widdowson, H G (eds.) *English in the world: teaching and learning the language and literatures*: 164–73. Cambridge University Press

Rampton, M B H 1987 Stylistic variability and not speaking 'normal' English: some post-Labovian approaches and their implications for the study of interlanguage. In Ellis, R (ed.) *Second language acquisition in context*: 47–58. Prentice-Hall, Englewood Cliffs, New Jersey

Ratner, N and Bruner, J 1978 Games, social exchange and the acquisition of language. *Journal of Child Language* 5: 391–401

Ravetz, J R 1971 *Scientific knowledge and its social problems*. Oxford University Press

Redfield, D L and Rousseau, E W 1981 A meta-analysis of experimental research on teacher questioning behavior. *Review of Educational Research* 51: 237–45

Richards, J (ed.) 1974 *Error analysis*. Longman

Rosen, H 1969 Towards a language policy across the curriculum. In Barnes, D, Britton, J, Rosen, H and the LATE *Language, the learner and the school*: 119–59. Penguin

Rosen, H 1978 Signing on. *The New Review* 4: 55–7

Rossner, R 1986 Editor's Note. *ELT Journal* 40(1): 1–2

Rowe, M B 1974 Wait-time and rewards as instructional variables. *Journal of Research in Science Teaching* 11: 81–94

Rubin, J 1975 What the 'good language learner' can teach us. *TESOL Quarterly* 9: 41–51

Sacks, H 1963 On sociological description. *Berkeley Journal of Sociology* 8: 1–16

Sacks, H 1972 On the analyzability of stories by children. In Gumperz, J J and Hymes, D (eds.) *Directions in sociolinguistics*: 329–45. Holt, Rinehart and Winston, New York

Sacks, H, Schegloff, E A, and Jefferson, G 1974 A simplest systematics for the organization of turn taking in conversation. *Language* 50: 696–735. Reprinted in Schenkein, J (ed.) 1978 *Studies in the organization of conversational interaction*: 7–55. Academic Press, New York

Sanday, P R 1982 Anthropologists in schools: school ethnography and ethnology. In Gilmore P and Glatthorn, A A (eds.) *Children in and out of school*: 250–53. Center for Applied Linguistics, Washington D. C.

Sanford, N 1981 A model for action research. In Reason, P and Rowan, J (eds.) *Human inquiry: a sourcebook of new paradigm research*: 173–81. John Wiley, Chichester

Saussure, F de 1959 *Course in general linguistics*. Philosophical Library, New York

Saville-Troike, M 1982 *The ethnography of communication: an introduction*. University Park, Baltimore

Schegloff, E A 1979 The relevance of repair to syntax-for-conversation. In Givon, T (ed.) *Syntax and Semantics 12: discourse and syntax*. Academic Press, New York

Schegloff, E A 1981 Discourse as an interactional achievement: some uses of 'uh huh' and other things that come between sentences. In Tannen, D (ed.) *Analyzing discourse: text and talk*: 71–93 GURT 1981, Washington D. C.

Schegloff, E A and Sacks, H 1974 Opening up closings. In Turner, R (ed.) *Ethnomethodology*: 233–64. Penguin

Schegloff, E A, Jefferson, G and Sacks, H 1977 The preference for self-correction in the organization of repair in conversation. *Language* 53: 361–82

Schinke-Llano, L 1983 Foreigner talk in content classrooms. In Seliger, H W and Long, M H (eds.) *Classroom oriented research in second language acquisition*: 146–65. Newbury House, Rowley, Massachusetts

Schmidt, R W 1983 The strengths and limitations of acquisition: a case study of an untutored language learner. *Working papers 2* 2: 87–114. Department of English as a Second Language, University of Hawaii at Manoa

Schumann, F E and Schumann, J H 1977 Diary of a language learner: an introspective study of second language learning. In Brown, H D, Crymes, R H and Yorio, C A (eds.) *Teaching and learning: trends in research and practice*: 241–9. TESOL, Washington D. C.

Schumann, J H 1978 *The pidginization process: a model for second language acquisition*. Newbury House, Rowley, Massachusetts

Schwartz, J 1980 The negotiation for meaning: repair in conversations between second language learners of English. In Larsen-Freeman, D (ed.) *Discourse analysis in second language research*: 138–53. Newbury House, Rowley, Massachusetts

Scollon, R 1976 *Conversations with a one-year old: a case study of the developmental foundation of syntax*. The University Press of Hawaii

Scollon, R 1981 The rhythmic integration of ordinary talk. In Tannen, D (ed.) *Analyzing discourse: text and talk*: 335–49. GURT 1981, Georgetown University Press, Washington D. C.

Seliger, H W 1977 Does practice make perfect? A study of interaction patterns and L2 competence. *Language Learning* 27: 263–78

Seliger, H W 1983 Learner interaction in the classroom and its effects on language acquisition. In Seliger, H W and Long, M H (eds.) *Classroom oriented research in second language acquisition*: 246–67. Newbury House, Rowley, Massachusetts

Seliger, H W and Long, M H (eds.) 1983 *Classroom oriented research in second language acquisition*. Newbury House, Rowley, Massachusetts

Shultz, J J, Florio, S and Erickson, F 1982 Where's the floor? Aspects of the cultural organization of social relationships in communication at home and in school. In Gilmore, P and Glatthorn, A A (eds.) *Children in and out of school*: 88–123. Center for Applied Linguistics, Washington D. C.

Simon, A and Boyer, E G 1970 *Mirrors of behavior*. Research for Better Schools, Philadelphia

Sinclair, J McH and Brazil, D 1982 *Teacher talk*. Oxford University Press

Sinclair, J McH and Coulthard, M 1975 *Towards an analysis of discourse*. Oxford University Press

Sinclair, J McH, Forsyth, I J, Coulthard, M and Ashby, M C 1972 *The English used by teachers and pupils*. Report to SSRC, University of Birmingham

Smith, B O and Meux, M O 1962 *A study of the logic of teaching*. University of Illinois Press, Urbana

Speier, M 1973 *How to observe face-to-face communication: a sociological introduction*. Goodyear Publishing Company, Pacific Palisades

Spradley, J P 1980 *Participant observation*. Holt, Rinehart and Winston, New York

Stenhouse, L 1975 *An introduction to curriculum research and development*. Heinemann, London

Stevick, E W 1980 *Teaching languages: a way and ways*. Newbury House, Rowley, Massachusetts

Stubbs, M 1976, 1983 *Language, schools and classrooms* (Second edition). Methuen, London

Stubbs, M 1983 *Discourse analysis: the sociolinguistic analysis of natural language*. Basil Blackwell, Oxford

Stubbs, M and Delamont, S (eds.) 1976 *Explorations in classroom observation*. John Wiley, Chichester

Tarone, E 1983 Some thoughts on the notion of 'communicative strategy'. In Faerch, C and Kasper, G (eds.) *Strategies in interlanguage communication*: 61–74. Longman

Thompson, J B 1984 *Studies in the theory of ideology*. University of California Press, Berkeley

Townsend, D R and Zamora, G L 1975 Differing interaction patterns in bilingual classrooms. *Contemporary Education* 46: 196–202

Trevarthen, C 1974 Conversations with a two-month-old. *New Scientist* 2, May 1974: 230

Trevarthen, C 1979 Communication and cooperation in early infancy: a description of primary intersubjectivity. In Bullowa, M (ed.) *Before speech: the beginning of interpersonal communication*. Cambridge University Press

Trueba, H T, Guthrie, G P and Au, H P (eds.) 1981 *Culture and the bilingual classroom: studies in classroom ethnography*. Newbury House, Rowley, Massachusetts

van Dijk, T A 1977 *Text and context*. Longman

van Lier, L A W 1984 Discourse analysis and classroom research: a methodological perspective. *International Journal of the Sociology of Language* 49: 111–33

van Lier, L A W 1985 Review of Seliger, H W and Long, M H (eds.) *1983 Classroom oriented research in second language acquisition*. *TESOL Quarterly* 19: 356–67

Varonis, E M and Gass, S 1985 Non-native/non-native conversations: a model for negotiation of meaning. *Applied Linguistics* 6: 71–90

Walker, R 1981 On the uses of fiction in educational research. In Smetherham, D (ed.) *Practising evaluation*: 147–65. Nafferton, Driffield

Walker, R and Adelman, C 1976 Strawberries. In Stubbs, M and Delamont, S (eds.) *Explorations in classroom observation*. John Wiley, Chichester

Weiner, S L and Goodenough, D R 1977 A move toward a psychology of conversation. In Freedle, R O (ed.) *Discourse production and comprehension*: 213–26. Ablex, Norwood, New Jersey

Wells, G 1981 *Learning through interaction*. Cambridge University Press

Wells, G 1985 *Language development in the pre-school years*. Cambridge University Press

Widdowson, H G 1981 ESP and the curse of Caliban. In Fisher, J C, Clarke, M A and Schachter, J (eds.) *On TESOL '80: Building bridges*: 50–60. TESOL, Washington D. C.

Widdowson, H G 1983 The learner in the language learning process. In Holden, S (ed.) *Focus on the learner: Bologna Conference 1983 organised by the British Council*: 7–12. Modern English Publications, London

Widdowson, H G 1984 Procedures for discourse processing. In *Explorations in Applied Linguistics*, Volume II: 97–124. Oxford University Press

Willis, J 1981 *Teaching English through English*. Longman

Wode, H 1980 Operating principles and 'universals' in L1, L2 and FLT. *IRAL* 17: 217–31

Yngve, V H 1970 On getting a word in edgewise. In *Papers from the Sixth Regional Meeting, Chicago Linguistics Society*: 567–77

Index